Ahron
# Bregman

## Israel's Wars

A history since 1947

Third edition

**Routledge**
Taylor & Francis Group

LONDON AND NEW YORK

First published 2000 by Routledge
2 Park Square, Milton Park, Abingdon, Oxon OX14 4RN

Simultaneously published in the USA and Canada
by Routledge
270 Madison Ave, New York, NY 10016

Second edition first published 2002
Reprinted 2003, 2004
Transferred to Digital Printing 2007
Third edition first published 2010

*Routledge is an imprint of the Taylor & Francis Group, an informa business*

© 2000, 2002, 2010 Ahron Bregman

Typeset in Joanna and Scala Sans by
RefineCatch Limited, Bungay, Suffolk
Printed and bound in Great Britain by
TJ International Ltd, Padstow, Cornwall

*British Library Cataloguing in Publication Data*
A catalogue record for this book is available from the British Library

*Library of Congress Cataloging in Publication Data*
A catalog record for this book has been requested

ISBN 10: 0–415–42436–4 (hbk)
ISBN 10: 0–415–42438–0 (pbk)

ISBN 13: 978–0–415–42436–3 (hbk)
ISBN 13: 978–0–415–42438–7 (pbk)

# Israel's Wars

For A. M., who
deserved a better end

# CONTENTS

# LIST OF ILLUSTRATIONS

## MAPS

## PLATES (Between pp. 142 and 143)

1.1 Jewish troops march in Haifa after its capture in the 1948 war.

1.2 Palestinians flee from their village near Haifa in 1948.

# PREFACE TO THE 2010 EDITION

Ten years since the first publication of *Israel's Wars* and eight since its second edition comes the current third edition. There have been many developments in the Middle East over these years which justify a new edition, not least an all-out war in 2006 between Israel and Hezbollah. Indeed, the main addition to this edition is a new chapter on that war and the period preceding it: the lengthy confrontation between the Israeli Defence Forces (IDF) and Hezbollah's guerrilla fighters in the Israeli security zone in southern Lebanon, which contributed to Israel's decision to withdraw from the area. Students of civil–military relations will find this latter episode particularly intriguing, as the methods used by then Prime Minister and Defence Minister Ehud Barak to outmanoeuvre those who opposed withdrawal, particularly the military establishment, are fascinating.

When the previous edition of this book went to print in 2002, the *Al-Aqsa intifada* was still in full swing. This war is not over yet, but the passage of time since its beginning in 2000 has lent us a better perspective on events and this, as the reader will see, is reflected in a substantially revised chapter on this period.

In the original version of *Israel's Wars* I hinted at the identity of the most important spy Israel's intelligence agency Mossad ever had in the Arab world, one who played a prominent role in the lead-up to the 1973 Yom Kippur War. I argued that he was a double agent who had, in fact, misled his Israeli masters and was, as I put it, the jewel in the crown of the Egyptian plan to deceive Israel before the 1973 war. I thus shifted the blame for the Israeli failure to realize that war was imminent from the IDF's Military Intelligence unit to Mossad, the agency that employed this spy. However, my concealed references to this mysterious man in *Israel's Wars* and other publications eventually led to a serious spat between us, where he dubbed my version of events 'a silly detective story' and I, in response, unmasked him; revealing that he was Ashraf Marwan, son-in-law of Egypt's President Gamal Abdel Nasser. We later mended fences, met and kept working relations for five years – I was an adviser on a book he was writing. But then came his mysterious death on 27 June 2007 – the very day we were due to meet for a chat. He either jumped to his death from the balcony of his flat in Mayfair, London – or was pushed. I pray that, in either eventuality, my unmasking him had nothing to do with his brutal death, but it was still much too painful for me to deal with this story again and I refrained from updating this section of the book. Those interested in this historically important episode might consider consulting the relevant chapter in my *A History of Israel* and the writings of Uri Bar Joseph of Haifa University.[1]

At Routledge UK, I would like to thank Vicky Peters, Eve Setch, Emily Kindleysides, Andrew Watts, James Benefield and free-lance copy-editor Monica Kendall. Thanks also to Tom Raw, Dr Massimiliano Fiore, Ruti Frensdorff and Donald Winslow for help with the images.

Ahron Bregman<br>London, 2009

# PREFACE TO THE 2002 EDITION

When I wrote *Israel's Wars*, in the late 1990s, my idea was to produce a relatively short volume which would provide a summary and evaluation of some five decades of Israeli–Arab wars. At that time – the post-Oslo era – my mood, like that of many others, was euphoric. I saw in Yitzhak Rabin's handshakes, first with Yasser Arafat in 1993 and then with King Hussein of Jordan in 1994 historic events so powerful that they should, so I believed, in their symbolism alone, have put an end to the Arab–Israeli conflict. 'Never', I remember myself saying with much conviction in a lecture, 'will anyone be able to turn this wheel back'. I was wrong – like many others – for the wheel has been indeed turned back and as this edition goes to print, the most famous land in history is yet again engulfed in flames, with Israelis and Palestinians fighting each other in a war of planes and tanks, sniper shooting and ambushes, suicide bombings and assassinations. The patterns of this cruel war, the so-called *Al-Aqsa intifada*, have been shaped during its first year and although it is still in progress the picture is clear enough for us to chronicle the main turning points of this confrontation and analyse its nature. This has been done in the new chapter – The *Al-Aqsa intifada* – which is the main addition to this 2002 edition.

This revised edition also contains other new – never before published – material which sheds new light on one of the most mysterious episodes in Israel's war history – the *Liberty* Affair. USS *Liberty* was an American spy ship which was dispatched by Washington during the June 1967 war to monitor events in the Middle East. On 8 June, the fourth day of this war, Israel bombed *Liberty*, killing 34 men and wounding 171. The attack has been a matter of controversy ever since and over the years there have been speculations on whether the Israeli attack was premeditated – planned and deliberate – aimed at preventing *Liberty* from following up events, particularly that Israel was massing forces in Galilee in order to seize the Golan Heights, or whether it was – as the Israelis have always claimed – a 'tragic case of misidentification'.

A short but significant recording of a conversation over the radio link between Israeli pilots and the Air Force headquarters during the attack on *Liberty*, published here for the first time, shows beyond doubt, that the Israelis *did* know, even in the initial stages of their strike on *Liberty*, that this was an American vessel. Nevertheless, and in spite of the *positive* identification of the ship as American, they continued with naval attacks until they put *Liberty* out of action.

This revised edition of *Israel's Wars* has been aimed particularly at the general reader and consequently much of the scholarly apparatus has been removed. For details of the archival and other sources on which the book is based readers are invited to consult the original 2000 edition.

Ahron Bregman
London, 2001

# PREFACE

This book is the result of a suggestion made by Jeremy Black, general editor of *Warfare and History*, who thought that an account of Israel's wars would be a useful addition to the series. Its publication was delayed by an invitation to act as a consultant and write the companion book for a six-part BBC Television documentary about the Arab–Israeli conflict (*The Fifty Years War: Israel and the Arabs*). This has proved a benefit since, in the course of my work on the series, I came across material which I could never otherwise have obtained.

*Israel's Wars* is, first and foremost, an overview of Israel's wars with the Palestinians and Arabs. I start with the 1947–8 Jewish–Palestinian struggle for possession and mastery of the land of Palestine, and conclude with the Israeli–Palestinian confrontation which took place between 1987 and 1993, the so-called *intifada* and its sequel – the *Al-Aqsa intifada* of 2000. In between I examine Israel's wars with its Arab neighbours, principally Egypt, Jordan, Syria and the PLO in Lebanon, in the years 1948, 1956, 1967, 1968–70, 1973 and 1982.

*Israel's Wars* is not, however, only about battles and fighting, but also about the people of Israel, a nation-in-arms, who are, it is often said, 'soldiers on eleven months' annual leave'. By looking at more than five decades of Israeli–Palestinian–Arab conflict we can see that the Israelis, in spite of tremendous difficulties, have for many years demonstrated an extraordinary willingness to carry the burden, pay high taxes, endure long military service, and fight both in wars and between them. But after, and as a result of, the Six Day War of June 1967, as I shall demonstrate, Israelis became more critical of their leadership, dissent grew, and there was also a pronounced tendency to reject the idea that preparations for war need always be at the expense of social services and justify indifference towards domestic problems. Still, in spite of growing dissent and criticism, the Israelis remained, in the post-1967 war period, loyal to their leadership, always rallying behind it in times of war. The turning point, however, came during the 1982 war in Lebanon when, for the first time in Israel's history, national solidarity showed signs of breaking down, and while the battle was still in progress Israelis protested against the war, and some even declared their refusal to take part in it. This unprecedented challenge and decline in the motivation of Israelis to serve gathered pace after the Lebanon war and reached a peak during the *intifada*, the Palestinian revolt in the occupied territories between 1987 and 1993, and then as of 2000.

I link this trend mainly to a reduction in the level of the external threat to Israel's existence, and suggest that during the first two or three decades of the state, a strong sense of external threat, fresh memories of the Holocaust and collective ideals and priorities had stiffened the will of Israelis to serve, fight and sacrifice. This determination was strengthened by the leadership's success in cultivating the image of Israel as a small defenceless state surrounded by evil Arabs bent on her destruction; and, ironically, by the Arabs themselves, who played into their hands by exaggerating their own military capability and talking of dismantling the Jewish state, wiping it out and driving the Jews into the sea. However, with the external danger subsiding, the gradual disappearance of the Holocaust generation and a general shift from collective ideals and priorities to individual ones, there was also a decline of will among Israelis to serve and bear the burden, as was made very clear in Lebanon in 1982 and during the intifada.

This book on Israel's wars is designed to be rather more than a chronicle of events. There are frequent pauses to examine how things operate and for what reasons; and I often go beyond the task of narrative and description to comment and explain, so that the reader can elicit from the sequence of events some better understanding of how things turned out as they did.

The book also contains new – never before published – material. Perhaps most notable is the revelation that Anwar Sadat's right-hand man (who also worked for Sadat's predecessor President Nasser as confidante and member of his presidential staff) was an agent of Mossad, Israel's secret service. I expose, for the first time, the documents he passed to the Israelis which became the foundation of Israel's strategy before the Yom Kippur War ('The Conception') and claim that from being an agent working exclusively for Mossad, he later became a double agent and worked also for Sadat, who sent him, on the eve of the Yom Kippur War, to meet the head of Mossad in London and to mislead him regarding the time Egypt would open fire.

I have always believed that while one can learn history from documents, articles and books, it can be better understood if heard from those who have made it, for motives and personalities are important in the making of history. And though a person's recollection tends to be clouded by later events, oral history is still an important complement to the written word; a personal context sometimes sheds light on political decision-making better than the most detailed of documents. In the last decade or so, in addition to sieving through piles of written material, I have had the opportunity to meet many who have taken part in making the history about which I am writing here. Their names are too numerous to mention, but I should like to thank in particular the following, from whom I have benefited most: Meir Amit, Moshe Arens, Ehud Barak, Haim Bar Lev, Mordechai Bar On, Benyamin Begin, Yossi Beilin, Yossi Ben Aharon, Shlomo Ben Ami, Avigdor Ben Gal, Benyamin Ben Eliezer, Yosef Burg, Warren Christopher, Ben Zion Cohen, Avraham Dar, Robert Dassa, Uzi Dayan, Abba Eban, Rafael Eitan, Miriam Eshkol, Yeshayahu Gavish, Mordechai Gazit, Eli Geva, Benjamin Givli, Mordechai Gur, Eitan Haber, Yehoshafat Harkabi, Isser Harel, Yair Hirschfeld, Mordechai Hod, Yitzhak Hofi, Yehiel Kadishai, Lou Keddar, David Kimche, Yoseph (Tommy) Lapid, Tarje Rød Larsen, Yitzhak Levi-Levitza, Dan Meridor, Amram Mitzna, Shaul Mofaz, Uzi Narkiss, Yitzhak Navon, Benjamin Netanyahu, Marcelle Ninio, Meir Pail, Dan Pattir, Matityahu Peled, Shimon Peres, Leah Rabin, Yitzhak Rabin, Itamar Rabinovich, Gideon Rafael, Ran Ronen (Peker), Elyakim Rubinstein, Yehoshua Saguey, Yossi Sarid, Uri Savir, Amnon Lipkin-Shahak, Silvan Shalom, Shlomo Shamir, Yitzhak Shamir, Yaacov Sharett, Ariel Sharon, Yisrael Tal, Avraham Tamir, Yair Tzaban, Dov Weisglass, Ezer Weizman, Aharon Yariv, Dani Yatom, Re'havam Ze'evi, and Eli Zeira. Last, but certainly not least, my love and thanks go to Dana, and to my children Daniel, Maya and Adam, whose constant interruption is a good reminder that there is more to life than the long and lonesome business of writing.

Ahron Bregman
London, 1999

# 1

## THE 1947–9 WAR

### A CONFLICT IS BORN

'Some years', J. K. Galbraith once wrote, 'like some poets and politicians and some lovely women, are singled out for fame far beyond the common lot'.[1] For the Middle East in general, and for the people of Palestine in particular, 1948 was clearly such a year. It was the year in which the British Mandate for Palestine terminated, a Jewish state called Israel was established, thousands of Arab Palestinians became refugees, and regular armed forces of Transjordan, Egypt, Syria and other Arab countries entered Palestine-Israel and clashed with Israeli forces. Thus begun the first all-out Arab–Israeli war which – like the civil war which preceded it – revolved around land.

The ancient land of Palestine – small in size, covering some 10,000 square miles – formed a narrow strip stretching along the Levant. In the south it was separated from Egypt by the dunes of the Sinai desert, in the east it was bordered by the Syrian Arabian desert, and in the north it was marked by the city of Dan. Although described in the Bible as 'a land of milk and honey', Palestine was in fact a barren, rocky, neglected and inhospitable land with malaria-infested swamps. Nevertheless its strategic importance was immense, for it provided a bridge from Asia to Africa – a junction for traffic crossing from the south (Egypt) to the north (the highlands of Hittite Anatolia), to the east (Mesopotamian Anatolia) and to the west (Cyprus). Because of its strategic importance, Palestine had been, throughout its history, the battleground for military campaigns and invasions by the pharaohs, the kings of Assyria, Babylon and Persia, Alexander the Great, the emperors of Byzantium, the Arabs, the Crusaders, the Mamelukes and the Turks. Finally, British forces during the First World War had taken it from the Turks, who had ruled this land ever since Sultan Selim I occupied it in 1517.

It was under the British rule, which lasted from 1917 to 1948, that the struggle between Jew and Arab for the mastery and possession of the land of Palestine reached an unprecedented peak. A *modus vivendi* between the two peoples in Palestine had been always hard to achieve, because here was a clash of *rights* – the claim of two races to one land – and thus any solution could be found only on the lines of least injustice. In their struggle to win the argument and the land, the Jews claimed that the rocky land of Palestine which they called *Eretz Yisrael* was their traditional and spiritual home, one promised by God to Abraham and 'to [his] posterity'. But the Arabs of Palestine also regarded Palestine as their rightful home, for 'posterity', as they saw it, also included themselves, since they were the descendants of Ishmael, Abraham's son by his concubine Ketirah. But it was more than a conflict between two rights, for the Jews felt that *Eretz Yisrael* was their only safe haven after years of persecutions and endless pogroms in their native countries. The Arabs of Palestine, on the other hand, resented the idea that they, the majority of whom were Muslims with no tradition of anti-Semitism, had to pay the price for evils committed against the Jews by others, often within European Christendom. They also argued that in contrast with the Jews, who had been moving in and out of Palestine and had always been the minority in this land, they – the Arabs – had never abandoned the land, and had for hundreds of years constituted the majority of its population. This was true, but as the years passed and Jews continued to arrive in Palestine, the demographic scales tilted steadily in their favour. There were Jews who had come to Palestine to die and be buried in the Holy Land, others who had immigrated to Palestine to escape persecution, and there were also Zionists who had immigrated to Palestine in order to build a new Hebrew society which they wished would be, as Dr Chaim Weizmann, a Zionist and chemist at Manchester University, put it, 'as Jewish as England is English or America is American'.

Scrutinizing the speeches and writings of Zionist leaders of the late nineteenth century and the beginning of the twentieth, one comes to the inevitable conclusion that some of the Zionist leaders did truly believe that Palestine was derelict and empty – 'A land without a people waiting for a people without a land' as the Anglo-Jewish writer Yisrael Zwangwill put it. This, it is worth noting, was not an unusual thought, for some early Zionists suffered from the common Eurocentric illusion that territories outside Europe were in a state of political vacuum. But there were also Zionists who did realize that an Arab community existed in Palestine – that people married, brought up children, quarrelled, loved and died – however, they took it for granted that the native Arabs would welcome the new arrivals, whose zeal and skill and, of course, money would help develop the barren land for the benefit of all of its inhabitants. Theodor Herzl, a Budapest-born Viennese journalist and the father of modern Jewish nationalism (Zionism), who in 1896 had published an 86 page book called *The Jewish State*, knew, as emerges from his writings, that Palestine was not an empty land. But he thought that the Jews could buy the land from Arab landlords and spirit the 'penniless [Arab] population [living on this land] . . . across the border by procuring employment for [the Arab population] . . . while denying [them] any employment in our country'.[2] It is easy with hindsight to criticize this way of thinking, but we should bear in mind that such thinking was not unusual in the age of colonialism, when the rights of indigenous inhabitants were often ignored.

Persecuted, and often encouraged by their leaders to leave their native countries, Jews began pouring into Palestine. From 1882 to 1903, some 20,000–30,000 Jews arrived to join the small Jewish community, mostly religious, living especially in Tiberias, Jerusalem and Safed; and in the short period between 1904 and the beginning of the First World War another 35,000 Jews were added. It is estimated that in 1917 about 85,000 Jews lived in Palestine alongside 600,000 Arabs. Jewish immigration to Palestine was relatively restricted under Ottoman rule because the authorities suspected that the Jews were being used as cat's-paw by the West, but with the defeat of the Turks during the First World War, Jewish immigration to Palestine increased. From the end of the war to 1923 another 35,000 Jews came mainly from Russia, and in the second half of the 1920s the flow of Jews increased, with 82,000 arriving between 1925 and 1930. Troubles in Europe, notably the rise of Nazism in Germany, meant that immigration to Palestine gathered momentum, with 200,000 arrivals between 1932 and 1938. Here it is worth remarking that many of these Jewish immigrants would have preferred to go elsewhere, especially to America, one of the most sought-after destinations for immigrants, but the gates to America were half-shut. Among other reasons, this was because the leaders of the Zionist movement exerted all the influence they could muster to make sure that the US did not open up immigration to these Jews for the simple reason that they wanted to herd these same Jews to Palestine.

The mounting influx of Jewish refugees had quite dramatic-ally changed the demography of Palestine, and the balance had begun to shift remarkably in favour of the Jews. Jews, who comprised only 4 per cent of the total Palestinian population in 1882, formed 13 per cent in 1922, 28 per cent in 1935 and about 30 per cent in 1939. By 1947 there were 608,230 Jews in Palestine compared with about 1,364,330 Arabs. Not all the Jews remained in Palestine, where harsh living conditions were hard to bear, and there were periods where more Jews actually left Palestine than entered. But of those who did remain there emerged the future Jewish-Israeli leadership: David Ben Gurion (Gruen), who had arrived from Poland in 1906 and later became the first Prime Minister of Israel; Levi Eshkol (Shkolnik) who had arrived from the Ukraine in 1909 and later became the third Prime Minister; and Golda Meir (Meyerson), who had arrived from America in 1921 and would succeed Eshkol to the premiership.

Demographic modification aside, a geographical transformation was also under way in Palestine; for Jews not only poured into the country but also bought large tracts of its land. For this purpose, The Jewish National Fund (*Keren Ha'Kayemet* in Hebrew) was established in 1901 with the task of buying land in Palestine, and in 1908 the economist and agronomist Arthur Ruppin set up at Jaffa the first Zionist office, which bought land from Arab landlords. So successful was the Jewish policy of purchasing land, that in 1935 the quasi-religious politician and leader of the Arab Palestinians, the Grand Mufti of Jerusalem, Hajj Amin al-Husseini, had to issue a *fatwa*, which is a decree or a religious order, defining Arabs who sold land to Jews as apostates to be denied burial in Moslem cemeteries. This was to no avail, even though the growing demand led to the value of property in Palestine soaring, Jews had mustered the money and bought large tracts of it. It is estimated that between 1920 and 1939 Jews acquired 845,198 acres in Palestine, most of which belonged to absentee landowners, and towards the end of the 1930s they possessed around 1,533,400 acres. From a modest fifty-five Jewish settlements in 1920, the number had rocketed to 218 in 1939.

It perhaps deserves mention that the Jews did not, as is sometimes alleged, 'rob' the Arabs or 'steal' their land, but rather they bought it from them for hefty sums of money. As for the Arab aristocracy of landowners who had sold the land to the Jews, they did so voluntarily and with open eyes, and they must have known that for the Arab peasants who had been living on their lands for generations this would be a devastating blow. Indeed it proved to be so, for when the new owners of the land voluntarily became hewers of wood and drawers of water and worked the land themselves (they called it: *Avoda Ivrit*, 'Jewish work') – as a means of recovering contact with nature and also disproving the slander of their detractors that they were fit only for commerce and not for labour – they inevitably deprived Palestinian labourers of employment.

What made matters far worse and increased the anxieties of the Arabs of Palestine, was the fact that the massive influx of Jews and their purchase of large tracts of land in Palestine was accompanied by a gradual commitment of the British government to the idea of establishing a 'national home' for the Jews in Palestine. Most notable was the Balfour Declaration, approved by the British cabinet and enshrined in a letter dated 2 November 1917, which was sent by the British Foreign Secretary Arthur James Balfour to a prominent member of the Jewish community in England, Lord Rothschild. In this short but most significant letter the British minister expressed the support of His Majesty's Government for the idea of establishing a 'national home' – a term undefined by international law and a complete novelty – for the Jewish people. The subsequent commitment that this should not 'prejudice the civil and religious rights of existing non-Jewish communities in Palestine' did little to dispel the fear of the Arabs for their own future. Indeed, it angered them, for they, who were referred to in this 117-word letter as the 'existing non-Jewish communities in Palestine', formed at this time the overwhelming majority of the population – they made up around 87 per cent of the total population while the Jews were only 13 per cent – and the land of Palestine was theirs in the generally accepted sense of the word. What the Arabs feared, and with hindsight we know that they were right, was that as soon as a large Jewish population had built up in Palestine, the idea of a Jewish 'national home' would turn into that of a Jewish state. The Arabs, though, found some comfort in the joint Anglo-French declaration which was issued simultaneously in Palestine, Syria and Iraq on 7 November 1918, stating that 'The goal envisaged by France and Great Britain . . . is the complete and final liberation of the peoples who have for so long been oppressed by the Turks . . . and the setting up of national governments'. This was taken by the Arabs as a pledge for Arab independence in Palestine.

The British promise to the Jews of a 'national home' in Palestine was turned into an international commitment when the League of Nations, on 24 July 1922, reiterated the British pledge in a document which assigned a mandate of Palestine to Britain. On this Arthur Koestler commented in *Promise and Fulfilment*: 'The League requisitioned Palestine from its [Arab] owners to provide the Jews with a permanent abode, and appointed Britain to act as billeting officer'.[3] The promise to the Arabs expressed in the joint Anglo-French declaration of 7 November 1918 was all but forgotten. For the Jews the pledge of the international community was a significant political victory, for after all, the Balfour Declaration was without legal force because Britain had no sovereign rights over Palestine, had no authority to dispose of the land and thus her declaration was no more than a statement of its intentions. But now with the Balfour Declaration incorporated into the Palestine mandate, the British promise had received explicit international recognition. One can only be puzzled by how little thought was devoted to the Arab Palestinians, who were the overwhelming majority in Palestine, and by how much was promised to the Jews, who were the minority, by both the British and later the international community in issuing, respectively, the 1917 Balfour Declaration and the 1922 British Mandate. The explanation seems to be that those who endorsed these critical documents and sealed the future of the two communities, had all been nurtured on biblical reminiscences of the eternal bond between the children of Israel and their promised land, and that they knew next to nothing of the Arab community of Palestine.

It is ironic that in their growing opposition to the Jews, the Arabs of Palestine were now led by prominent Palestinian clans and families who had sold their lands to the Jews through middlemen at high profits, and thus visited on the Palestinians the very problems which were now causing such tensions with the Jews. In fact, tensions between the two peoples had already risen dangerously in the early 1920s. On 3 April 1920, for example, which was the first day of Passover, Arabs attacked Jews in the old town of Jerusalem – these were called the Nebi Mussa disturbances – and on 1 May 1921, disturbances in Jaffa led to the killing of nearly 200 Jews and 120 Arabs. A few quiet years followed, but then on 23 August 1929, Jews and Arabs clashed in Jerusalem and the next day Arabs killed fifty-nine men, women and children in Hebron. Arab dissatisfaction reached its peak between 1936 and 1939, a period known as 'The Arab Rebellion', when they began a general strike which soon turned into clashes, mainly with the British who had allowed Jews to enter Palestine, purchase land and establish the infrastructure for a future state.

The British authorities, the caretakers of Palestine, crushed the revolt, but overall they failed to calm the situation in Palestine, because their tendency to veer first one way and then the other, and their policy of appeasement which in practice meant endorsing the claims of the stronger invited even more violence from the parties involved. Thus when the British had allowed Jewish immigrants to enter Palestine they angered the Arabs, and in their attempts to appease the latter they angered the Jews. British attempts to find a way out of the dilemma and offer solutions to which both Arab and Jew could agree came to little. In August 1936, for example, the British government entrusted Lord Peel (grandson of Sir Robert Peel, the nineteenth-century British Prime Minister) with the mission of recommending a solution to the problem in Palestine. After investigating the matter, Peel published his report on 7 July 1937. It proposed that Palestine should be partitioned between Arabs and Jews. While the Jews accepted the proposal, the Arabs of Palestine rejected it; they were not prepared to give up Palestine either in part or in whole, which in retrospect seems to be a grave error of judgement, for their insistence on having all the land resulted, as we shall later see, in their losing it all.

In the summer of 1939, with increasing tension in Palestine, the British summoned an Arab–Jewish conference to try and sort out their differences; but the conference quickly broke down. The British government then imposed its own solution, expressed in a White Paper of May 1939 stating that a final batch of 75,000 Jews was to be admitted to Palestine between 1939 and 1944, and that, after this, further entry of Jews would be subject to Arab approval. Additionally, it empowered the High Commissioner of Palestine to prohibit the sale of land by Arabs to Jews in specified areas. The White Paper caused an uproar among the Jews, who turned on the British and accused them of retreating from previous pledges. Here without doubt the British government had miscalculated, for they were imposing restrictions on Jewish immigration to Palestine at a time when Jews in Europe were the first targets of the Nazis. As a result of the White Paper, the Jewish underground organizations, including Irgun but mainly the small but violent Lehi (the so called 'Stern

Gang'), viciously attacked the British in Palestine soon rendering the mandate unworkable.

At the close of the Second World War and with the ending of their rule in India, Britain's primary motive for staying in the Middle East had gone, and there seemed little reason for the British to pursue a policy in Palestine — 'a hell disaster' as Winston Churchill once described it — that imposed financial burdens (there were 100,000 British troops there), was difficult to implement, and was increasingly unpopular both at home and abroad. A growing number of British politicians — and they had broad British public support — now urged the government to lay the Mandate at the feet of the United Nations Organization and thereafter evacuate the country with which Britain had no connection or tradition. And indeed, even before a final decision regarding Palestine was made, the British government on 31 January 1947 ordered the evacuation from Palestine of all British women, children and male civilians in non-essential jobs. About two weeks later, on 14 February 1947, the British Foreign Secretary announced that his government intended to refer the Mandate of Palestine back to the two-year-old United Nations, the successor of the League of Nations; he repeated the announcement to the House of Commons on 18 February, and it was debated on the 25th.

'The Palestine question' was put on the agenda of the UN, whose assembly met on 28 April and on 15 May to discuss the matter. It then decided to appoint a special committee, called UNSCOP (United Nations Special Committee on Palestine), to investigate conditions in Palestine and decide what recommendations should be made to Britain as Mandatory Power. The committee duly arrived in Jerusalem on 16 June, stayed for five weeks and met Jewish representatives; the Arab Higher Committee, the body representing the Arabs of Palestine, boycotted it, arguing that the departure of the British should be followed by one thing only, which was the establishment of an Arab state on the entire land of Palestine. The boycott was a grave error of judgement, for the absence of the Arab side made it easier for the Jews to put a forceful case before the UN committee for partitioning the land with the Arabs and having their own state on part of Palestine. It is sometimes alleged that, in fact, the real intention of the Jews was to have the whole of Palestine (including parts allotted to the Arabs), but that they wished to obtain it in stages – first get what they could from the UN and then expand it by force. This claim is supported, for example, by a letter of Ben Gurion to his wife, where he says: 'Establish a Jewish state at once, even if it is not in the whole land . . . the rest will come in the course of time'.[4] That the Jewish hidden agenda was indeed to occupy all of Palestine was also believed by leading Palestinians. At a meeting in September 1947 with a British official in Lebanon, where he was in exile, the leader of the Arab Palestinians, Hajj Amin al-Husseini, said: 'No form of partition . . . would finally satisfy the Zionists. Whatever they got would merely be a springboard from which to leap on more'.

Back in Geneva, the UN committee produced a report of 67 printed foolscap pages in which it recommended that the Mandate for Palestine should be terminated at the earliest practicable date. But the committee was divided with regard to the nature of the regime which should be set up after the British departure. A minority of three suggested a federal state, and a majority of eight was in favour of passing a 'Judgement of Solomon' which would partition the land between Jews and Arabs but maintain the economic unity of Palestine.

On 29 November 1947 the matter was brought before the General Assembly of the UN, which voted 33 to 13, with 10 abstentions, in favour of Resolution 181 to partition Palestine. Britain abstained, all the Islamic Asian countries voted against, and both the USA and USSR – the latter regarding Britain as a greater menace than the USA in world politics – voted in favour. According to the UN partition resolution, the 10,000 square miles of Palestine was to be divided between Arabs – then numbering 1,364,330 including 127,000 Bedouin – who were to retain 4,300 square miles, and Jews – then numbering 608,230 – who were allotted 5,700 square miles. Jerusalem and Bethlehem were to come under United Nations control.

For the Jews this was a significant political victory, which could be compared in magnitude only to their success in obtaining the Balfour Declaration of 1917. For the Arabs of Palestine, however, the vote for partition was a devastating blow; they vowed to oppose it by force and called for a three-day protest in Palestine. In Haifa, where 70,000 Arabs were living alongside 70,000 Jews, an Arab gathering took place where a leading Palestinian, Sheikh Sabri Abdeen, announced: 'If the Jews are going to take our land then by God we will throw them into the sea' and he pointed to the Mediterranean which was only a few hundred metres away to the cheering, clapping and shooting-in-the-air of the crowd.[5] In such a charged atmosphere, the more moderate Palestinian Arabs such as the Nashashibi family (many of this moderate clan had previously been assassinated by fellow Arabs during the 1936–9 Arab rebellion), the Nablus group and the communists who were more willing to accept partition were silenced.

With the benefit of hindsight, it is obvious that the failure of the Arabs to accept the 1947 UN partition proposal was a colossal historical mistake, as was their previous rejection of the Peel partition plan of 1937. If they had accepted either, they could have had an independent Palestinian state alongside Israel. But this, as we know, was not to be the case.

## CIVIL WAR IN PALESTINE

Although significant, the UN partition resolution did not envisage the immediate creation of either a Jewish or an Arab state on the land of Palestine. Yet, rather than easing tension, the resolution to partition the land and the subsequent British decision,

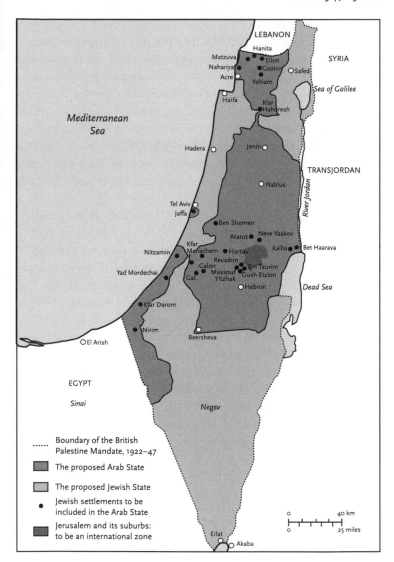

*Map 1* Palestine 1947: the UN Partition Plan

made on 4 December 1947, to depart on Friday 14 May 1948, had increased tensions between the peoples of Palestine and 'it was as if on a signal Arabs and Jews squeezed the trigger and exchanged fire'.[6] On 15 December 1947, Lieutenant General Sir Alan Cunningham, the British High Commissioner for Palestine, sent a top-secret memorandum to the British Colonial Secretary Arthur Creech-Jones, outlining the situation in Palestine in fearful detail. 'Situation now is deteriorating', he wrote, 'into a series of reprisals and counter-reprisals between Jews and Arabs, in which many innocent lives are being lost, the tempo of which may accelerate'.[7]

The initial phase following the UN resolution to partition Palestine was characterized mainly by Arab attacks on Jewish convoys and street fighting on the Jaffa–Tel Aviv border and in the Old City of Jerusalem. This was not yet a full-blown civil war but rather skirmishes and a vicious circle where an action was followed by a reprisal with disturbances and clashes between Jews and Arabs spreading to all parts of Palestine.

With all its energy directed to the evacuation and removal of some 210,000 tons of stores and a huge retinue of colonial administrators, the British in Palestine, under the command of Sir Gordon Macmillan, chose to stand aside and to protect only their own evacuation routes. Britain now simply washed its hands of the problems of Palestine and refused to assume responsibility for implementing the UN partition plan. And with the 'policeman' standing aside, the condition of Palestine deteriorated into anarchy, with Jews and Arabs fighting out their differences in what gradually slid into an all-out civil war which was to last about five months.

## The opposing forces at the outbreak of the civil war

On the eve of the civil war in Palestine, Jewish forces comprised Haganah, which was the largest underground organization of the

Yishuv, the Jewish community, and two smaller dissident organizations: the *Irgun Zvai Leumi*, better known as 'the Irgun' and *Lochamai Herut Yisrael*, known also as 'the Lehi' (or 'The Stern Gang'). The Haganah comprised 45,000 men and women, about 2,100 of them in the Palmach, making up the striking force of the organization. In the Irgun and the Lehi there were about 3,000 fighters and, although independent of Ben Gurion's Haganah, the two small organizations often coordinated their actions with the Haganah, as they did in the notorious battle at Deir Yassin. Expecting a strong Arab response to the UN resolution to partition the land of Palestine, the Jewish leadership under Ben Gurion began mobilizing the whole community, and just a day after the UN resolution it issued a decree calling on men and women between the ages of 17 and 25 (those born between 1922 and 1930) to service. On 22 January 1948, the Jewish leadership ordered that all those born between 1931 and 1932 were not to leave the country; a month later all those born between 1908 and 1932 were ordered to come forward and enlist. On 3 February, all Jews aged between 19 and 23 (born between 1925 and 1929) were called to serve. The new recruits were not ordered to join a specific underground organization – this could have caused an immediate controversy – rather to enlist to *Sherut Ha'am* (literally: 'Service of the Nation').

The Arab force in the civil war was made up of four components. First was the Arab Liberation Army (ALA), which had around 4,000 volunteers from Palestine and the neighbouring Arab countries, mainly Iraq and Syria. The ALA was organized and equipped by the Military Committee of the Arab League and was trained at the Syrian training centre, Katana. It marched into Palestine on 20 January 1948 from Jordan, and operated from two locations: Galilee, where it had two battalions comprising between 1,500 and 2,000 men; and Samaria, just west of the Jordan river, where it deployed about the same number of men.

The second element of the Arab force consisted of between 1,000 and 1,500 volunteers from the 'Moslem Brothers' and Egyptian youth organizations who had crossed from Egypt to Palestine, and operated in the southern part of the country and in and around Majdal (now called Ashkelon) and Yibne (now called Yebne).

The third element, some 5,000 men, was led by Abdall Quader al-Husseini, a relative of the Mufti of Jerusalem and perhaps the most charismatic and ablest Arab leader in Palestine; he was operating in the Jerusalem, Ramallah and Jericho areas. Husseini's force comprised irregular bands and masses of villagers – the Palestinian element was strong – and it also had some European elements, that is volunteers from Britain, Yugoslavia and Germany who had joined the Arab Palestinians in their fight against the Jews. Another Arab group, 3,000 at most, was led by Hassan Salemeh, who had been trained in Germany, had been parachuted into Palestine, and was operating in the Jaffa-Lydda-Ramleh area. All in all, the number of Arab para regulars, irregulars and volunteers can be estimated at 25,000–30,000 men; their weakness, though, was a lack of cooperation and central control.

## Aims and fighting

The principal aim of the Jews in Palestine in the period immediately after the UN resolution to partition Palestine, was to gain effective control over the territory allotted to them by the UN and to secure communication with thirty-three Jewish settlements which, according to the UN plan, fell outside the proposed Jewish state. For although the UN had partitioned the land between Jews and Arab Palestinians, there were still Jewish settlements which were to remain within the Arab area and, on the other hand, Arab villages on land allotted to the Jews. In contrast to Arab villages within Jewish areas, which were self-reliant, the Jewish settlements relied heavily on outside supplies, which made the keeping open of routes a necessity for them. Another aim of the Jewish forces was to prepare the ground for what seemed to be an inevitable invasion of neighbouring Arab regular armies the moment the British left Palestine. The General Staff of the Jewish forces devised what became known as 'Plan Dalet' (*Tochnit Dalet*), the principal objective of which was to consolidate control over areas allotted to the Jewish State and also to seize strategic positions to make it possible to block regular Arab armies in case they marched into Palestine. What is significant about 'Plan Dalet' – it was distributed to field commanders on 29 February and became a directive to all units on 10 March 1948 – is that, apart from envisaging the occupation of strategic positions, it also allowed for the occupation of Arab villages, towns and cities and, where necessary, the expulsion of their inhabitants. This, we should comment here, was a blank cheque for Jewish forces to expel Arab Palestinians, as indeed happened in the ensuing days of the war.

The Palestinians' strategic aim during the civil war was negative in nature, namely to prevent the implementation of the partition plan by disrupting and strangling Jewish lines of communication, and by cutting off Jewish settlements from localities and positions that were already occupied. These opposing aims of Jews and Arabs led to the 'battle of the roads' which raged in Palestine during the first half of 1948, with Jewish forces attempting to gain control of the communications roads and the Arabs of Palestine seeking to prevent them from achieving this.

In the initial stages of the civil war the Arabs gained the upper hand and succeeded in dictating the pattern of the struggle. By March 1948 they had cut off the entire Negev – allotted to the Jews by the UN – from the coastal plain, as well as most of Western Galilee and the Jerusalem area; they also succeeded in isolating many Jewish settlements within these regions from one another. So successful were these operations that the Arabs of Palestine came close to reaching their principal aim when, in

March 1948, British Colonial Secretary Creech-Jones told the British House of Commons that the Palestine situation was 'rapidly becoming insoluble' and on 19 March proposed that the UN rescind partition in favour of trusteeship. The US administration, too, frustrated by the deteriorating situation in Palestine, had joined the British call and declared, in mid-March, that since partition was hard to establish, a trusteeship should replace it. Only the Soviet Union remained constantly in favour of partition possibly because Moscow calculated that the creation of a Jewish State would undermine Western relations with the Arab States and thus provide for the Soviet Union a means of extending its influence in the Middle East, or even that a socialist Israel would become an ally. Anyway, the British-American view, aimed at replacing partition with trusteeship, dismayed the Jews, who saw their dream of establishing a state on the land allotted by the UN slipping away.

But soon the civil war began to take a new shape. In April 1948, with the war at its height, an attempt by the Arab Liberation Army to cut off the Haifa region and the Valley of Jezreel from the coastal plain failed (4 April) and Jewish forces proceeded with their own offensive, which proved to be eminently successful. In central Palestine, they broke open the road to Jerusalem ('Operation Nachshon', 3–15 April) and this allowed supplies of food and ammunition to get through to the Jews in the city. Elsewhere, all Arab towns and villages, and the mixed cities within the territory designated for the Jewish state, were overrun in rapid succession. Tiberias was captured on 18 April, and the vital port of Haifa fell into Jewish hands on 22–3 April. Most of Haifa's 70,000 Arabs fled, many to Acre, others to Lebanon. Between 25 and 27 April, Irgun forces attacked the all-Arab town of Jaffa, which was meant to be included in the future Arab state. At first they were checked by British troops, but once the British had left, Irgun forces took the town (13 May 1948) whose original 90,000 inhabitants were reduced to only 5,000

– most of them fled to Gaza by sea. In northern Palestine, the town of Safed was occupied, and on the night of 13–14 May all Western Galilee came under Jewish control. The all-Arab town of Acre – like Jaffa it was meant to be included in the future Arab state – was besieged by Jewish forces and capitulated on 17 May. The Arab forces in Palestine were now bewildered by defeat, and retreated, with their leadership confused and disorganized.

## Massacres and refugees

The civil war in Palestine was vicious, cruel and littered with atrocities. It involved immense human suffering and a degree of blatant brutality never before seen in Jewish–Arab relations in Palestine, which had usually seen the two peoples living side-by-side in relative peace. On 31 December 1947, taking revenge for the killing of six of their fellows by the Irgun, Arabs attacked and killed thirty-nine Jews at the Haifa oil refineries. The Haganah responded in kind, attacking the village of Blad-el-Sheikh, where it killed more than 60 Arabs, including women and children. At the beginning of February 1948, more than ten Arabs and two British policemen were killed in an explosion near the Jaffa Gate in Jerusalem and, on 22 February, 60 Jews were killed by a car-bomb explosion on Jerusalem's Ben Yehuda street. The Jewish leader David Ben Gurion, visiting the scene, blamed Jewish thugs for this. As he put it: 'Such a destruction . . . I could not recognize the streets . . . But I could not forget that our thugs and murderers (meaning members of the Irgun and the Lehi) had opened the way', that is, brought about this Arab reaction by their own terrorist actions.[8] On 11 March, 17 Jews were killed and forty were injured by a bomb in the courtyard of the Jewish Agency in Jerusalem and, on 9 April, 110 Palestinians – men, women and children – were killed by Jews in the small village of Deir Yassin just west of Jerusalem, at least 25 of them being massacred in cold blood. Four days later, on 13 April, the Arabs took revenge by attacking a Jewish convoy of medical staff on its way to Mount Scopus, leaving 77 dead.

What is so significant about the civil war in Palestine is that it was then that what became known as 'the Palestinian refugee problem' started. With its leadership and the middle class – those who had the money to do so – leaving Palestine to take what they believed to be temporary refuge in neighbouring Arab countries, and with the Jews advising the poorer Palestinians to follow suit and using force to expel the others – the Arab Palestinians moved out of Palestine. Exaggerations by Arab leadership of Jewish atrocities, as happened after the events at Deir Yassin, was also a catalyst, leading the Palestinians to flee whenever a Jewish soldier was seen approaching their village.[9]

The demographic scales were now tilting in favour of the Jews, and with the *en masse* departure of the Arabs, Jews became the majority in the land of Palestine. While there was no explicit decision by the Jewish leadership to expel the Palestinians, there was nevertheless a tacit agreement that this should be done. In a meeting with military commanders, Prime Minister Ben Gurion said: 'In each attack [against Arabs] it is necessary to give a decisive blow, ruining the place, kicking away the inhabitants'.[10] It is estimated that about 750,000 Palestinians left Palestine during the war (160,000 remained behind) and their homes were taken by new Jewish immigrants; as Ben Gurion recorded in his war diary: 'New immigrants [we] put in Arab houses'.[11] This was the method the Jewish leadership employed to absorb the new Jewish immigrants who, in spite of the ongoing civil war, poured copiously into Palestine.

Although highly successful, the period which had followed the UN partition resolution was for the Jews in Palestine, many of whom were European refugees, traumatic. During the six months from November 1947 to mid-1948, 1,308 Jewish soldiers and 1,100 civilians perished.[12] This is a very high toll, given the relatively low number of Jews in Palestine and the relatively short duration of the fighting.

## PROCLAMATION, END OF BRITISH MANDATE AND REGIONAL WAR

On 14 May 1948, Prime Minister David Ben Gurion recorded in his war diary: 'At four in the afternoon the Jewish independence was proclaimed and the state [of Israel] was established', and he added 'Its fate is in the hands of the armed forces'. From the thirty-two-minute ceremony where he had declared the establishment of Israel, Ben Gurion went straight to the 'Red House', the headquarters of the Israeli forces on Tel Aviv beach, to discuss with his military commanders the deteriorating situation. Declaring a state was a bold and courageous move, given the threat of Arab neighbouring states to prevent by force the establishment of a Jewish state, even on that part of Palestine which had been allotted to the Jews by the UN. It also seemed, at the time, a suicidal move, given that US Secretary of State George Marshall had warned the Jews that America would not consider itself responsible for the consequences of their declaring a state and would not 'bail you out' if attacked by Arab neighbours.[13]

That Friday night, just half an hour before midnight, Lieutenant-General Sir Alan Cunningham, the seventh and last British High Commissioner for Palestine, sailed in HMS *Euryalus* from the bay of Haifa for England. The birth of the State of Israel and the end of more than thirty years of British rule in Palestine took place on a single day. In fact, the state of Israel was proclaimed even *before* the official termination of the Mandate. The reason being that the Mandate was due to expire on Friday at midnight, and because this was during the Jewish Sabbath, it was decided to bring forward the proclamation ceremony. These two events were significant for two main reasons. First, they came to symbolize the transformation of the status of Jews in Palestine from a community to an independent state, soon to be recognized by the international community. Second, these two events were the catalyst which transformed a strictly localized conflict – until the departure of the British and the proclamation of Israel the Jewish–Arab struggle had remained essentially a communal war – into a full-blown regional confrontation which also involved neighbouring Arab states and their regular armies.

That night, American President Harry Truman recognized the Jewish state. This was a major development, and vital for Israel, because neither the UN decision to partition Palestine nor Ben Gurion's unilateral declaration of independence gave any international status to the Jewish state. A recognition by a superpower – as the United States was after the Second World War – meant that, at least symbolically, the newly established state of Israel was accepted into the family of nations. At five in the morning on 15 May, while giving his positive reaction to the American recognition in a Tel Aviv radio studio, Ben Gurion could hear the Egyptian bomber planes overhead.[14] By now the Arab Legion, consisting of four well-trained regiments, was already on the march into the West Bank, an area allotted to the Palestinians by the UN. It was dispatched to there personally by King Abdullah who just a few minutes before midnight arrived at the eastern side of the Allenby bridge. With the formal expiry, at midnight of the British Mandate, the King took out his pistol, fired a shot into the air and shouting "Forward" he dispatched his troops across the Jordan river to the West Bank. That day, which was a Saturday, the Egyptian government sent a telegram to the President of the UN Security Council, announcing that Egyptian armed forces had entered Palestine and were engaged in 'an armed intervention'. On Sunday 16 May the Arab League sent a cablegram making similar statements on behalf of the Arab states.

By world standards the war which was now developing in Palestine–Israel was a small-scale, primitive confrontation conducted by poorly-equipped and ill-trained units. For his invasion of Russia – 'Operation Barbarossa' – in 1941, Hitler had assembled 160 divisions; in the Palestine war the biggest unit to take part in battle was a brigade, and actual fighting often involved smaller units. The German armoured strength in the Barbarossa invasion totalled 3,550 tanks; in the Palestine war the Israelis had no tanks at all and the Arabs had only a few primitive ones. Nevertheless, for the parties involved, in particular for the Israelis, the war was perceived, rightly or wrongly, as a life-or-death struggle. It was a war fought all over the country in separate battles – a see-saw struggle with many changes of fortune.

It is worth looking at the forces, Israeli and Arab, which were now confronting each other in Palestine, to demolish what is perhaps the biggest myth with regard to this first all-out Arab–Israeli war.

## Forces and weapons

Contrary to popular belief, the 1948 war between Israeli forces and the invading regular Arab armies was not one between 'the few [Israelis]' and 'the many [Arabs]', or, as it is often put, a clash between David (Israel) and Goliath (the Arabs). The root of this popular, though utterly erroneous, notion lay in the Israeli practice of referring to the potential of the Arabs rather than to the actual number of troops they put into the field. By confusing the issue, the Israeli leadership, in its war of words and attempts to gain the sympathy of the world and its own people, had for many years knowingly ignored the fact that ratios among adversaries do not merely reflect population ratios, and that a high degree of manpower mobilization can make up for the quantitative demographic inferiority of a small nation like Israel. Indeed, during the 1948 war, Israel had mobilized almost its entire resources and ablest population, while the more numerous Arabs had utilized only a small fraction of their huge potential.

The number of Israeli troops committed to battle on the eve of the Arab invasion was more or less equal to that of the Arabs, but then, while the number of Arab troops increased only slightly, the number of Israelis grew steadily and dramatically. A breakdown shows that the total strength of the invading Arab armies was about 23,500 troops, made up of 10,000 in the Egyptian army, 4,500 in the Arab Legion of Transjordan, 3,000 Syrians, 3,000 Iraqis and 3,000 Lebanese and Arab Liberation Army (ALA) troops; there was also a token contingent from Saudi Arabia. Compared with these numbers, Israel, as Ben Gurion notes in his diary of the war, had committed a total of 29,677 men and women to battle. But then, with the progressive mobilization of Israeli society and the average monthly arrival of 10,300 new immigrants, the number of available fighters steadily grew. On 4 June 1948, the number of Israeli troops was, according to Ben Gurion, 40,825; and on 17 July it grew to 63,586. On 7 October 1948, these numbers swelled to 88,033, and by 28 October reached more than 92,275. On 2 December the number of Israeli soldiers on the field was 106,900; on 23 December it stood at 107,652, and on 30 December the number had risen to 108,300 (10,259 of them women). Jewish volunteers from abroad – Mahal – also joined, and although their number was relatively low, at most 5,000, they nevertheless provided valuable technical expertise. By the end of the war Israel's fighting force was larger in absolute terms than that of the Arabs, and as John Bagot Glubb correctly observed:

> the common impression that the heroic little Israeli army was fighting against tremendous odds (one army against seven armies was one of the expressions used) was not altogether correct. The Israeli forces were, generally speaking, twice as numerous as all the Arab armies put together.[15]

In weaponry and firepower, however, the Arabs had a clear edge. The total inventory of the Haganah at the start of the war consisted of 22,000 rifles of various calibres, 1,550 light and medium machine guns, 11,000 largely home-made submachine guns, 195 three-inch calibre infantry mortars, 682 two-inch mortars, 86 PIAT (Projector Infantry Anti-Tank – a crude man-portable device of armour-piercing explosive charges) and five old 65mm field guns. A few tanks and aircraft still awaited shipment in Europe. Egypt, according to Israeli estimates, had 48 field guns, 25–30 armoured cars, 10–20 tanks, and 21–25 air-craft. Iraq had 48 field guns, 25–30 armoured cars, and 20 aircraft. Syria had 24 field guns, 36 armoured cars, 10–20 tanks and 14 aircraft. Jordan had 24 field guns and 45 armoured cars; and Lebanon 8 field guns and 9 armoured cars.

But as in manpower, so with weaponry; as the war progressed the balance steadily tipped in favour of the Israelis. A fund-raising mission by Golda Meir to America raised $50 million, which was used to buy arms, and ships loaded with weapons were purchased and sent to Israel by such people as Ehud Avriel. In New York, a team headed by Teddy Kollek – later the long-serving Mayor of Jerusalem – bought aeroplanes, took them to pieces and, with the help of the Mafia, and under the nose of the FBI, shipped the precious weapons to Israel. Israelis not only purchased weapons, but they also took measures to prevent the Arabs from adding arms to their own arsenals. In Bari, Italy, on 9 April 1948, Israeli agents executed 'Operation Booty 1' and sunk the ship Lino, which was packed with 8,000 rifles designated for Syria. Also in Italy, on 18 September 1948, Israeli agents broke into a garage where they destroyed four aeroplanes which were awaiting shipment to Egypt. Additionally, Israel developed its own weapons industry, which included chemical and biological weapons.[16]

There were, apart from manpower and equipment, other fac-tors which affected the character of the battle. The invading Arab armies had the advantage of being fresh in comparison with the Israelis, who were exhausted after five months of bloody civil war in Palestine. Moreover, the invading armies were relatively homogenous, with commanders and troops communicating in the same language, while the Israelis suffered language difficulties, as many troops were new immigrants, who could not speak Hebrew. The weather also played an important part. The summer of 1948 was extremely hot and harsh, and Israeli troops, many of whom had just arrived from cold Europe, found it too oppressive.[17] While the invading Arab armies had the tactical advantage of surprise, the Israelis had the advantage of interior lines of communications and fortified settlements which provided useful bases of operations.

Turning to the fighting itself, we see not only that the Arab invaders were inferior in numbers to the Israelis, but also that they failed to coordinate their moves and to prepare themselves properly for war. They also underestimated the determination of their opponents, all of which explains their total failure to dislodge the Israelis.

## Fighting

The invading Arab armies of Syria, Iraq, Lebanon, Egypt, Transjordan and a contingent force from Saudi Arabia had started from different directions, heading towards the heart of the Jewish state and the lands allotted to the Palestinians by the UN in November 1947. Had they coordinated their operations better and concentrated their offensive, the outcome of the struggle could have been different. In the event, however, there was coordination neither of operational plans nor of movement and concentration of forces, reflecting both the lack of common interest of the invaders and the divided purposes in the minds of the Arab leaders, who were suspicious of each other's intentions. All regarded Jordan's King Abdullah with intense suspicion, and rightly so, for the King was far more concerned to seize the land west of the river Jordan, which had been allotted to the Palestinians, than to destroy Israel. Abdullah even dispatched his Prime Minister to the British Foreign Minister to explain that his intention was only to take the West Bank to which Bevin replied: 'It seems the obvious thing to do. But don't go and invade the areas allotted to the Jews'.[18] The British commander of the Arab Legion later confirmed that the Jordanian troops were indeed instructed 'To occupy the central and largest area of Palestine allotted to the Arabs by the 1947 partition'.[19] This is a most significant statement, for it shows that rather than five Arab armies attacking the Israelis, there had been only four – Egypt, Syria, Iraq and Lebanon – and rather than intending to destroy the newly born state of Israel, the Arab Legion had crossed the Jordan river with the aim of partitioning the land by seizing the territory allotted by the UN to the Palestinians.

Lack of coordination among the invading forces is reflected in testimonies of Arab troops who took part in this war. Mohsein Abdel Khalek, a captain in the Egyptian army and later a prime minister of that country, recalls how

> The Jews were attacking us from the flank that the Iraqis were supposed to be protecting. We discovered that the Iraqi army had withdrawn, without even telling us. We had to shorten our lines, else the Egyptian army would have been destroyed. It was the turning point in the war.[20]

Thus, although Israel suffered war on three fronts, she fought in effect separate enemies among whom there was little coordination. The invading armies also suffered from lack of preparation – they had simply neglected to prepare themselves for such an operation. The Egyptian army, for example, which was considered the most powerful of all Arab regular armies, had less than two weeks to prepare itself for the war and everything had to be improvised in haste. Abdel Ghani Kanout, an Egyptian officer during that war, recalls: 'We went to the front on horseback . . . we did not have enough food for the horses so we had to send them back during the war. So overnight my unit was transformed from a cavalry unit to an infantry unit'.[21] Worse still, the invading Arab armies had a poor opinion of the Jews and underestimated their strength and determination. Adel Sabit, a cousin of King Farouk and the liaison between the King and the Arab League, recalls: 'We were complacently expecting the Jews to run away the moment they saw us . . . we thought it would be a pushover'. And Mourad Ghaleb, another Egyptian officer: 'We thought that the Jews were not courageous . . . not fighters'.[22] And Lieutenant-General John Bagot Glubb, the British commander of the Arab Legion: '[The Arabs] believed themselves to be a great military people, and regarded the Jews as a nation of shopkeepers. . . . [The Arabs] assumed that they would find no difficulty in defeating the Jews'.[23] The Israelis, however, determined to win the war – for they felt themselves with their backs to the wall – exploited the confusion on the Arab side, and after less than four weeks of fierce fighting they had managed to withstand the initial critical moments of the invasion.

While the fighting was still raging, important organizational and structural changes were taking place in the Israeli forces. Mobilization was completed, and on 31 May 1948 Prime and Defence Minister Ben Gurion published an Order of the Day officially establishing the Israeli Defence Force (IDF, or *Tzhal* in Hebrew) as the sole armed force of the state. This meant that the Irgun and the Lehi – the dissident underground groups led, respectively, by Menachem Begin and a committee of Lehi members, Nathan Yelin Mor, Yisrael Eldad and Yitzhak Shamir – had to disband and its men and weapons to be incorporated into the IDF, the nucleus of which was the Haganah. Disarming the dissidents and restoring law-abiding habits – taking the law into one's own hands had become a custom hallowed by patriotism throughout the decades of British rule in Palestine – was not an easy task for Ben Gurion's government. Indeed, the attempt to dissolve the dissident groups and divert their weapons to the IDF led to a severe deterioration of relations between these organizations and the government, to the point where a Jewish civil war seemed imminent. But this was avoided thanks to the willingness of Irgun's commander, Menachem Begin, to call off his troops and agree to their complete integration with the IDF; the Lehi would be disbanded in September 1948.

The first three crucial weeks of fierce fighting between Arabs and Israelis ended in a truce which was negotiated by the Swedish UN mediator Count Folke Bernadotte. The Arabs had objected to stopping the fighting on the grounds that the Israelis might exploit the respite to regroup, strengthen their defences and obtain weapons. The Israelis, on the other hand, welcomed the possibility of a truce so that they could snatch a breathing space and reorganize themselves. Fearing UN sanctions, the Arabs reluctantly accepted the truce which came into effect on 11 June 1948 at 10 a.m. Four days later on 15 June Ben Gurion recorded in his war diary the arrival of ten 75mm guns, ten light tanks with 37mm guns, 19 65mm guns and four 20mm automatic guns. During the truce a highly centralized command system was also set up, and from his office in Tel Aviv, Ben Gurion's orders passed through GHQ to the four regional commands – North, Centre, East and South – which were functioning as operational fronts.

As the time approached for the truce to expire, the Arab League Political Committee met in Cairo and decided, under pressure from the Egyptian Prime Minister Nokrashy Pasha, to renew the fighting with the Israelis. Efforts by the UN mediator Count Bernadotte to renew the truce failed, and he recorded in his diary: 'They [the Arabs] totally rejected my proposal to agree to prolong the truce'.[24] Upon realizing that the truce would not be renewed, the Israelis took the initiative and struck on 9 July,

two days before the ceasefire was due to expire. Now – as the
Arabs rightly feared when they objected to having a truce – the
Israelis were even better organized and equipped with new
weapons.

Fighting – particularly concentrated in the area of Tel-Aviv –
was raging for ten successive days during which the battle clearly
went in Israel's favour. Led by a young military commander,
Moshe Dayan, later a chief of staff of the Israeli army and defence
minister, Israeli forces occupied the Arab towns of Lydda (11–12
July) and Ramleh (12 July) – both of which had been allotted to
the Arabs by the UN Partition Plan – expelling their 50,000
inhabitants and thus making more space for settling new Jewish
immigrants. This major expulsion of Palestinians was carried
out with the tacit approval of Premier Ben Gurion, as is recorded
by Yitzhak Rabin – then a military commander who took part in
the operation – in a piece which was censored from his
published memoirs:

> We walked outside [the headquarters], Ben Gurion accompany-
> ing us. Allon [the commander of central command] repeated
> his question: 'What is to be done with the [Arab] population [of
> Ramleh and Lydda]?' Ben Gurion waved his hand in a gesture
> which said: 'Drive them out!' Allon and I had a consultation. I
> agreed that it was essential to drive the inhabitants out. We
> took them on foot towards Bet Horon road. . . . The population
> did not leave willingly. There was no way of avoiding the use of
> force and warning shots in order to make the inhabitants
> march the ten to fifteen miles to the point where they met with
> the Arab Legion.[25]

One of those expelled was George Habash – years later the leader
of the Popular Front for the Liberation of Palestine (PFLP):

> They directed us to a specific road . . . there were road blocks
> manned by Israeli soldiers every 100 metres to make sure that

no one diverted. This went on until we arrived at the outskirts
of Lydda (now Lod). There we found a large number of [Israeli]
soldiers. They put us in rows and started searching each person, a body search . . . they were not just looking for weapons
but also tried to take money.[26]

The expelled Arabs were not allowed back to their homes, for
what the Israelis wanted was to have the land without its
inhabitants so they could establish an exclusive Jewish community. In a meeting of the Israeli cabinet on 16 June 1948,
Prime Minister Ben Gurion told ministers: 'War is war. We did
not start the war. They did. Do we have to allow the enemy back
so they could make war against us? They lost and fled and I will
oppose their return also after the war'.[27]

On 19 July 1948, a second UN truce came into effect, but by
this time the Israelis were well on the offensive, while the Arabs
were exhausted and demoralized and had no alternative but to
sue for a truce. Military commander Rabin recorded in his
memoirs: '[The Arabs] did not incline to renew the war . . . we
estimated that the Egyptians were not interested in renewing
it'.[28] But to build on their previous successes, the Israelis now
wished to continue the struggle and to fight on, especially in
the Negev, which could provide Israel with much space to
accommodate Jewish immigrants.

On the night of 15 October, under the command of Yigal
Allon, an Israeli army launched – in breach of the truce – 'Operation Yoav' which was aimed at breaking into the Negev.
Beersheva, the capital of the Negev, fell into their hands on 21
October, and two months later, on the night of 22–3 December,
they attacked again; and later, on 5–10 March 1949, they
struck again in the Negev, reached Eilat and occupied it. This
was significant for, by seizing Eilat, Israel had driven a wedge
between the east and the west Arab world, thus preventing Egypt
from having a direct land bridge to Jordan. In the north of the

country, during 29–31 October 1948, four Israeli brigades had penetrated into Lebanon and moved up to the Litani river, destroying on its way the Arab Liberation Army, as well as Lebanese and Syrian units – this was 'Operation Hiram'.

All in all the war lasted one year, three months and ten days and cost Israel $500 million, compared with $300 million for the Arabs. There had been three separate rounds of fighting between December 1947 and March 1949, interrupted by two truces imposed by the UN. The Israeli forces occupied about 2,500 square miles of Arab land, which was added to the 5,600 square miles allocated to them by the UN in November 1947. According to the UN partition resolution, about 55 per cent of the land was to be given to the Jews and 45 per cent to the Arabs, but when the war ended Israel controlled almost 80 per cent of the land. Israel – odd though it seems – had managed to keep these occupied territories without serious protest or international outcry – this was not to happen again in future wars. Egypt retained the Gaza Strip, and Jordan's King Abdullah the West Bank of the river Jordan, which he annexed to his kingdom in 1950. For all practical purposes Palestine was partitioned; not, however, as the UN had envisaged, between Jews and Arab-Palestinians, but rather between the Israelis and the Arab states which had, apparently, invaded the land in support of the Palestinians. These last were the big losers in this war, for they had become refugees in camps in Gaza, the West Bank, and other neighbouring Arab states.

When the war ended, Israelis and Arab representatives of the invading armies met on the island of Rhodes where, as Moshe Dayan of the Israeli delegation later recalled, 'Good food, spring weather, enchanting scenery . . . hundreds of butterflies of all sizes and colours' lent a 'fairy tale air' to the tough negotiations on achieving armistice agreements between the opposing parties.[29] The talks were tough because there was no clear victor in this war. Israel had withheld the Arab invasion and beaten Lebanon and Egypt, but both Syria and Jordan had done well. The Syrian army had managed to cross the international border – agreed between France and Britain in 1923 – and occupy land which had been allotted by the UN to the Jewish state. The Arab Legion, as has been shown, seized the West Bank and kept East Jerusalem. Thus in contrast, for instance, to the situation after the First World War, where the victors were able to impose 'peace' on Germany at Versailles, here there had been no clear winner, and reaching an agreement had to involve give-and-take between the parties.

Nonetheless, on 24 February 1949, Egypt was the first to sign an armistice agreement with Israel, and on 23 March 1949, after Israel agreed to pull out of 14 Lebanese villages it had occupied during the last stage of the war, Lebanon signed on the dotted line. On 3 April 1949, after four weeks of negotiations, Israel and Transjordan signed an agreement. Negotiations between Israel and Syria ended when, under international pressure, Syria was forced to agree to withdraw its forces from the land it had occupied west of the international border, which now became a demilitarized zone; Israeli and Syrian representatives signed on 20 July 1949. Iraq, however, refused to sign an armistice agreement with Israel, and its forces on the West Bank were replaced by those of the Transjordan Arab Legion, with some of the land under Iraqi occupation being transferred to Israeli hands.

The armistice agreements were seen as temporary settlements which would later be replaced by permanent peace agreements. But the conflict between Israel and the Arabs and Palestinians was bound to continue, for the great problem which had caused the war in the first place – the struggle between Jews and Arab Palestinians for mastery of the land – was still unresolved at the war's end. Worse still, the war had created a particular problem that was to fester and provoke unrest for more than 50 years: the Palestinian refugees.

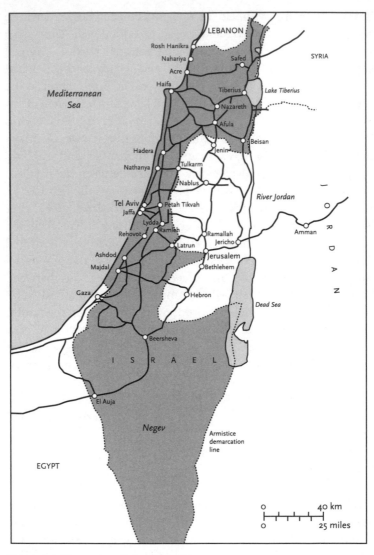

*Map 2* Israel 1949: armistice lines

## THE IMPACT OF WAR ON THE ISRAELIS

'The War of Independence' or 'The War of Liberation', as the Israelis refer to the 1947–9 war, was perceived by them as a life-or-death struggle. But with the benefit of hindsight we can state that if any danger of extinction did exist – when the country's fate was still in the balance – it was only during the very short period between 15 May 1948, the day the regular Arab armies invaded, and 11 June, the day the first UN truce came into effect. This three-week period was the time when there was still a clear Arab superiority in weaponry and firepower – though as we have shown, not in manpower – and when it was also unclear how the freshly recruited Israeli soldiers, many of whom were newly arrived immigrants, would perform. However, once the Israeli forces had checked the Arab onslaught, absorbed new weapons, increased their own weapons production, and trained immigrants and volunteers, the worst was over and Israeli superiority in manpower and weapons combined with short internal lines of communication and high motivation to defeat the Arabs.

That said, this bloodiest of all Israel's wars was to have a most profound and longstanding impact on the psyche of the people of Israel. A particularly significant effect of the war on the collective spirit of the Israelis concerned the fact that it was fought only a short time after the terrible tragedy that had befallen the Jewish people in Europe, with the massacre of 5.4 million of them at the hands of the Nazis.[30] Moreover, in sharp contrast to most of Israel's future wars, the majority of the Israeli population was effectively on the front-line, facing war on its doorstep and exposed to bombardment by enemy aeroplanes; Tel Aviv was bombed 15 times, with several hundred civilian casualties.

The war cost Israel 5,682 dead, 20 per cent of them civilians and about 8 per cent women. This amounts to about 1 per cent of the total Jewish population in Palestine-Israel, and is indeed a high ratio if compared, for example, to the number of casualties in the First World War, where France lost 34 per thousand, Germany 30 per thousand, Austro-Hungary 10 per thousand, Britain and Italy 16 per thousand, and Russia 11 per thousand. Taking into consideration that the First World War was nearly three and a half times as long as the 1948 war – 51 months compared with 15 – then it can be said that the ratio of Israeli dead compared with the population was more than Germany's and closer to France's. There were 1,260 women widowed, 2,290 children orphaned and 3,000 soldiers wounded, of whom as many as 360 became mentally ill, which is as high as Britain during the First World War.

The loss of so many young men – the fittest of their society – was perhaps the main feature of this war, but ironically, it had very little long-term effect on the growth of the Israeli population. A war like this, in which many perish, often causes a reduction in the number of marriages and inevitably leads to a sharp dip in the birth rate. But in Israel, the destruction of an entire generation did not lead to what had happened in Europe after the First World War – a 'surplus of women', or rather a 'deficit of men'. The reason for the absence of this problem after the 1948 war was that the death of so many men was compensated for by the waves of new immigrants arriving in Israel, which in 1948 amounted to 118,000, in 1949 to 239,000 and in 1950–1 to 343,000. In crude terms, for every Israeli killed, several more Jews had come. And thus although in 1948, the most hard-fought year of the war, the number of marriages went down to 10.85 per thousand – compared with 12.98 per thousand in 1947 – it went up (and again in spite of the sheer number of young men who died) in 1949 to 13.40 per thousand (even higher than in 1947!), and up again to 14.54 per thousand in 1950. The annual birth rate, which between 1947 and 1948 went down from 30.55 per thousand to 26.31 per thousand, had risen in 1949 to 29.95 per thousand and went up further in

1950. The young Israeli nation demonstrated its resilience, and a closer look shows that in all walks of life there had been little change, even during the most intensive months of the war. The number of deaths in the Jewish population (excluding deaths resulting directly from the war) was stable: 6.36 per thousand in 1946; 6.58 per thousand in 1947; 6.46 per thousand in 1948; this shows that in spite of the dreadful war the standards of medical care remained intact. Jerusalem was under siege, but there was no hunger, and social life continued to function more or less normally.

Nevertheless, the war provided succeeding generations of Israelis with plenty of material for mythology and legend with which to nourish their future. But not all that was told was strictly true. The Israeli soldier emerging from this war was portrayed as a fighter always playing a fair game – a sort of an English gentleman who even in the heat of the battle never stabs his enemy in the back. In reality, however, the Israeli soldiers, contrary to the myth, had behaved no differently from many other armies – they looted, expelled, massacred and raped. In Acre a group of Israeli soldiers raped an Arab woman, killed her father and injured her mother; and this, as we learn from the war diary of Prime Minister Ben Gurion, was not an isolated case.[31]

The experience of the war stamped a sense of unity and common destiny on the psychic fibre of the Israelis, who had emerged from it with a new national consciousness, a unity of purpose overriding party conflict and internal feuds. What further cemented unity and emphasized the common destiny of the people of Israel was the huge effort which had followed the war to commemorate those who had died. The Ministry of Defence assembled details of those who perished and produced 4,520 obituaries, collected in a book entitled *Yizkor* ('Remembrance'). Another official memorial was *Gevilei Esh* ('Scrolls of Fire'), which included 455 items: poetry and stories written by those who had died. It was after this war that the term *Mishpachat*

*Ha'schol*, meaning 'The Family of Breavement', was coined to emphasize that the entire nation was one family grieving its dead. The number of memorials erected to commemorate the dead had reached 1,321 by the mid-1950s; at least one out of every three dead soldiers was individually commemorated.

Gunther Rothenberg, in *The Anatomy of the Israeli Army*, summarizes the story of the 1948 war of independence in a fine passage: 'Both the realization that his life and that of his family literally were at stake . . . fuelled by the pronouncements of Arab politicians about a "war of extermination" stiffened the will [of Israelis] to fight'.[32] And this will to fight was further strengthened by the dominant presence of the Holocaust generation. For as Bernard Lewis correctly observed in *Semites and Anti-Semites*:

> For most Jews, that genocide was the most shattering event in their history . . . the central experience of their personal lives, and their thoughts and actions are dominated by the knowledge that what has happened once can happen again, and by the determination that it must not.[33]

Indeed, feeling that they were with their backs to the wall facing enemies determined to destroy them, and with the experiences of the Holocaust still fresh in mind, Israelis in the coming years would continue – as they had done during the first war with the Arabs – to rally behind the flag and its leadership, to take up arms when asked, and to fight with determination and desperation, believing themselves to be fighting for their very survival.

# 2

# A NATION-IN-ARMS

## 1949–67

In the days, months and years that followed the 1948 War of Independence, the Israeli government had to face two supreme tasks. The first was to absorb the tide of destitute, physically and mentally handicapped Jewish immigrants, who poured copiously into the country following the British departure and Ben Gurion's announcement that the 1939 White Paper and all immigration laws based upon it were null and void. Ben Gurion's statement was reinforced by the 'Law of Return' which was passed by the Knesset on 5 July 1950 and said that: 'Every Jew has the right to immigrate to the country'. This became one of the most important laws ever passed by the Israeli parliament, for it opened the gates of Israel and enabled every Jew to come and join in the attempt to build a nation and a state and to become automatically one of its citizens.

During the first seven and a half months of the state's

existence, 101,819 Jewish immigrants arrived, and they were added to in 1949 by 239,076 new arrivals, in 1950 by 170,597, in 1951 by 172,245 and between 1952 and 1955 by 92,204 Jews; in addition there were 88,338 Jewish births during these last four years. Entire Jewish communities had left their homes and countries of origin and immigrated to Israel. But rather than being a voluntary step, it was often one of desperation, for the truth is that the majority of these Jews, especially those living in Middle Eastern countries, were pushed out of their native countries by outraged Arabs humiliated by the victory of the Jews in 1948, rather than being attracted by the newly established Jewish state. Thus the entire Yemenite Jewry, a total of 49,000, was transferred to Israel in 'Operation Magic Carpet' in 1949, and the majority of Iraqi Jewry, a total of 100,000, were airlifted to Israel in 'Operation Ezra and Nehemiah' between May 1950 and December 1951. The Jews of Iraq formed a unique case, for they were harassed not only by the Iraqi authorities but also by Israeli agents who, in April 1950, pretending to be anti-Jewish Iraqis, threw hand grenades at the Dar al Bayda coffee house where Jews used to meet, then repeated the same exercise at the US Information Centre where young Jews often came to read, and in March 1951 struck again just outside the Masuda Shemtov synagogue. This unusual method of frightening away the Jews so that they would leave Iraq and immigrate to Israel seemed justified at the time, given that the *raison d'être* of a Jewish state and one of its paramount goals was to gather the Jews from all over the world and bring them to *Eretz Yisrael*. Survivors of the European Holocaust also arrived in Israel after being held in internment camps in Cyprus, because the British, as long as they were still in Palestine, would not grant them entry visas. Others had arrived from Eastern Europe, where, unlike Western Europe, the post-Nazi era did not bring a decline in anti-Semitism through compassion for the victims, but rather an increase directed principally against those Jews seeking to return to their homes. By 1951, 100,000 Jews from Poland and 120,000 from Romania had settled in Israel in addition to the Jewish communities of Bulgaria (37,444 had arrived between 1948 and 1955), Czechoslovakia (18,297 had arrived between 1948 and 1955), Yugoslavia, and the greater part of Turkish Jewry.

Yet these Jews, coming from the four corners of the world, had little in common – their diets were different, their cultures unique, and they used different languages, one group often unable to communicate with the other. At the first census in 1949 Jews listed more than 20 different European and Asiatic languages as their media of speech. Together they formed a very fragmented community, and while absorbing and providing them with the barest necessities of life – food, housing, clothing – was the government's main task, transforming them from individuals and close-knit communities into a cohesive Israeli society was also of paramount importance.

The other task of the Israeli government was to reorganize the Israeli military and transform it into an efficient, professional body capable of defending the fledgling state. In fact, it was necessary to build it from scratch, for when hostilities ended most of the forces that had won the 1948 war, about 100,000 troops, were demobilized and the armed forces had now effectively ceased to exist. Worse still, weapons and ammunition were in short supply, the remaining forces were under-equipped and military standards were appalling. Rebuilding and equipping the IDF was an urgent task, and there was no time to indulge in leisurely preparations for war because a renewal of hostilities with the Arabs seemed inevitable. The General Staff – led in the postwar period by Chief of Staff Yigael Yadin – had predicted that Israel 'should expect another war with the Arabs', and Premier and Defence Minister Ben Gurion agreed with this assessment, recording in his diary: 'The Arab states were beaten by us. Could they forget that? 700,000 [Jewish] men had beaten

30 million [Arabs]. . . . Could they forget such a humiliation?'[1]
In the Foreign Ministry a file named 'The renewal of war' was
opened as early as July 1949.

These two tasks – absorbing and transforming the people of
Israel from individuals into a cohesive society, and building a
new army – were interconnected. A healthy, cohesive society
was needed in order to provide the resources – both human and
material – to build a highly motivated armed force capable of
winning future wars, and armed forces, in turn, seemed at the
time to be the best instrument to turn a fragmented community
into a nation and society. 'Even the English nation', Ben Gurion
observed, '[was no more than] tribes [which were] different
from each other. . . . And only after hundreds [of] years of evolu-
tion did they become one nation . . . we [Israelis] do not have
hundreds of years and without this instrument – the army – we
will not become a nation'.[2] What Ben Gurion had in mind was
an army which should be a school for society, namely an organization which would be 'not only the fortress of our security', as
he put it, 'but also [serve as] an educational force for national
unity' where Jews from different cultures would mix together
and become 'friends and partners with the native born'.[3]

## BUILDING AN ARMY – CREATING A MELTING POT

The civilian is a soldier on eleven months' annual leave.
(Chief of Staff Yigael Yadin)

Ben Gurion's notion of an army which was an instrument to
build a nation and cement the fragmented Israeli society can best
be illustrated if the army is seen as a bottleneck through which
almost all Israeli citizens, including women, must pass during a
compulsory military service. While undergoing this experience
Israelis live together, learn to know each other and about each
other, communicate in the same language – obviously Hebrew –

and are all indoctrinated with the common and ultimate goal of defending their homeland, Israel, from enemies bent on destroying it. Furthermore, the 'bottleneck experience' is reinforced when Israelis, after experiencing compulsory military service, continue to see and meet each other when they are called every year for routine security duties, training and wars. For even after becoming civilians, the Israelis, as Chief of Staff Yadin once put it, remain 'soldiers on eleven months' annual leave'. Such a life experience – it has been calculated that almost every Israeli male devotes at least six full years of his life to military service and almost every woman between one and two full years – inevitably creates a strong bond between society and the military to the point where the society is the army and the army is a mirror of society, or as it is often put: 'the IDF is the people of Israel in uniform'.

In attempting to create a military system based on almost the entire Israeli society, Ben Gurion opted for the Swiss model. In this, a small nucleus of regular and conscripted personnel trains, maintains depots and command structures, and carries out routine security duties. This nucleus is also available in the event of an emergency, and is the body responsible for holding the ground and absorbing a potential surprise attack by the enemy until the main bulk of the armed forces which consists of reservists, namely civilians who were previously trained as conscripts, takes over. The advantage of this system which so attracted Ben Gurion is that it both provides for an adequate defence of the state in times of war, and allows an ordinary functioning of the economy in peacetime.

The new IDF, which was reorganized after the 1948 war and which was modelled closely on the Swiss military system, was established with three tiers. The first tier, the standing army, contains 30 per cent of the total available manpower and is composed of conscripts subject to universal and compulsory military service. During this period of service, conscripts are trained and specialize in specific areas: armour, artillery, air force, navy, and so on. In times of war, this component is given, as in the Swiss system, the mission of absorbing an enemy's first strike and if necessary of being the first to move into enemy territory. The second tier of the new IDF is the reserve body. Composed of civilians who have completed their period of compulsory service, the reserves provide the quantitative component of the IDF, which reverses the numerical advantage of the Arab troops in favour of the Israelis and bridges the gap between peacetime and wartime manpower requirements. In fact, the main feature and also the object of this new military system is the production of a substantial reserve with which to expand the active army in war. The third tier of the military system is the professional component composed of career personnel, most of whom serve in the air force and the navy. It was clear from the start, that if this system, which is based overwhelmingly on civilian reserves, was to function properly, it would have to rely heavily on a first-rate intelligence service, capable of providing an alert early enough for reserves to be called up, mobilized and join the regulars; a big investment was therefore put into creating an effective army intelligence service. Chief of Staff Yadin who, under the close supervision of Ben Gurion, had carried out the task of building the new IDF, often compared it to an iceberg with only its tip, namely its regular and the professional components, visible, while the iceberg itself, namely the reserve component, based on almost the entire society, was hidden.

To enable the government to mobilize the entire society – for this was the implication of having a military system based on civilian reserves as the main component of the wartime order of battle – in June 1949 the Knesset passed 'Hok Sherut Bitachon Leumi'. Under the provisions of this national service law, which has been amended throughout the years but basically remains unchanged, men and women who were found physically and mentally fit were liable to service at the age of 18; the period of service to be modified in accordance with defence requirements. The law also stipulated that upon terminating a period of compulsory service the authorities could call men and women to serve in the reserve force, either to be trained in new methods or to participate in military actions. The law also allowed a semi-military framework called *Gadna* ('youth brigades') to prepare boys and girls of 14–18 to become soldiers. Thus by law almost the whole of Israeli society between the ages of 14 and 55 was enlisted.

There were, however, a few exemptions. The law stipulated that Arab citizens living in Israel – meaning those who had not left during the 1948 war and were living under Israeli military rule until after the 1967 Six Day War – should be exempted. The reason for that was that the makers of the law felt they had to keep guns away from a potential fifth column, and also to absolve the Arabs of Israel from a dual loyalty to the Jewish state and to their fellow Arabs. That said, Christians and Bedouin were allowed to volunteer, and indeed many of them chose to serve in the IDF. Responding to political pressure from orthodox religious parties and a demand to replenish the pool of Torah scholars after the Holocaust, Ben Gurion also agreed to exempt 400 top students of religious institutions (called *Yeshivot*). In addition, girls of orthodox background were allowed to sign a declaration stating that military service was incompatible with their upbringing.

To the Knesset, which had voted overwhelmingly for this law, Ben Gurion explained that it aimed 'to prepare the entire people for defence; to give the youth – Israeli born and immigrant – pioneering and military training, to maintain a permanently mobilized force adequate to withstand a surprise attack and hold out until the reserves were mobilized'.

## ARMING THE IDF AND PERFECTING THE SYSTEM

Equipping the new IDF, though crucial, was no easy task given the stress and burden caused by the need to absorb the massive influx of immigrants. But then, as we have already noted, a 'second round' with the Arab world seemed certain, and the Israeli government felt obliged to make its first priority the buying of arms and equipping the IDF. Thus, in the period between March 1949 and December 1951, it procured some 216 planes, 21 tanks, 46 naval vessels, 19 armoured vehicles, 102 half tracks, 591 cannons, 23 torpedo boats, 403 heavy machine guns, 11 medium machine guns, 5,135 rifles, seven sub-automatic rifles and 3,453 pistols. At the beginning of 1952 the IDF had a total of 420 planes, 61 tanks, 85 naval vessels, 221 half tracks, 19 armoured vehicles, 1,007 canons, 24 heavy mortars, 23 torpedo boats, 561 heavy machine guns, 1,428 medium machine guns, 6,039 automatic rifles, 57,526 rifles, 530 sub-automatic rifles and 5,208 pistols. This might appear to be an unimpressive arsenal, but compared with the tiny stockpile of arms the Israelis had only four years earlier, it was indeed a most impressive amount of weapons to have been assembled within a relatively short period of time.

As with arms, so it was with training – expensive but essential. Mobilization in future wars, so the Israeli planners had stipulated, would have to be very different from the way it was carried out during the 1948 war, where mobilization was gradual and months had passed before the army reached full strength. In future wars Israeli society would have to mobilize much more efficiently – reserves moving quickly to the battle fronts and the rapid transference of cars, vehicles and other resources from the citizenry to the IDF. Those segments of society which did not join the front-line fighting force, mostly women, the young and the old, were to flock into factories, offices and voluntary services, to hospitals and to schools in order to take the place of men so that mobilization would not wreck the economy.

Military manoeuvres and training got under way immediately after the 1948 war, and this was regularly reported in the papers – which were tightly controlled by the state – presumably in order to induce a sense of belonging among Israelis and also to make a show of strength and deter potential adversaries. The IDF magazine *Ba'machane*, reported, on 17 October 1949, that 'When the men were called up to take part in the summer military manoeuvres . . . they were not the only ones who were called to the flag. Recruitment calls were also issued for animals'. It was, in other words, almost the entire society which was called to serve – even animals.

In spite of the hardships and austerity and the fact that the economy was in a desperate condition, Chief of Staff Yadin was able to hold three large-scale manoeuvres involving more than 100,000 reserves. The first major exercise, which was called 'Manoeuvre A', took place in 1950 and was aimed at testing the call-up system by using two types of calls up – 'silent calls' in which officers called up reserves by telephoning them; and an open mobilization where reserves were summoned to join their units by codes broadcast over the radio. In 1951 two other extensive exercises, 'Manoeuvre B' and 'Manoeuvre C', took place, in which reserve formations were physically deployed and took up positions to test the system under two different scenarios: one in which Israel had suffered a surprise attack, and another in which Israel had itself launched a pre-emptive strike. For although the Israeli doctrine of warfare based on pre-emptive strike and the transfer of war into enemy soil was developed only after the 1956 Sinai campaign, in the early 1950s the advantages of this method for a small state like Israel were already becoming clear.

The manoeuvres had proved beyond any doubt that the new IDF functioned properly and its reserve component – that is, the society as a whole – had cooperated fully. This was crucial, given that for such a system to function properly – with men leaving their jobs and other obligations and also transferring their private cars to the army – full public cooperation was essential.

## A SENSE OF INSECURITY AND PUBLIC COOPERATION

After the 1948 war the government of Israel could count on the public to rally behind it and cooperate fully, both in paying high taxes for defence and also in devoting much time to carrying out routine military duties. What ensured the public's full cooperation was its strong sense of insecurity, caused partly by Arab actions, which seemed to be aimed at harming Israel, and partly by the tendency of the Israeli leadership to exaggerate the external danger posed by the Arabs.

Palestinian infiltration, for example, had strongly affected the public mood. Palestinians, now living as refugees in camps in the Gaza Strip, Jordan, Syria and Lebanon, would enter Israel through its penetrable borders. These incursions, especially in the early 1950s, were not, however, aimed at re-occupying the land these people had lost a few years earlier, but rather at returning to villages and homes in order to collect possessions and crops in abandoned fields, and also to steal from Israeli farms. In fact, much of this non-violent Palestinian infiltration was encouraged by Israel's policy of repatriation, which extended rights to close family members separated by the war to return home. Since, in order for a person to be eligible for this scheme, there had to be some member of their family remaining in the country, a method was developed by which Palestinian women and children infiltrated Israel and thereafter applied for permission for members of their families to join them. IDF figures show that in 1952, 16,000 cases of Palestinian infiltration occurred; in 1953 there were 7,018 cases; in 1954, 4,638; in 1955, 4,351; and during the first months of 1956, 2,786 cases. Israel's policy was determined and ruthless – its armed forces shot the infiltrators. This policy was aimed at deterring Palestinians from attempting to return to their homes, thus preventing a trickle of return turning into a flood which would then endanger the Jewish character of Israel.

But not all Palestinian infiltration was non-violent, and there were infiltrators who sought to carry out acts of sabotage and kill Israelis. IDF figures show that in 1950, 19 Israelis were killed and 31 were injured by Arab marauders. In 1951 the figures were 48 and 49 respectively; in 1952, 42 and 56; in 1953, 44 and 66. Palestinian violent actions had gathered momentum from April 1955, when groups of guerrilas called fedayeen were established in the Gaza strip under Egyptian intelligence supervision, with the aim of striking at Israel. All in all, between 1949 and 1956 Israel lost 486 lives, including 264 civilians; and 1,057 were injured, including 477 civilians.

In absolute terms this was surely not a heavy toll for a country whose population exceeded 1.5 million, but as Avner Yaniv rightly observed in *Deterrence without the Bomb*:

> The damage was perceived as extensive ... in terms of people's state of mind. Incidents leading to death and injury of Israelis by Arabs who had crossed over from the neighbouring countries created a pervasive sense of insecurity. People became afraid to travel at night – even, in certain areas, in broad daylight.[4]

Israeli leaders often exaggerated the danger of Arab infiltration, as did, for example, minister Yitzhak Ben Aharon when declaring in the Knesset that Arab infiltration 'Endangers our very existence'. Inevitably, such statements increased rather than eased the public's sense of insecurity, and as Sir John Bagot

Glubb, the British commander of the Arab Legion, the army of the state of Transjordan, correctly observed:

> One of the most dangerous aspects of this unrestrained [Israeli] propaganda was the effect which it seemed to be having on the Israeli public. They [the Israeli government] complained that the inhabitants of their frontier colonies could not sleep at night. This is scarcely to be wondered at, if they read the Israeli Press, which daily described the most bloody (but fortunately often fictitious) battles [between Israeli forces and the infiltrators].[5]

To counter Palestinian violence, the Israelis devised a policy which became known as the 'doctrine of retaliatory action'. One of the features of this policy was to hit hard in response to even a small provocation, and also to strike at the countries from which the perpetrators had come so as to put pressure on hosting Arab governments to prevent incursions of Palestinian fighters into Israel. The killing, for instance, of an Israeli mother and her two young children in Yahud in 1953, led to a massive Israeli retaliatory action in Kibia which resulted in the deaths of 69 Arab civilians. The killing of an Israeli cyclist near Rehovot led to an equally massive Israeli retaliatory action against the fedayeen in Gaza on 28 February 1955, in which 38 Egyptian soldiers were killed and 32 wounded.[6] An Egyptian attempt to demolish Israeli water devices near the border with Gaza led to Israeli retaliation against the Khan Yunis police fort on 31 August 1955, in which 72 Egyptians were killed and 58 wounded. When Syrians fired at Israeli fishermen on the Sea of Galilee, the Israelis retaliated on 11 December 1955, ('Operation Kinneret') killing 54 Syrians, wounding nine and capturing 30.[7]

Israel's retaliatory doctrine neither curbed infiltration nor eased public insecurity. In fact, it achieved precisely the opposite effect for, by reacting massively and disproportionately to even minor Palestinian provocations, the Israeli leadership instilled in the public a mistaken impression that a big and continuous war was being waged between Israeli troops and the fedayeen.

Another reason for a growing sense of insecurity among Israelis was what seemed to be an Arab intention to strike at and destroy Israel. While true at times, this has not always reflected reality. In fact in the early 1950s, Arab leaders were less concerned with their struggle with Israel than was reported at the time. In Egypt, for example, the Free Officers who overthrew King Farouk in July 1952 did not even mention Israel in their manifesto, which dealt only with social reforms. Nevertheless in the mid-1950s, policies taken by Egypt which had little to do with Israel were often seen by the Israelis as aimed at harming them. On 27 September 1955, for example, Egypt's President Nasser concluded his arms deal with Czechoslovakia under which Egypt was to receive large amounts of weapons including tanks, field guns, anti-aircraft guns, jet bombers and even 120 MiG-15 fighters. At first this failed to make an impression on the Israelis, and Prime Minister Moshe Sharett did not even bother mentioning it in his personal diary, where he would record almost every event. It took Sharett no less than three days to convene a special session of the government to discuss the matter.

But soon this arms deal was causing considerable panic, with every paper in Israel running headlines such as 'A time of danger, a time of opportunity' and 'Anything could now happen along Israel's borders'. In Ma'ariv, 2 October 1955, Azriel Carlibach, a senior journalist, published an editorial warning of Egyptian aggression. Davar, the paper controlled by the Labor movement, declared in its 2 October editorial that 'The arms were purchased solely for planned aggression against Israel. . . . The Egyptian ruler and the other Arab rulers believe it their right to foreclose Israel's possibility of self-defence, just as they deny the very existence of our state'. In the Knesset around this time Ben Gurion, now a defence minister under Sharett, announced that

> The rulers of Egypt seem to have concluded that it is easier to win victories on the foreign policy front than to reform the unfortunate and shameful domestic situation, and in order to gain Arab hegemony the tyrants of Egypt have apparently decided that the easier and cheapest way is by attacking Israel.

On 10 October, Ya'acov Meridor of Herut declared that the Czech arms deal 'put into question the future of our nation here, our very existence and well-being'. Prime Minister Sharett announced from the podium of the Knesset: 'From here in this house, in this our capital, we call on the citizens of Israel, to the Jewish people throughout the Diaspora, and to the entire world for weapons for Israel', and elsewhere he said 'We [Israelis] must now pull together to mobilize all our capabilities which may be limited but are not insignificant . . . to take a stand and defend the ramparts'. The Knesset declared its concern about the large quantities of weapons supplied to Egypt which 'will be directed by Israel's enemies against her . . . The Knesset charges the government with mobilizing the people and the state against the dangers'.

The view that Nasser meant to attack Israel at that time was, in my judgement, mistaken. Nasser had no precise plans of aggression; at best he had an intention of doing so, which he held in common with most Arabs. And while such an arsenal in the hands of an Arab state undoubtedly presented a potential threat to Israel, we now know – and it is likely that the Israeli leaders knew at the time – that Nasser's arms deal was more a protest against the Baghdad Pact than against Israel. This pact, of 24 February 1955, of mutual cooperation between Iraq and Turkey, in which Britain and Iran joined and the US supported with arms and money, was part of American Secretary of State John

Foster Dulles' policy of containing Soviet expansion by clear contractual deterrents that would prevent Soviet penetration of the Middle East. Nasser, who saw himself as the leader of the Arab world, regarded the pact as an attempt to divide the Arabs. Hence, as the Israeli diplomat Abba Eban observed, the acquisition of weapons was 'above all Nasser's response to the Baghdad Pact', and agression against Israel was 'at most, a subsidiary motive'.[8]

Was the Israeli government exaggerating the danger of weapons in Nasser's hands in order to rally its people behind it? This is hard to answer. It is probable that it was assumed by Israeli leaders that almost any jet could take off and bomb towns in Israel, and that all these weapons could be used against Israeli targets, and that they would be used. But it also might well be that in addition to this, Israeli leaders assumed that exaggerating the external danger was not a bad idea after all, for it would rally the nation behind it. Indeed, on the day of the Knesset debate on the Egypt–Czechoslovakia deal, a young boy came to the Ministry of Defence offices in Tel Aviv asking to see the Minister. When he was directed to one of the clerks, the boy gave him a handful of small coins that he had been saving for his Bar Mitzvah, to buy defensive weapons for Israel; the next day an old woman appeared offering her own contribution of a gold bangle. Former Chief of Staff Yadin added to the sense of urgency when he called on Israeli parents to 'buy an iron cloth for the defence of your children'. Soon, prices of weaponry systems were published in the daily papers and the public was invited to 'buy' them for the IDF. The Israeli Teacher Association donated money to 'buy' a jet plane and a tank, while Haifa Council 'bought' a torpedo boat for the navy. Ramat-Gan Council 'bought' a transport plane and 100 parachutes and the Discount Bank of Israel collected money to 'buy' a tank, as did representatives of the public in the town of Ramleh, who called the tank they had 'purchased' 'Ramleh I'. And with the public fully cooperating, the government moved to consolidate the donations by establishing the 'Voluntary Defence Fund' into which old and young poured money. Calls on the public to help in order to face the Egyptian threat had gathered momentum with Prime Minister Sharett's announcement that the decisive military advantage which would soon be held by a nation intent on laying Israel to waste, endangered the state and each and every Israeli citizen. He then declared that 'it is time to work for the defence of Israel'. Playing the Holocaust card, the leadership went so far as to announce that the lesson of Jewish history, reinforced by the experience of the Holocaust, was simple – a Jewish state must be able to protect itself. Defence Minister Ben Gurion told the public that President Nasser's aim was to strike at Israel because he had been humiliated in 1948, and Chief of Staff Moshe Dayan called the Egyptian leader 'a military dictator'. In ten days, IL5 million had been collected to buy arms for the IDF.

Mordechai Bar On, an intelligent and well informed observer, who served as Moshe Dayan's head of bureau, wrote in a fine passage:

> For most Israelis, the conflict shaped since the War of Independence had limited their perspective. Their images had crystallized during the hostilities of 1948; if this was how one began reckoning history then the conflict in the mid-1950s could only be seen as one between a defensive Israel, protecting its very existence and the belligerent Arabs, intent on Israel's destruction. This view provided Israel's security establishment with two important assets: a wide public consensus on security issues and total civilian willingness to fight in the wars.

Indeed, a wide public consensus on security enabled the Israeli leadership to channel substantial sums of money into defence and spend increasing proportions of the national income on armaments, without raising any significant opposition from tax-payers. In 1950 the defence budget amounted to $87.6 million; in 1951 it was $151.5 million; in 1952 it was $75.5 million; and in 1953 the figure was $68.8 million. Defence expenditure as a percentage of government expenditure grew dramatically from 23.0 per cent in 1952 to 34.9 per cent in 1956. That the government could spend so much on arms, while at the same time demanding that the public 'tighten its belt' and live an almost Spartan life, is a clear indication that it had strong public support. Furthermore, as Bar On correctly observed, given the Israeli sense of insecurity, the government could be sure that if called to the flag, Israelis would cooperate fully and take up arms to defend themselves. Indeed, this proved to be the case in the autumn of 1956.

## A MAJOR TEST

The 'Kadesh War' – Kadesh after the desert post where the Israelites had rested on their way to the promised land – or as it is better known, the 'Sinai Campaign', was the largest military operation undertaken by the IDF since the 1948 war. It was sparked by President Nasser's announcement on 26 July 1956 that his government had decided to nationalize the Suez Canal Company. Nasser offered to compensate the company's share-holders, mainly France and Britain, and said he would use the income from the canal to build the Aswan Dam, at an estimated cost of $1.3 billion, a project that Egypt needed for irrigation and for power. Nasser's announcement came in response to American Secretary of State John Foster Dulles' announcement, made on 19 July, that no American aid for the building of the Dam would be forthcoming, and that American and British participation in financing the High Dam of Aswan through the World Bank was not 'feasible in present circumstances'. This meant that Washington had reversed its previous pledge to support the project. It had done so, among other reasons, because of Nasser's growing links with the Soviet Union and his fierce campaign against the Baghdad Pact.

Nasser's nationalization of the Suez Canal drew together two previous colonial powers – France and Britain – who resented the idea that with Nasser's nationalization of the Suez Canal Company they – who had acquired a concession to operate the Suez Canal for 99 years after its opening, that is until 1968 – would be dependent for their major supplies, especially of oil, not on an international waterway over which they had direct control, but on Nasser's goodwill. In London and Paris, Nasser's action was seen as a major threat to their far-flung maritime economic interests east of Suez.

Soon after Nasser's announcement, France and Britain began considering the use of force to regain control of the Suez Canal. Israel – odd as it seems – was also invited to join the anti-Nasser coalition, and saw in the possibility of war against Egypt an opportunity to achieve its own aims, which were not at all, however, connected with the Suez Canal, but rather with the Straits of Tiran.

The Straits of Tiran were Israel's primary route to East Africa and Asia, but for several years had been blocked by Egyptian batteries deployed at Sharm el-Sheikh. Troubles had started in 1953 when Egypt had detained, for the first time, a Danish cargo ship en route to the Israeli port of Eilat. In September 1953 the Egyptians treated a Greek vessel in the same way, and on 1 January 1954 they opened fire on a small Italian cargo vessel en route to Eilat. For the Israelis, interference with freedom of navigation through the Straits posed not only an economic but also a political danger. For the Israelis were haunted by the fear that the West, in its anxiety to lure Egypt into a pro-Western alliance, would force Israel to cede the Negev so as to facilitate territorial continuity between Egypt and the Fertile Crescent. Settling the Negev and keeping the port and town of Eilat bustling with activity might have prevented such demands, but for this to succeed Israel needed the Straits to remain open. On 6 May 1955, Ben Gurion had declared that blocking the Straits was for Israel a *casus belli*, and when the blockade continued he went so far as to threaten, in an interview given to the *New York Times* on 29 September 1955, that if Egypt failed to lift the blockade within a year, Israel would use force to open the Straits. And now, following Nasser's nationalization of the Suez Canal and the building of an anti-Nasser alliance which contemplated military action, Israel saw an opportunity to achieve this aim. Military action against Nasser could also be beneficial to Israel for two further reasons: first, it would enable Israel to strike at the Egyptian army before it assimilated the weapons Egypt had acquired through the September 1955 deal with Czechoslovakia. Second, it would enable Israel to hit and destroy the fedayeen bases in the Gaza Strip, which had been their jumping-off points for attacks on Israel.

A period of consultation and planning involving Israeli, French and British representatives had resulted in a simple military plan: Israel, as the eastern flank of a Franco-British attack, would provide a pretext for a French and British intervention by attacking Egypt towards the Suez Canal. On being appraised of this, the British and the French governments would make two appeals to the governments of Egypt and Israel. To Egypt: (a) halt all acts of war; (b) withdraw all troops ten miles from the Canal; (c) accept temporary occupation of key positions on the Canal by the Anglo-French forces to guarantee freedom of passage through the Suez canal. To Israel: (a) halt all acts of war; (b) withdraw all troops ten miles to the east of the Canal. It was obvious that Israel, which was party to this plan, would agree, though it was stipulated that Nasser might refuse to withdraw, in which case France and Britain would use force to take over the Suez Canal.

On 22 October, Prime and Defence Minister Ben Gurion, accompanied by his two principal lieutenants, Chief of Staff Dayan and director-general of the defence ministry Shimon Peres, flew to Sèvres in France to finalize the joint military plan. On 25 October, Dayan recorded in his diary:

> We can sum up the situation today as follows: 1. The prime minister and defence minister, David Ben Gurion, has given approval in principle to the campaign and its aims. 2. Our forces will go into action at dusk on 29 October 1956, and we must complete the capture of the Sinai Peninsula within seven to ten days. 3. The decision on the campaign and its planning are based on the assumption that British and French forces are about to take action against Egypt.[9]

To the Israeli cabinet, on 28 October, Ben Gurion presented Israel's aims as follows:

> We are interested, first of all, in [opening] the Straits of Eilat [to Israeli shipping] and the Red Sea. Only through them can we secure direct contact with the nations of Asia and East Africa. . . . The main thing, to my mind, is freedom of navigation in the Straits of Eilat. As far as the Gaza Strip is concerned. . . . If I believed in miracles I would pray for it to be swallowed up in the sea. All the same, we must eradicate the fedayeen bases and secure peaceful lives for the inhabitants of border areas.[10]

The Israeli forces for the campaign, as detailed by Chief of Staff Dayan, comprised an armoured brigade – the 7th, with two tank battalions; two mechanized armoured brigades – the 27th and 37th; a paratroop brigade – the 202nd, and six infantry brigades – the 1st, 4th, 9th, 10th, 11th and 12th. Except for the 7th and 202nd, all were reserve formations. Given that the majority of forces were reservists, this campaign was to be a major test for the new IDF. To maintain security, Dayan delayed mobilization for most units until the last moment, and the initial mobilization which had begun on 26 October was carried out by messengers. Two days later on 28 October, an open mobilization was ordered, and once the radio call-up was used, units rapidly filled up and moved to the front.

The attack on Egypt was launched at 4.59 p.m. on 29 October, with Israeli aircraft dropping 385 parachute troops of the 890th battalion at the Israeli end of the Mitla Pass, some 30 miles east of the Suez Canal. Simultaneously, the rest of the 202nd para-troop brigade, under the command of Ariel Sharon, had embarked on an overland advance of 190 miles across central Sinai towards Mitla to link up with its parachute battalion 28 hours later.

The campaign was quickly and easily won by the Israelis, who had managed to occupy the entire Sinai Peninsula within 100 hours, and reach and open the Straits of Tiran to Israeli shipping by occupying Sharm el-Sheikh. Israel had destroyed the Egyptian forces in Sinai at a cost of 172 killed, 700 wounded and four prisoners of war. Egypt suffered thousands of deaths, great num-bers of wounded and 5,581 prisoners of war. The IDF, and par-ticularly its reserve component, seemed to have conclusively proved its efficacy. The scores of thousands of civilians, who in the years preceding the war had trained within the constraints that a reserve system involved, in particular the limiting of train-ing time, did not seem to have affected adversely the IDF's per-formance in battle. An army of civilians had proved itself capable of fighting a brief, intensive war. The logistical system, too, had withstood the demanding conditions of such a war. Israeli forces elsewhere took advantage of the fog of battle to finish the uncompleted job of the 1948 war. As the head of Northern Command Yitzhak Rabin testified: 'exploiting the war with the Egyptians ... I have solved one problem in the north [of Israel] ... I have transferred about 2,000 Arabs, who were a major security problem . . . to the eastern side of the Jordan [river]'.[11]

The Sinai campaign proved that the panic caused in Israel by the Egyptian–Czech arms deal was premature; the Egyptians had failed to assimilate the weapons, and Israel had captured great quantities of them.

While this brief war was a major test for the armed forces as far as mobilization and fighting practices were concerned, it had little impact on Israeli society as a whole. This was because it was perceived as a 'campaign' by the Israelis, and was seen as not much different from the major large-scale retaliatory actions which had taken place against Egypt and Jordan in the period leading up to it. More importantly, the campaign was short, decisive and successful, and as the old proverb goes, 'nothing succeeds like success'.

After the storm came a strange calm. Israel withdrew from the territory it had occupied, including Sharm el-Sheikh, and, in general, the next decade or so was a period of relative peace and tranquillity, especially along Israel's border with Egypt. It was a period in which Israel had the time to devote to producing some order from the chaos of war and social upheaval. Israeli society after the Sinai campaign became much more cohesive and self-assured, and was able to concentrate on consolidating its position in world affairs and at home.

That said, the consciousness of a severe external threat to its very existence remained. Nasser, after what seemed to be a victory over France and Britain, became much more confident, and also felt growing resentment towards Israel for having attacked him. As a result, his anti-Israeli declarations became more pronounced than in the early 1950s, although, as we have said, he avoided unrest on his border with Israel. On 4 October 1958 Nasser endorsed the anti-Semitic *Protocols of the Elders of Zion*, which was the spiritual basis of European and especially Nazi anti-Semitism, thus arousing the deepest fears of the Israelis, many of whom were Holocaust survivors. Five years later in 1963, Nasser joined Iraq's President Abdul Salam Arif in signing a communiqué proclaiming that 'The aim of the Arabs is the destruction of Israel'. On 11 July 1965, Nasser declared: 'The final account with Israel will be made within five years if we are patient. The Moslems waited 70 years until they expelled the Crusaders from Palestine'. With such threats and intimidating declarations, and with the warnings of Israeli politicians that such statements should be taken very seriously indeed, the Israeli public rallied behind its leadership and was willing to carry on the burden of paying high taxes so that there would be no cuts in the defence budget, to leave jobs and families to take up routine training, and to agree to serve for long periods. For as one observer put it:

> Rightly or wrongly, most Israelis were convinced that the Arabs were bent on destroying their state and that they were fighting with their backs to the wall. For them there could be no retreat because there was no place to retreat to and in every war the individual soldier believed that he was fighting for the life of his family, his home, and his nation.[12]

# 3

## THE SIX BAD YEARS

### 1967–73

## A POWDER KEG

The outbreak of war in the spring of 1967 shocked Israelis to the core, for it came, to speak bluntly, as a bolt from the blue. And it is only because this war was so remarkably successful that no demand was ever made – as was to be the case after the 1973 war – to investigate the politico-military establishment, whose superficial optimism and complacency had led Israelis to believe that war was a remote and unlikely event. That the Israeli leadership was totally relaxed about the security situation in the period just before this war, is well illustrated in the following extract from a report written by Walt Rostow, National Security Adviser in Lyndon Johnson's administration, of his meeting with Israeli Ambassador Abraham Harman on 31 January 1967:

Israeli ambassador Harman came in yesterday . . . to share his observations on the mood in Israel. His theme was basically that Israel faces an economically difficult situation over the next three years or so . . . he said most Israeli leaders feel the long-term security situation is under control.[1]

The view in Israel in the first half of 1967 was that its most implacable foe, President Nasser of Egypt, was unlikely to embark on a full-scale war. This opinion rested upon a theory that proved to be utterly erroneous; it was that as long as *la crème de la crème* of Nasser's forces, eight brigades in all, was still involved in the civil war in Yemen, supporting the Republicans against the Royalists, he would not dare to attack Israel. Complementary to this assessment was the view that neither Syria nor Jordan would open fire without the active participation of Egypt, which not only had the most powerful army but which was also in a geographical position to impose on Israel its traditional nightmare – a war on more than one front. And because the Israeli theory that war was remote was based heavily on the continuing Egyptian presence in the Yemen, the eyes of its intelligence services were fixed on airfields in Yemen and Egypt to check whether Egyptian troops were being brought back home, for their return to Egypt would be a strong indication that the prospects of war were higher than before. But in the first half of 1967 the Egyptian elite forces were still bogged down in the Yemenite civil war – they would return to Egypt only *after* the 1967 war – and in Israel it seemed as if the relatively calm situation along the Israeli–Egyptian border would continue unabated.

In stark contrast with the relatively calm relations between Egypt and Israel, the latter's relations with Syria were volatile and, in the period up to the 1967 war, characterized by a series of mounting tensions and skirmishes. There were three bones of contention between Israel and Syria. The first of these was over water. Israel wished to divert water from Lake Kinneret (also known as the Sea of Galilee) down south to the Negev desert where water was scarce. It was vital for Israel to develop the Negev, because this was its most unpopulated area, and it contained valuable resources such as uranium. Perhaps more important was the fact that a Negev which was dotted with Jewish settlements and factories would, so the Israelis hoped, put an end to the persistent calls on Israel to cede parts of the desert to the Arabs and allow Egypt to establish a land bridge with Jordan. But without water Israel could not develop the desert, and this is why she built a pipeline, partly open, called *Ha'movil Ha'artzi* (National Water Carrier) to divert water from the north to the south. The Syrians, however, objected to this project – their aims, after all, were opposite to those of Israel – and as the water sources, mainly from the Hatzbani and Banyas rivers, were in their territory, they attempted to divert the water before it reached Israel. This in turn had led to exchanges of fire in which Israeli tanks and aeroplanes hit and destroyed Syrian tractors and other machinery assembled to divert the water. This happened in four major border clashes: 17 March 1965, 13 May 1965, 12 August 1965 and 17 July 1966. Israel did manage to transfer water to the Negev, but the water project was a constant source of tension between the two countries.

The second bone of contention between Israel and Syria, and a persistent source of trouble in the region, was the support which the Syrian regime was giving to Palestinian paramilitary groups to cross into Israel and terrorize its citizens. This often led to Israeli military retaliatory actions aimed at forcing Syria to curb incursions from her territory. But while the authorities in both Jordan and Lebanon had taken tough measures to curb such infiltrations from their own countries into Israel, the Syrian leadership had extended its support to the Palestinian paramilitary groups. This led Yitzhak Rabin – he had taken over as Israel's Chief of Staff in January 1964 – to state on 12 May 1967 that the retaliatory actions Israel had directed against Jordan and

Lebanon to force them to curb terrorist attacks on Israel, were not an effective measure as far as Syria was concerned because, as Rabin put it, 'In Syria . . . the authorities themselves activate the terrorists'. He went on: 'therefore, the aim of any [future Israeli military] action against Syria will be different from the actions which Israel has taken against Jordan and Lebanon'.[2] This statement – although given to the small and unimportant IDF Magazine Ba'machane – was regarded in Arab circles as an Israeli intent to harm Syria. As Nasser later put it: 'Israeli commanders (meaning Rabin) announced they would carry out military operations against Syria in order to occupy Damascus and overthrow the Syrian government'.[3] Although Premier and Defence Minister Levi Eshkol – he had taken over from Ben Gurion in June 1963 – criticized Rabin for issuing statements which increased tensions in the region, he had himself fuelled Arab anxiety by issuing similar declarations (Nasser: 'on the same day . . . Eshkol made a very threatening statement against Syria'). Eshkol's bizarre behaviour had little to do with Israeli–Arab relations, but rather with his own relationship with Chief of Staff Rabin and the attempts of each of them to outdo the other and impress upon the Israeli people that they were tough on the Arabs. Such declarations put President Nasser under strong pressure because of the defence pact between Egypt and Syria – signed on 4 November 1966 – which committed Egypt to helping Syria if it was attacked by Israel.

The third bone of contention between Israel and Syria was over control of the demilitarized zones (DMZs). These were three areas west of the international border (agreed in 1923 between French mandatory Syria and British mandatory Palestine) which Syria had occupied during the 1948 war. Under intense international pressure, the Syrians were obliged to withdraw and to agree to these lands becoming demilitarized zones without defining their sovereignty. The Israelis – who had signed up to this arrangement voluntarily rather than under a

Diktat – later regretted this, and attempted to regain control over
these lands by provoking the Syrians and then taking advantage
of military clashes to expand control over the DMZs. In a candid
interview, former Chief of Staff Moshe Dayan had openly admitted that Israel, rather than Syria, was responsible for 'at least 80
per cent' of the clashes that had occurred in the DMZs between
1949 and 1967.[4] Perhaps the most serious clash between Israeli
and Syrian forces just before the June 1967 war occurred on
7 April 1967. On that day an exchange of fire in the DMZs
escalated into an air battle in which Israeli planes shot down six
Syrian MiG fighter planes, two of them on the outskirts of the
capital Damascus. This was a humiliating defeat for Syria and,
again, it put Nasser of Egypt under intense pressure to come to
Syria's assistance.

To sum up, in the spring of 1967 Israeli–Egyptian
relationships were relatively calm, in contrast with the tense
Israeli–Syrian situation. As we shall now see, what ignited
the Israeli–Syrian powder keg into a full-blown war which would
also involve other Arab states, notably Egypt, was a Soviet lie.

## THE SPARK – A FALSE SOVIET REPORT

In the literature, there are two competing views on relationships
between the superpowers – the USSR and the USA – and the
local states in the Middle East during the period of the Cold War
(1945–89). One view maintains that throughout these years the
local states had their own domestic and regional agendas which
they tried, in their different ways, to make the Cold War serve.
The other view is that the Middle Eastern powers had been mere
pawns in a game played by the superpowers. The 1967 war has
often been explained in terms of the first view, and the answer to
the question of who first raised the storm and launched the
march of events which ended in the short but decisive confrontation between Israelis and Arabs and which almost led to direct

US and Soviet intervention, was clear: it was Nasser. New evidence, however, shows that this was not the case, and in fact what really sparked this confrontation was a Soviet attempt to exploit the local states in order to score points in its confrontation with the US.

To understand how this came to happen we should go back to 13 May 1967, the date on which Anwar el-Sadat, speaker of the Egyptian parliament, was on an official visit to Moscow. When the visit was over Sadat was seen off at Moscow airport by Vladimir Semnov, the Soviet Deputy Foreign Minister, and it was then that Sadat heard from Semnov that according to Soviet intelligence, 'Ten Israeli brigades had been concentrated on the Syrian border' ready to strike at Syria; in Cairo the same message was delivered to President Nasser by the Soviet ambassador. Against mounting tension between Israel and Syria – which, as we have seen, was caused by statements from Israeli leaders and troubles in the DMZs, notably the shooting down of six Syrian fighter planes on 7 April – the Russian information was taken very seriously indeed. Nasser now felt he had to act, for he had long been under intense pressure and criticism from Jordanian and Saudi Arabian radio stations for not doing enough to support fellow Arab states. This is why, at a late-night meeting with his deputy and commander of the Egyptian armed forces, Field Marshal Abd el-Hakim Amer, and Sadat, who had just returned from Moscow, Nasser ordered to dispatch two divisions across the Suez Canal and into the Sinai, with the aim of distracting Israel from what seemed to be, according to the Soviet report, an imminent strike at Syria. It is important to note here that Sinai was Egyptian territory, and although the move was unusual there was nothing wrong with sending Egyptian troops there. In fact, seven years earlier, on 18 February 1960, Nasser had taken similar action, dispatching an armoured division and three infantry brigades – quite a substantial force at the time – into the Sinai to hint to the Israelis that they should leave Syria alone after they had attacked it at a place called Tawfik. But the difference between the two occasions was that in 1960 the Egyptian mobilization into the desert had been quiet and secret, whereas this time Egyptian troops on their way to Sinai marched through the streets of Cairo chanting: 'We are off to Tel Aviv'.[5]

In addition to dispatching troops into the desert, Nasser sent his Chief of Staff Mohammed Fawzi to Damascus, entrusting him with two missions: first to confirm the Soviet information about the apparent Israeli mobilization, and second to coordinate moves with Damascus. In Syria, Chief of Staff Fawzi went with Syrian General Anwar Al-Kadi to inspect the border, but found nothing unusual. He later recalled: 'I was seeking confirmation about the Israeli troops, but when I arrived on the border I didn't find anything unusual . . . I looked at the latest aerial photos, but again I didn't find anything unusual.'[6] The Syrians – they too had been informed by the Russians of the apparent Israeli mobilization – had sent reconnaissance planes which reported back that 'there was no massing [of Israeli troops] on the border [with Syria]'.[7] The Israelis, in turn, dismissed reports of mobilization as false, and Prime Minister Eshkol even suggested that the Soviet ambassador in Tel Aviv, Leonid Chuvyakin, join the head of the Mossad, Meir Amit, in touring the border between Israel and Syria to see for himself that the Soviet allegations were unfounded; Chuvyakin, however, declined the offer. Neither in Israel nor in Syria had the foreign press reported any mobilization, which, as Abba Eban, Israeli Foreign Minister at the time, found odd, for:

> The mobilization of 'Eleven to thirteen Israeli brigades', to say nothing of their concentration on a narrow front, would have had a conspicuous effect on Israel's life. No newspaperman or foreign mission in Israel could have been unaware of it. The disruption of normality in so many families would have been registered in all the chanceries and newspapers of the world.[8]

Israel, as everyone now knows, did not move any forces to its border with Syria, and it is widely acknowledged that the Soviet report, which for a long time has been one of the most puzzling features of the run-up to the 1967 war, was false. An explanation of Soviet motives in issuing a false report is now possible, thanks to recent testimonies of such people as Evgeny Pyrlin, head of the Egypt department in the Soviet foreign ministry at the time the report was released. According to Pyrlin the reason why this crucial and most damaging report was issued was because the Soviets wanted to spark a war between Israel and its Arab neighbours, believing that

> even if the war was not won by our [Arab] side a war would be to our political advantage because our side would demonstrate its ability to fight with our weapons and with our military and political support.[9]

That this was all part of the ongoing Cold War between the superpowers is also confirmed by the extraordinary report of a CIA agent, who had heard from a KGB agent that by releasing the report and instigating a full-scale Arab–Israeli war,

> The USSR wanted to create another trouble spot for the United States in addition to that already existing in Vietnam. The Soviet aim was to create a situation in which the US would become seriously involved economically, politically, and possibly even militarily and would suffer serious political reverses as a result of siding with the Israelis against the Arabs.[10]

This evidence provides striking proof that, contrary to popular belief, the 1967 war was not instigated by the local states – neither Egypt nor Israel – but rather by the USSR as part of its competition with the US for world influence and supremacy.

Oddly enough, and in spite of Fawzi's findings that Israel had not mobilized troops on its border with Syria, Nasser did not call his divisions back from the Sinai – in fact he went so far as to reinforce them by dispatching more troops to the desert. Furthermore, on 16 May he instructed UN troops, which since the 1956 war had been deployed on the Egyptian side of the border (Israel would not allow them to deploy on her side of the border) and in Gaza and Sharm el-Sheikh, to leave their posts. Even though these UN troops were not strong enough to prevent either Israel or Egypt attacking the other, they were a symbol of non-belligerence and their removal was seen, and rightly so, as a further escalation of an already critical situation. We should point out, however, that Nasser's action was qualified, for what he did was order the removal of UN troops solely from their positions along the Egypt–Israel border, and not from Gaza or Sharm el-Sheikh, which controls passage through the Straits of Tiran. As Nasser put it in a later interview: 'I did not ask U Thant [the UN Secretary General] to withdraw UN troops from Gaza and Sharm el-Sheikh . . . but only from a part of the frontier from Rafah to Eilat'.[11] Here, however, U Thant acted hastily and foolishly, insisting that either all UN troops remain in their positions, or that they leave altogether. Nasser – he could not back down on the UN issue without loss of face in the eyes of the world and his own people – took the latter option.

A week later, on 23 May, Egypt's president took yet another step, which raised the temperature of an overheated situation to boiling point, by ordering the closure of the Straits of Tiran to Israeli shipping. At a meeting with pilots at Bir Gafgafa air base, Nasser said:

> The armed forces yesterday occupied Sharm el-Sheikh . . . under no circumstances will we allow the Israeli flag to pass through the Gulf of Aqaba . . . if Jews threaten war we tell them 'you are welcome, we are ready for war. Our armed forces and all our people are ready for war'. . . . This water is ours.[12]

As has already been shown, the Straits of Tiran were perceived by Israel as a vital interest, and closing them meant bottling up Israel and hampering both vital imports – mainly oil from Iran – and exports. Closing the Straits, as we have made clear, also threatened Israel's ability to develop the Negev. The issue, however, was not only economic but also political, for the Straits had become a test of prestige for both Israel and Egypt. We should recall that after the 1956 campaign in which Israel occupied Sharm el-Sheikh and opened the blocked Straits, it was forced to withdraw and return the territory to Egypt. At the time, members of the international community pledged that Israel would never again be denied use of the Straits of Tiran. The French representative to the UN, for example, announced that any attempt to interfere with free shipping in the Straits would be against international law, and American President Dwight Eisenhower went so far as publicly to recognize that re-imposing a blockade in the Straits of Tiran would be seen as an aggressive act which would oblige Israel to protect its maritime rights in accordance with Article 51 of the UN Charter. Reluctantly, Israel accepted these diplomatic guarantees as a bad second-best substitute for the material security of actual occupation of the Straits. But on 1 March 1957, prior to the withdrawal of Israeli troops, Foreign Minister Golda Meir stated Israel's position before the UN General Assembly in unmistakably clear terms. She said:

> Interference by armed force, with ships of Israeli flag exercising free and innocent passage in the Gulf of Aqaba and through the Straits of Tiran will be regarded by Israel as an attack entitling it to exercise its inherent right of self-defence under Article 51 of the Charter and to take all measures as are necessary to ensure the free and innocent passage of its ships in the Gulf and in the Straits.[13]

Yet in May 1967 Nasser ignored all this, and in the full knowledge that the Israelis were likely to react violently, he declared
the Straits closed to her shipping. That he did so with open eyes
we know from Anwar Sadat, who later testified how Nasser had
said to his colleagues, whom he had brought together to decide
on the closure of the Straits: 'Now, with the concentration of our
force in Sinai the chances of war are fifty–fifty but if we close the
Straits, war will be 100 per cent certain'.[14] What is also puzzling
is that Nasser took such a drastic move without consulting either
Syria or Jordan.

The historian A. J. P. Taylor once said that 'the greatest
decisions are nearly always the ones most difficult to explain',
and indeed, Nasser's fateful decision to close the Straits will long
remain one of the most puzzling features of the 1967 war, and it
may never be possible to learn for certain what his motives were.
Nevertheless, two possible explanations can be offered to the
question why he had decided on this action in the knowledge
that for Israel this was a *casus belli* and the Straits represented a
supreme national interest, their use being a right which it would
assert and defend whatever the sacrifice. The first explanation,
simple and straightforward, was probably best stated by Sadat –
he would succeed Nasser in 1970 – who wrote that 'Nasser was
carried away by his own impetuosity'.[15] Yet there may be a
deeper explanation, and that is that in a matter of days Nasser's
motive had changed from that at the start of the crisis, which
was, following the false Soviet report, the attempt to distract the
Israelis from attacking Syria, to a totally different aim, which was
to take advantage of the growing crisis to reverse the post-1948
situation in the southern Negev and Eilat.

We should remember that at the end of the 1948 war, and
after armistice agreements between Israel and Egypt (but not
with Jordan) were concluded and signed, Israel breached these
agreements by sending troops to Eilat and occupying it. This was
significant, for by seizing Eilat Israel prevented Egypt and Jordan

from having direct land access to each other. In *Al Ahram* on 7 January 1966, Mohamed Hassanian Heikal, a versatile journalist and intimate of Nasser whose writing frequently reflected the thinking of his president, wrote that it was most regrettable that in 1948 Israel had taken Eilat and thus created a 'wall' between the east and the west Arab world. He then added that in any future war with Israel, Egypt must attempt to pull down this wall and restore the pre-1948 situation in the vicinity of Eilat. It seems that now, with a crisis under way, Nasser decided to take advantage of the situation and achieve his long-held aim of reversing the situation in Eilat. What supports this interpretation is that the specific deployment of Egyptian forces in the desert appear instrumental to achieving such a task. We shall now examine this.

## ON THE BRINK OF WAR: THE OPPOSING FORCES AND THEIR OBJECTIVES

By 1 June – roughly two weeks after Nasser's first mobilization of troops into the desert – the Egyptian forces in the Sinai comprised seven divisions and a strength of 100,000 men. In addition, an infantry brigade was deployed at Sharm el-Sheikh, in control of the Straits of Tiran but not physically blocking it. It is a puzzling but little-known fact that Egyptian troops never blocked the Straits, which remained open before and throughout the crisis. As regards weaponry, the Egyptian forces were equipped with nearly 1,000 tanks, 900 guns of various calibres, 419 aircraft, four missile boats and two submarines. Yet contrary to popular belief, these forces were not deployed in attacking positions but rather on strictly defensive lines. That said, the one force which was ready to strike in the event of war, and thus was deployed in jump-off places, was Saad el-Shazli's, which was not, however, aimed at moving on Tel Aviv, but rather at striking in the direction of the southern tip of the Negev and Eilat in order to pave the way to establishing a land bridge between Egypt and Jordan. All other Egyptian forces in the Sinai were required to seal and isolate the operational area by blocking potential Israeli thrusts and thus enabling the Shazli force to accomplish its mission.

The Syrian army, which was also now fully mobilized, comprised between 50,000 and 60,000 men with at least 200 tanks of operational capacity and 100 Soviet aircraft, including thirty-two modern MiG-21s. The military aim of the Syrian forces was to occupy eastern Galilee and defend the Golan Heights from any Israeli attempt to seize them.

Jordanian forces were also fully mobilized and deployed. King Hussein's army was 56,000 strong and its main strength lay in its two armoured brigades – the 40th and 60th – mustering some 200 Patton tanks. These were deployed in a counter-attack role in the Jordan valley around the Damiya bridge in the north and near Jericho in the south; their aim was to defend the West Bank and East Jerusalem. A Jordanian–Egyptian force was also deployed in the salient of Latrun, just west of Jerusalem on the way to Tel Aviv. On 30 May, the King and President Nasser signed a joint defence pact. It meant that an attack on one country was seen as an attack on the other, which was required to come to the rescue. The King and the President also agreed that, in the event of war, Jordan's forces would be placed under Egyptian command.[16]

Other Arab forces which were assembling against the Israelis included an Iraqi division, which took up positions on Jordanian territory, and two Iraqi squadrons which were advanced towards the Jordanian border and were thus closer to Israeli territory. Small token forces from other Arab countries, including Algeria and Kuwait, were sent to Egypt, and a small Lebanese army was also deployed.

Israel – whose main strength was its reserve force – had started mobilizing on 16 May and moved to full mobilization on

19 May; this was completed by the 20th. The forces were deployed in line with operational plan 'Anvil', which was a defensive posture, but one also designed for a speedy switch from defence to counter-offensive. Regarding Egypt as its main adversary and hoping that both Syria and Jordan would keep out of the battle, Israel had concentrated the bulk of its armed forces in the desert, leaving only scanty forces to fend off any attack on other fronts.

Israel's forces in the Sinai were organized into three divisions; the most northern was commanded by the diminutive Yisrael Tal, and consisted of two armoured brigades in which there were a total of between 250 and 300 tanks. Also under Tal's command and led by Colonel Rafael ('Raful') Eitan was a paratroop brigade supported by a battalion of Patton tanks. The second Israeli division in the Sinai, based entirely on reserves, was commanded by the veteran Abraham Yoffe and consisted of two armoured brigades equipped with Centurion tanks. The third and most southern division was a mixed force which included an armoured brigade, two paratroop battalions, an infantry brigade, six battalions of artillery and a combat engineer battalion. It was commanded by the robust Ariel Sharon. In addition to these forces there were several independent combat groups: a mixed infantry armoured brigade in the rear of El Kuntilla; the 55th paratroop brigade headed by Mordechai Gur, and a naval task force. Totting up the balance sheet (Table 3.1), it can be seen that the Arab armies had clear superiority both in human and material resources.

The crux of all Israeli military operations in the desert was the offensive, for the strength of the Israeli Defence Force – despite its name – was in attack. Since the 1956 campaign, the IDF had been trained as an assault force whose doctrine of warfare was based on two principles: first, a pre-emptive strike by the air force, and second, the transfer of the war into enemy territory.

Table 3.1 Comparison of IDF and Arab forces

|  | IDF | Arabs |
| --- | --- | --- |
| Armoured brigades | 10 | 18 |
| Paratroop brigades | 9 | 53 |
| Tanks | 1,300 | 2,500 |
| Artillery pieces | 746 | 2,780 |
| Fighter jets | 247 | 557 |
| Ground-to-air batteries | 5 | 26 |

The first military plan, drawn up immediately after Nasser's closure of the Straits of Tiran, visualized the movement of Israeli troops into the Gaza Strip with the aim of seizing it and then using it as a bargaining card to compel Nasser to open the Straits of Tiran. But opinions were divided as to the merits of such a plan. Moshe Dayan – he would later become Defence Minister – strongly opposed it on the ground that the Gaza Strip was not important enough for Nasser to be willing to trade it for ending the blockade of the Straits. In a private meeting with the Chief of Staff, Dayan told Rabin that the plan to capture the Gaza Strip in order to compel Nasser to open the Straits would not work, and added 'What will we then do with all these Arabs (meaning the Palestinian refugees of the Gaza Strip)?'[17]

Under Ezer Weizman – he was then chief of operations, and on 24 May temporarily replaced the sick Chief of Staff Rabin – this plan was substantially modified. Now codenamed 'Atzmon Murchav', it visualized the occupation of the Gaza Strip and from there an advance of troops to occupy El Arish, and thence along the northern coastal axis to reach the Suez Canal. When Rabin returned to full service – he was absent for forty-eight hours and rumours said he had suffered a nervous collapse under the intense strain of the previous few days – he ordered the war plans to be recast. The air force was now to launch a pre-emptive strike to be followed by a simultaneous thrust of the three divisions in the northern part of the Sinai, in the area between Rafah and Umm Kataf, to break through into the desert and engage the Egyptian forces. Tal's forces operating in the northern sector were to occupy Gaza, El Arish and Rafah, which – controlling a natural passage of approximately ten miles between the sea and the dunes to the south – was considered a critical location as the jumping-off point for other forces into the heart of the Sinai. In the southern sector, Sharon's forces would take Abu Ageila and the Kuseima strongholds, two separate but mutually supporting bases. Sandwiched between Tal's forces in the north and Sharon's in the south, Yoffe would advance over dunes that had been considered to be almost impassable for tanks, and engage the major Egyptian armoured formations in central Sinai before moving deeper into the desert to seal the Mitla and Giddi passes against retreating Egyptian forces. From there the divisions would be ready to move up to the Suez Canal upon receiving new orders.

## ISRAEL – A SOCIETY UNDER PRESSURE

In Israel, meanwhile, the danger of war aroused increasing anxiety, and what came to be known as the 'waiting period', where forces were fully mobilized and the country came almost to a standstill, was nothing but a war of nerves. With news of the closure of the Straits of Tiran, anxiety turned to panic because after years of warnings by its leaders that a closure of the Straits meant war, Israelis could expect nothing but war. Threatening declarations by Arabs fuelled Israeli anxiety. In a speech before unionists on 26 May – just three days after announcing the closure of the Straits of Tiran – Nasser declared: 'The battle [with Israel] will be a general one and our basic objective will be to destroy Israel', and later:

> I was told at the time that I might have to wait seventy years. During the crusaders' occupation, the Arabs waited seventy years before a suitable opportunity arose and they drove away the crusaders. . . . The whole question then, is the proper time to achieve our aims. We are preparing ourselves constantly.[18]

In Damascus in the meantime it was announced that the time was ripe 'to liberate Palestine', and a Syrian delegation was reported to be heading to Cairo to coordinate military plans. The defence pact signed between Egypt and Jordan on 30 May – despite the inveterate hostility between the two countries – indicated to the anxious Israelis that this time the Arabs meant war and that Israel was totally isolated and faced a disaster. This all had a strong effect and awakened old memories of the Holocaust; as military commander Uzi Narkiss – he would later lead his forces to occupy Jerusalem – recalled: 'Auschwitz (the death camp where Jews were executed) came up. It never happened before. [Israelis] said . . . "we are surrounded, no one will help us, and God forbid if the Arabs armies invade, they'll kill us" '.[19] Such was the panic that it was reported that Holocaust survivors were rushing to pharmacies to buy poison tablets lest they fell into the hands of the enemy. Rumours were rife, and we now know that these were based on fact, that the authorities had estimated 10,000 dead and, as we also now know, the Chief Rabbi, Shmuel Goren, demanded the preparation of coffins and sent his men to inspect public parks which would potentially become huge cemeteries in the event of war.[20] In My Country, Abba Eban describes the mood in Israel at that moment in time: 'A sense of vulnerability penetrated every part of the Israeli consciousness like an icy wind. As Israelis looked around, they saw the world divided between those who were seeking their destruction and those who were doing nothing to prevent it'.[21]

With tensions mounting and the mood becoming desperate, there was strong public pressure on Premier Eshkol to allow Ben

Gurion back as either Prime Minister or Defence Minister. This was because Ben Gurion, the father of modern Israel, had led Israel through the 1948 and 1956 wars and was considered an expert in military affairs, while Eshkol was more of a finance expert. It did not matter to the Israelis that by now Ben Gurion was relatively out of touch, for what they sought was a strong, charismatic leader, and it seemed that Ben Gurion was the right man for this role. But relationships between Eshkol and Ben Gurion were at a low ebb, and Eshkol – an earthbound man and realist by nature, who had invested heavily in buying arms for the IDF in the years before this crisis – bitterly opposed having his predecessor in the cabinet. He said to those who pressurized him to invite Ben Gurion into his cabinet: 'These two horses can no longer pull the same cart'.

But on 28 May came an event which forced Eshkol to give way to public demand and political pressure. That Sunday he personally took to the airwaves to address the nation, and as he delivered his speech and as Israel heard it over the radio – there was not yet television in Israel – Eshkol stumbled over the words.[22] He read his speech so badly and gave so poor a performance that it left the worst impression. It should be pointed out, however, that Eshkol's was more a failure of presentation and delivery than of substance, for there was nothing wrong with the speech itself – but such was the national mood that the effect of such a poor delivery was devastating. After his speech, which came to be known as *Ha'neum Ha'megumgam* ('the stammering speech'), Eshkol was widely criticized.

Now under growing pressure, Eshkol had no other option but to relinquish the defence post and offer it to Moshe Dayan, former chief of staff of the IDF and now a politician in Ben Gurion's small Rafi party. With the nomination of Dayan, it seemed as if the brake had been released and that the IDF – it could not remain mobilized indefinitely without wrecking Israel's economy – would be ordered to take action.

## THE EVE OF WAR

On 2 June, Dayan met the IDF high command, and after being presented with the latest war plans he introduced three changes; the first related to the Straits of Tiran. We should recall that the last straw for Israel had been Nasser's decision to close the Straits to Israeli shipping; therefore Dayan held that in the event of a war breaking out, the Straits of Tiran must be opened. His instructions were that while the decisive thrust should be – as already planned by the military – in the direction of the heart of the Sinai desert, there should also be a thrust towards Sharm el-Sheikh to open the Straits. It was necessary to give such an instruction, for although the Straits were the main issue during the 'waiting period', by now the military planners preferred to concentrate on deciding how to engage the bulk of the Egyptian army in the desert and break its backbone. Dayan's second change to the operational plans dealt with the Gaza Strip. According to the military plans which were originally approved by Eshkol before the nomination of Dayan to the post of Defence Minister, Israeli forces were tasked with occupying the Gaza Strip. It was, in fact, Minister of Labour Yigal Allon – who was normally on the worst of terms with Dayan – who persuaded Eshkol that Israel should take the Gaza Strip and transfer its Palestinian refugees to Egypt. But to this Dayan objected strongly, for he held that the entire international community would turn against Israel if it attempted to transfer the Palestinians. Perhaps more importantly, he considered the Gaza Strip to be a place that 'bristled with problems . . . a nest of wasps', a place which Israel should not occupy if it did not want to be 'stuck with a quarter of million Palestinians'. Therefore, in this crucial meeting with the military high command, Dayan ordered that the Gaza Strip should not be occupied, and as he later wrote in his memoirs: '[the plan] now before us received my approval . . . there would be no conquest of the Gaza Strip'.[23] It is of historical interest to note here that Dayan was not the first to warn of the danger of occupying the Gaza Strip. In 1956, after Israeli troops had occupied the densely populated Strip, Prime Minister Ben Gurion said that he regarded Israel's rule over this compact mass of 'unreconciled people' as being 'as dangerous as dynamite placed at the foundation of the state'. The third element in the war plan which Dayan recast was the Suez Canal. Dayan held that if Israel occupied the Canal and deployed forces on its eastern bank, a mere 180 metres from Egyptian troops, Nasser would not operate the Suez Canal and he would resume the war against Israel; Dayan therefore gave orders that the troops should stop short of the Suez Canal. The restrictions which Dayan had imposed with regard to the Gaza Strip and the Suez Canal were clear and precise; as Aharon Yariv, then director of military intelligence later told the author: 'Dayan said to the General Staff: "I give you now the instruction of the defence minister: 1. To hit the Egyptian army. 2. Not to reach the [Suez] Canal. 3. Not to enter [the] Gaza [Strip]" '.[24] Dayan's observation that if Israel occupied the Suez Canal the war would continue and if it took the Gaza Strip it would 'be stuck' with too many Palestinian refugees was, as we now know, a deadly accurate forecast of the shape of things to come. One wonders why no one other than Dayan had similar insights, and furthermore how, given such a prophetic sense, Dayan later, as will be shown, gave way and agreed to allow the generals to occupy the Gaza Strip and reach the bank of the Suez Canal.

But still, on that crucial night of 2 June 1967, in the light of Dayan's instructions, a new plan codenamed 'Nachshonim' was prepared and its object was defined as 'Occupying Sinai up to the line of El Arish-Jabel Libini-Bir Hasna-Kuseima . . . eliminating the Egyptian forces in this zone and being ready to continue development of the offensive into the heart of the Sinai'. From this newly devised plan two previous military aims were omitted: occupying the Gaza Strip and reaching the Suez Canal.

## BACK TO THE SUPERPOWERS

On 25 May, Nasser dispatched his Minister of War, Shams el-Din Badran, to Moscow to head an Egyptian delegation. Its mission was to obtain Soviet approval for Egypt to strike at Israel, and also to request a supply of war material.[25] Nasser rightly assumed that whoever struck first would enjoy the advantage of surprise and hold the initiative, but he also recognized that acting without Soviet permission would be risky; Moscow might refuse to restock his arsenal after the war, and might also refuse to extend much needed political support. Badran and his delegation met Prime Minister Alexei Kosygin and explained that Egypt wished to strike at Israel. To this Kosygin replied: 'We, the Soviet Union, cannot give you our consent for your pre-emptive strikes against Israel. . . . Should you be the first to attack you will be the aggressor . . . we are against aggression . . . we cannot support you'.[26] It is indeed puzzling that the Soviets, who had instigated the crisis in the first place by spreading the lie that Israel was mobilizing her forces on its border with Syria, were now attempting to control the situation and rein back Egypt.

On his return to Cairo, Badran reported to Nasser that the Soviets would not allow Egypt to strike and would not provide it with much-needed war material, but would intervene in the war on Egypt's side if America were to intervene on behalf of Israel.[27] Nasser was careful to abide by the Soviet instructions and told his military commanders that Egypt would have to absorb a first strike by Israel. He insisted on this in the face of strong opposition, especially from the commander of the air force, General Sudki Mahmoud, who pleaded with him that such a policy 'will be crippling. . . . It will cripple the armed forces'.[28]

Israel was also warned by the US not to take military action. In a tough conversation with Israel's Foreign Minister, US President Lyndon Johnson warned Abba Eban that: 'Israel will not be alone unless it decides to go it alone'. And in a late night meeting in Tel Aviv John Haydon, the CIA representative in Israel, warned Mossad Chief: 'If you strike, the United States will land forces in Egypt to defend her'.

On 30 May Israel sent former general and head of the Mossad, Meir Amit, to Washington. His mission was to see how Israel's view of the crisis compared with that of the American intelligence community (mainly the CIA), to see what would be Washington's response if Israel took action, and also to find out if any preparations had been made to put together an international armada – this had been proposed by British Prime Minister Harold Wilson – which would attempt to sail through the Straits of Tiran in defiance of Nasser's blockade. By this time the sole chance of preventing a general war lay in such an action, and given that, as we have already mentioned, the Straits were declared closed but were not in fact physically blocked (this of course was not known at the time), it might well be that such an armada could have passed without being fired on or even stopped, and war could have been averted. But this was a vain hope. In Washington, Amit found that the plan to set up a joint task force, composed of the principal maritime powers committed to the freedom of passage through the Straits of Tiran, had not even reached the launching stage. He also met Dean Rusk, American Secretary of State, who 'could not agree more' with Amit's assessment of the gravity of the situation.[29] Amit also had three private meetings with James Angleton, the CIA's longtime liaison with the Mossad, from whom he learnt that the Americans would welcome it if Israel were to 'strike [at Egypt]'. To Robert MacNamara, Amit said that he intended to recommend to his government that they launch an attack, to which the American Secretary of Defence replied: 'I read you loud and clear'.[30]

Thus it all came back to the superpowers. The USSR, which had instigated the crisis in the first place by issuing a false report, now showed the 'red light' to the Egyptians, warning them not to be the first to strike, though promising to intervene if America joined the war. As for the Americans, they had shown an 'amber light' to the Israelis ('I read you loud and clear'), which was interpreted by the head of the Mossad as a 'green light' to go to war. Following Amit's report, the Israeli cabinet decided to order the IDF to attack Egypt.

## THE ATTACK ON EGYPT

A successful air strike was crucial for the overall victory of the Israelis. This was aimed at curbing Egypt's capability to strike at Israeli cities and, perhaps more importantly, to achieve air supremacy over the desert, which would make Egyptian defeat certain. The air operation, codenamed 'Moked', began at 7.45 a.m., as Egyptian pilots were having their breakfast, on Monday 5 June 1967. The air strike took a very roundabout approach, flying via the sea and coming in from the west. While the first wave of Israeli aeroplanes – 183 in all – was making its way to Egypt, the entire command of the Egyptian armed forces, including Marshall Amer and Minister of War Shams el-Din Badran, were also in the air on their way to inspect Egyptian units in the Sinai; to ensure their safe passage and that they were not fired at by their own people, the radar system in Egypt was shut down. This tragi-comic episode, in which the Egyptian command is airborne, the radar system is shut down and Israeli fighter-bombers are on their way to targets in Egypt, symbolizes, perhaps more than anything else, the inefficiency of the Egyptian command, and demonstrates that part of Israel's stunning success resulted from the recklessness, blind folly and ineptitude of the enemy's political-military leadership.

'Operation Moked' was extraordinarily successful and led to a sensational and dramatic victory for the Israeli Air Force (IAF). Within 190 minutes the backbone of the Egyptian air force was broken – 189 Egyptian aeroplanes were destroyed, mostly on the ground, in the first wave of attack, and by the end of the first day of war a stunning 298 Egyptian planes lay in ruins. Back in his headquarters Marshall Amer was trying to piece together a new plan from the wreckage. He ordered the air force to hit back at the Israelis, but the reply he received was that the little that remained of the air force was unable to carry out any meaningful operation. Nasser was later to complain bitterly that the Israeli air strike eventually came not from the direction his guns were pointing, but from behind: 'They came from the west', he said, 'when we expected them to come from the east'.

Backed by complete air superiority, the three Israeli divisions thrust into the desert to engage the Egyptian forces, which were incessantly pounded by Israeli planes and were no match for the Israeli ground forces. Meanwhile, the spokesman of the IDF announced that since the early hours of the morning Israeli forces had been engaged in fierce fighting with Egyptian forces which had started 'advancing towards Israel'; this was not quite true for, as we now know, the Israelis rather than the Egyptians were the first to open fire.

The retreat of the Egyptian army, though unavoidable, was hasty and chaotic. A skilfully conducted step-by-step withdrawal could have saved lives, or at least proved less costly, but in the event the retreat was very disorderly, with small and uncoordinated groups of troops trying to escape on foot through the desert dunes in the direction of the Suez Canal. The end result was disastrous – for while 2,000 Egyptian troops were killed fighting the Israelis, 10,000 perished in the retreat.

As Israeli forces gave chase in an attempt to cut the Egyptian lines of retreat, they drew closer to the Suez Canal, which Defence Minister Dayan had on the eve of the war ordered them not to occupy. At one point Dayan, thinking that his troops had already reached the Canal, issued orders to pull back. But then, under strong pressure from his Chief of Staff, who argued that militarily it was better to stop at the Canal, Dayan reversed his decision and allowed the troops to resume their advance and reach the bank of the Suez Canal.[31] Furthermore, following the shelling of the Israeli settlements of Nachal Oz, Kisufim and Ein Ha'shlosha from inside the Gaza Strip, Dayan was requested to allow troops to enter the Strip and silence the enemy's fire. Again, Dayan gave way and allowed forces to enter Gaza, even though a few days before he had said that it 'bristled with problems', was 'a nest of wasps', and was a place which Israel should not occupy if it did not want to be 'stuck with a quarter of million Palestinians'.

Why Dayan gave way and allowed the armed forces to dictate the stopping line is a question to which there will never be a definite answer. But any clues may lie more in the character of Dayan than in any strategic consideration. For although Dayan was renowned as a brave soldier and almost a prophet because of his foresight, he was, on the other hand, too much the pessimist, often failing to fight for his ideas with colleagues or to impose his will on his subordinates; as was the case in the war in the Sinai, where he allowed short-term tactical considerations to disrupt his realistic policy.

## JORDAN

On the Jordanian front war started at 9.45 a.m. on 5 June, as King Hussein's guns opened fire along the border with Israel and Jordanian troops attempted to occupy the United Nations headquarters and other positions in Jerusalem. On this morning the Israelis delivered a message to the King, saying: 'This is a war between us and Egypt. If you stay out we will not touch you'.[32] Upon receiving this message, the King – he was at air force headquarters – said: 'Jordan is not out. Jordan is already engaged'.[33] This is understandable, for with Palestinians making up half of his population, if Hussein had stood aside his kingdom could have disintegrated. In addition, the King may have feared that he would miss the boat if he did not join the war, for in the early hours of 5 June, a message was received from Egypt's Marshall Amer, saying: 'approximately 75 per cent of the enemy's aircraft have been destroyed or put out of action . . . our troops have engaged the enemy and taken the offensive on the ground'.[34] This of course was a lie, but the King could not have known that. After all, Nasser had also called to say that Egypt was doing well. He said to the King – and we know exactly what he said because his conversation was intercepted and recorded by the Mossad – 'We have sent all our aeroplanes against Israel. Since early this morning our air force has been bombing the Israeli air force'.[35] This too was a lie, for while talking with King Hussein, Nasser already knew that his air force was totally destroyed. We know this because just *before* calling the King, Nasser had talked with President Boumedienne of Algeria, to whom he announced that the Egyptian air force was totally destroyed, and asked if he could spare a few aircraft. In his talk with the King, Nasser also urged that he join him in issuing 'an announcement concerning the British and American participation' in the war. This was clearly aimed to drag in the Soviets, for, as we should remember, the USSR had promised Egyptian Minister of War Badran that, if America joined the war, Russia would come in on Egypt's side.

Israel's response to the Jordanian attack was immediate and devastating – it destroyed Jordan's two air force bases and in 51 sorties totally crippled its small air force, before moving to occupy the West Bank and Jerusalem. This was a terrible defeat to King Hussein. He later recalled how he was standing on a hill watching his defeated troops:

> My troops were coming back in small groups, very tired. Many of them were saying: 'Please, your Majesty, find us some air cover and we'll go right back'. Of course, everything was over by then and I remember asking all these boys to move on to Zarka, so we could begin to reorganize whatever remained

... I saw all the years that I had spent since 1953 trying to build up the country and army, all the pride, all the hopes, destroyed ... I have never received a more crushing blow than that.[36]

## THE LIBERTY AFFAIR

With the war in full swing an incident occurred which would dent Israeli-American relationships for years to come. This was the Israeli air and naval attack on the United States spy ship USS Liberty, which resulted in the death of 34 US men and the wounding of some 171.

From the start of the Middle East crisis Washington was keen to follow up events in the region. But the Israelis, contrary to popular belief, were reluctant to cooperate with the Americans by sharing crucial information and intelligence. The Americans installed a radar on the roof of their embassy in Tel Aviv in order that they could, by using their own means, detect Israeli air activity and report back to Washington on the start and progress of the war. The Israelis, however, found out about the 'Igloo' which popped up on the roof of the American embassy and, on the morning of 5 June, when their warplanes were about to implement Moked, Israeli intelligence personnel climbed on roofs surrounding the embassy and jammed the radar, thus preventing the Americans from knowing that war was under way. Eager, however, to follow up events in spite of Israel's obstruction, the Americans dispatched an intelligence ship, USS Liberty, to the fighting area to monitor the progress of the battle and report back home. But on 8 June, at 1:58, while Liberty was sailing approximately twelve-and-a-half miles off the coast of the Sinai peninsula, in the vicinity of El Arish, she was attacked by the Israelis. The strike was carried out by two Mirage aircraft each making three runs on the ship and, as the first flight finished strafing Liberty with cannon and machine guns at 2:04, a second flight of two Super Mystere aircraft continued the attack by dropping bombs on the American ship.

Over the years there have been speculations on whether the Israeli attack was premeditated – planned and deliberate – aimed at preventing Liberty from following up events, particularly that Israel was mobilizing forces in Galilee in order to seize the Golan Heights, or whether it was – as the Israelis have always claimed – 'a tragic case of misidentification'.

However, from recordings of the conversation over the radio system of Israeli pilots during the attack on Liberty, it can be revealed here, for the first time, that the Israelis did know after the attack of the Air Force on the ship and before the Navy moved in to deliver the knock-out, that this was an American vessel. In these audio tapes, which are in the author's archive, one can overhear the following conversation between Colonel Shmuel Kislev, then Commander Air Control, sitting two seats away from General Hod, Chief of Israeli Air Force during this war, and Israeli pilots on 8 June 1967 at 2:14 p.m.:

PILOT  What country [does the ship belong to]?
COLONEL KISLEV  Most probably American.
PILOT  What?
COLONEL KISLEV  Most probably American.

Nonetheless, and in spite of the positive identification of the ship as American, 12 minutes later, at 2:26 p.m, three Israeli Motor Torpedo Boats led by a certain Moshe Oren arrived on the scene, stopped at a distance and flashed light signals to Liberty. When they came under fire from Liberty gunners the Israelis responded, at 2:31 – that is 17 minutes after the positive identification of the ship as an American – with a torpedo and strafing run on the ship. Five torpedoes were fired at Liberty and four minutes into the attack a single torpedo hit the ship, instantly killed 25, and put Liberty out of action. The Israeli official narrative that 'it was

only a helicopter, sent after the attack in order to render assistance . . . which noticed a small American flag flying over the
target' and that it was only 'at that stage that the vessel was
finally identified as a . . . ship of the US Navy' was a lie.[37]

## SYRIA

Elsewhere, on the Golan Heights, war did not start until 8 June.
In fact the Syrians, after perceiving the fate of Egypt and Jordan,
preferred to keep out of the battle, and when asked by the King
of Jordan to provide air support they replied that all their aircraft were on training missions and not a single aircraft was
available.

At first Israel refrained from attacking Syria because Defence
Minister Dayan felt that if Israel struck, the Soviets might
intervene on behalf of the Syrians. He also felt that if Israel
occupied the Golan Heights it would never be willing to give
it back and the conflict with Syria would continue for years. In
the end, however, Dayan gave way, reversed his previous order
not to attack, and authorized the occupation of the Golan
Heights; in fact he did not even contact the Chief of Staff, who
was sleeping at home in the belief that the war was over, but
picked up the phone and issued an order to strike. We will
probably never know why Dayan reversed his decision; it may
be that he feared that after the war he would be blamed for
not taking advantage of the situation to hit at Syria, with
whom Israel had hostile border relationships. According to
Dayan, his change of mind was made following intelligence
information indicating that the Syrians would not resist if Israel
struck. We now know what was not known even to Dayan at the
time – that his prediction, that the Soviets might intervene
alongside the Syrians to stop the Israeli advance on the Golan,
almost materialized; Soviet planes in the Ukraine were preparing
to attack Israeli military targets and Soviet submarines were

approaching the shores of Israel.[38] We do not know why they did not attack.

With Egypt and Jordan crippled, the IDF could concentrate all its strength on Syria, which was clearly no match for the Israeli air and ground forces. 'We dropped everything on the Golan Heights', recalls former IAF commander Mordechai Hod: 'In two days we dropped more tha[n] we had dropped on all Egyptian airfields [throughout the war]'.[39] According to Syrian General Abdel Razzak Al-Dardari, who commanded four Syrian brigades on the Golan Heights,

> On that morning the Israelis moved ahead. . . . There was a sudden panic and there was an order to withdraw to the south. The pull-out was done in total chaos . . . the retreating soldiers had left their weapons behind and were almost running home. Some were running home even before the Israeli soldiers had come anywhere near their positions . . . there was no air cover nor an Egyptian front to distract the Israelis.[40]

In spite of UN pressure on Israel to stop the war, and rising tensions between Washington and Moscow – the latter threatening to 'take any measures to stop Israel, including military' – the Israelis had managed to occupy the Golan Heights.

## EUPHORIA AND DIVISION

The speed of the operation staggered the world, and the Israelis, whose immediate reaction to the stunning victory was euphoria and jubilation as a spontaneous expression of relief that the worst – what seemed to be an imminent second Holocaust – had not materialized and instead Israel had gained a victory with relatively few casualties. Indeed, in six days the battle was over, and by then Israeli troops were less than 50km from Amman, 60km from Damascus and 110km from Cairo. Israel now controlled an area of 88,000 square kilometres compared with 20,250 before the war, or 18 times the area which was allotted to the Jews by Lord Peel in the first partition plan for Palestine of 1937. The Sinai desert, the Gaza Strip, the Golan Heights and the West Bank now provided Israeli cities with a buffer zone, dramatically reducing the danger of Israel's extinction by a surprise Arab attack.

The victory had a special historic meaning because of the capturing of territories central to the religious mythical past: the Old City of Jerusalem with the Western Wall, which is the remnant of the ancient Jewish temple destroyed by the Romans; and the West Bank, which is part of biblical Eretz Yisrael and where such sites as Machpela are situated. For Israel's religious community, the occupation of these territories established the relationships between what they define as 'People, God and Promised Land', strengthening their sense of Jewish identity.

But the occupation of Arab lands also sowed the seeds of conflict and division within Israeli society; this was apparent immediately after the war, when a fierce debate regarding the future of the occupied lands broke out. A society, which only three weeks before was huddling together and fearing for its very existence, was now beginning to split between those who wished to cling to the occupied lands and those calling for it to be given back in return for peace and reconciliation. But it was more than a debate regarding occupied territories, for in the postwar era, with what seemed to Israelis to be a reduction of external danger because of their newly acquired strategic depth, a whole range of problems began to surface. As Abba Eban, a diplomat and a good observer, has written:

> As the pressure of war . . . died down, some of the latent tensions in Israeli society came to the surface. The turbulence took many shapes and expressions but the common factor was the growth of dissent . . . [Israelis now] rejected the idea that

external dangers justified inertia or apathy towards domestic imperfections.[41]

What became crystal clear in the post-1967 war period was that Israeli society was essentially a diverse, turbulent organism which tended to have a monolithic aspect only when facing urgent external danger. And this is precisely what made the 1967 war such a turning point in the life of the Israeli nation and society. For while the war seemed to remove a great external danger to Israel – whose cities were now far from the front – it also, ironically, removed the cement which had kept the people of Israel together. And although, in the postwar era, opinion polls indicated the overwhelming popularity of the national leaders, with those in charge of defence policies supported by staggering percentages, the government was challenged as never before by its citizens. This criticism quickly gathered momentum and reached an unprecedented peak during the War of Attrition along the Suez Canal.

## 'THE FORGOTTEN WAR OF ATTRITION' 1968–70

The Egyptian army, we should remember, though badly beaten and crippled, had not been destroyed in the 1967 war, nor did the Egyptian leadership lose the appetite to reorganize itself to hit back at the Israelis, who were now deployed on the other side of the Suez Canal. In this regard, Defence Minister Dayan's observation, made on the eve of the 1967 war, that occupying the Suez Canal would mean the continuation of war with Egypt, proved prophetic.

On 22 June 1967, less than two weeks after war ended, President Nasser told the Soviet President: 'Because the Israelis are now in Sinai, we are building our defences on the west bank of the [Suez] Canal. If the Israelis refuse to leave peacefully, sooner or later we'll have to fight them to get them out'.[42] Moscow was

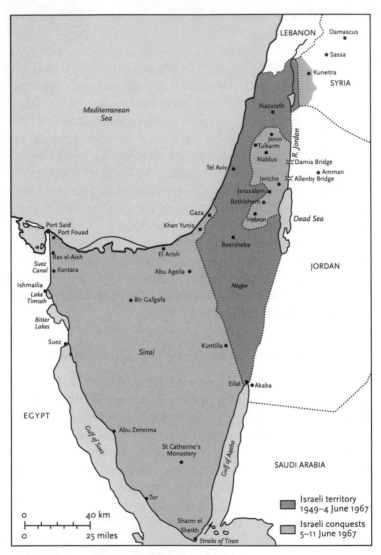

*Map 3* The 1967 Six Day War: Israel's conquests

sympathetic, promising Nasser: 'Soon you will have a larger number of fighter aircraft than you had before the [1967] invasion'.[43] In fact, by the second day of the 1967 war, Moscow was supplying both Egypt and Syria with weapons; 544 airlifts and 15 cargo ships transferred nearly 48,000 tons of military equipment to both countries. Egypt, whose air force was in ruins, had received 25 MiG-21 aircraft and 93 MiG-17s, followed by another transfer of 40 MiG-21s and six MiG-21s equipped for training purposes; it also received 38 Sukhoi aircraft, as well as 100 tanks. Between 1,000 and 1,200 Soviet advisers also arrived in Egypt to help assimilate and indeed operate the new weapons. As early as February 1968, General Fawzi, the new commander in chief of the Egyptian army, announced that the armed forces had reached 70 per cent of their strength before the outbreak of the June 1967 war.

The first major incident between Egypt and Israel after the Six Day War took place on 21 October 1967, when an Egyptian destroyer torpedoed and sank the Israeli destroyer Eilat in international waters off Port Said. Israel retaliated by shelling Egyptian oil refineries close to the city of Suez and setting alight the adjoining oil storage tanks. Clashes along the Suez Canal had developed into artillery duels between 8 September and 26 October 1968, where in two massive barrages Egyptian artillery inflicted heavy casualties on the Israelis. Israel's ground forces retaliated both along the Canal and deep into Egyptian territory. The air force blew up several bridges on the Nile, and paratroops, landing deep inside Egypt, destroyed the electricity transmission station at Naj Hamadi. By carrying out raids into Egyptian territory Israel signalled that it would not confine its retaliations to the Canal area. To some extent these raids compelled the Egyptians to call off their attacks, and led to a relatively calm period from November 1968 until March 1969.

It is important to note here that these clashes, the majority of which were initiated by Egypt, were not random incidents caused by local trigger-happy military commanders, but rather part of a well-planned Egyptian military programme which envisaged a total war against Israel in three main phases. The first of these was called the 'holding out' or the steadfastness stage; the second was the 'state of deterrence' and the third was to be a total 'war of attrition' against Israel. In a speech on 21 January 1969, Nasser explained: 'The first priority, the absolute priority in this battle, is the military front, for we must realize that the [Israeli] enemy will not withdraw unless we force him to withdraw through fighting'.[44] A month later, in February 1969, Nasser said to the council of ministers:

> We should go ahead this year and escalate the situation with Israel and in particular step up the commando operations in Sinai because, as part of the War of Attrition, such operations have a significant impact on the enemy's military deployment and morale. Operations of this sort will force the enemy to keep large numbers of troops under arms, which runs counter to his military policy and stretches his capabilities.[45]

In military terms, the first priority of the Egyptian armed forces, to put it in crude terms, was to cause Israel to bleed to death. As General Fawzi explained to the council of ministers:

> [Our intention is] first to provoke bloody clashes with the enemy with the aim of killing the largest possible number of enemy personnel; that is to say, priority will be given to [weakening] Israeli manpower in preference to weapons and equipment, because loss of lives causes greater concern to the Israeli military command.[46]

To impose on Israel what came to be known in Egypt as *Hareb el Istinzaf*, namely the 'War of Bloodshed', was a shrewd way to tackle the Israeli occupation of the Sinai, for Nasser was right in assuming that the close-knit, highly-sensitive-to-casualties Israeli society could hardly sustain a long and bloody contest – a war of positions – in which it would lose soldiers on a daily basis. The Egyptian plan was to hit at the Israelis not only militarily, but also psychologically: to hit the soft spots of Israeli society.

## THE BAR LEV LINE

Indeed, as the war dragged on and the number of casualties mounted, the Israeli General Staff was obliged to seek ways of protecting the troops along the Suez Canal. This led to the construction of a defensive line of fortifications named after then Chief of Staff Haim Bar Lev. The line was a chain of thirty-two strongpoints (*Ma'ozim*) stretching 180km from Ras el-Aish in the north to Port Tawfik in the south. Each fort had firing positions, as well as a courtyard big enough to hold a few tanks and allow soldiers enough space to carry on with their daily lives and routines. A paved road linked the strongholds, and a sand ramp was built between it and the canal to prevent the Egyptians from observing the movements of troops inside the forts. Between the fortifications there were observation posts and tank emplacements. Bunkers were built which were covered by thick layers of fill and stones. Between 7 and 12km east of the line, 11 big strongholds (*Ta'ozim*) were constructed. The Bar Lev line on the edge of the water, as Haim Bar Lev explained to the author, was 'only one component of a system which relied on defence in depth'.[47] Troops stationed in the line had to serve as the eyes and ears of this system and, in case of emergency, to summon tanks and activate other resources which were deployed behind them in the depths of Sinai.

IDF opinion was divided regarding the idea of constructing a line of defence along the Suez Canal, and it is curious to see how closely this debate resembled that which had taken place in

France regarding the construction of the Maginot line. In the French case it was the young Charles de Gaulle and a few other military commanders who attacked the idea of the Maginot line, saying that tanks and warplanes, armoured divisions and fleets of bombers had revolutionized warfare and that the advantage would in future lie with the state that could concentrate highly mechanized and fast moving strikepower. Within the Israeli command, it was mainly Generals Sharon and Tal who strongly opposed the building of the line, arguing similarly to De Gaulle, that the advantage would lie with those armies that could man-oeuvre and concentrate forces at crucial points in the battlefield, and that the offensive was more in tune with Israel's character and its forces. They also argued that the depth of the Sinai desert occupied in the previous war would enable the IDF to sell ground to gain time, practise shock-absorbing tactics and delay any offensive until the reserves were mobilized. Their bottom line was that the Bar Lev line would force Israel to fight pos-itional warfare, which would be catastrophic to her. But then, what Bar Lev had in mind, as he explained to the author, was not a Maginot line of defence, with a braking function, but rather a line to offer cover to troops under bombardment and reduce the number of casualties. Bar Lev then enforced his will and the line of defence was built and completed in March 1969. We now know that the objectors to the line were probably right, for the Bar Lev line played into the hands of the Egyptian army, which was thus able to proceed with Nasser's plan and impose an all-out war of attrition on the Israelis.

In March 1969, after a relatively calm period, Egypt resumed the war and carried out massive barrages of the Bar Lev line, with 35,000 shells being fired between 8 and 10 March. To this attack and those which followed, Israel's response was to send ground forces to carry out deep penetration raids. On 28 July paratroopers and naval commandos captured the rock fortress of Green Island, the southern hinge of the Egyptian air defence network, and destroyed its radar and anti-aircraft installations; this opened the way for Israeli aircraft to bomb Egyptian positions. On 9 September 1969, an Israeli seaborne force crossed the Gulf of Suez and landed not far from the Egyptian port of Zafarana, from where it moved for almost ten hours along the coastal road towards Suez, destroying installations on its way before returning home. On 26 December, Israeli forces carried out an operation against a new P-12 radar installation to detect low-flying planes, some 250 miles south of Suez; technicians dismantled the radar and a helicopter carried it back to Israel for examination. But all this was to no avail – the war continued with undiminished fury, the number of Israeli casualties mounted, and uneasiness spread within Israeli society.

## THE STRATEGY OF DEEP PENETRATION

Unable to put an end to the War of Attrition, and under strong public pressure to stop the bloodshed caused by this static war of positions, the IAF was dispatched to execute 'Operation Boxer', a massive air bombardment of Egyptian positions along the Suez Canal.[48] This was no more effective. Egyptian shelling of the Bar Lev line continued, and the black announcements, often carrying a photograph of a young soldier, continued to appear daily in the Israeli press. This lowered morale and spurred the Israeli military-political leadership to look for other ways of ending the war. The military command then devised a new strategy of deep penetration by the air force, aimed at bombing positions deep within Egypt, thus relieving pressure on Israeli troops along the Canal.[49] As Defence Minister Dayan put it: 'The first and foremost aim of the deep penetration strategy is to make it easier for the [Israeli] defence forces to hold the ceasefire line'.[50] The plan to bomb deep into Egypt was much helped by Israel's recent purchase of Phantoms and Skyhawk fighter jets.

The IAF began its bombardment on 7 January 1970 by attacking Egyptian military camps, including the Headquarters of the Suez Canal, some 30km northeast of Cairo. Throughout January and February 1970, raids were focused on military targets near the cities of Ismailia, Cairo, Insha and Hilwan, and between 1 January and 18 April 1970, the period of the bombing campaign, the IAF flew 3,300 sorties and dropped 8,000 tons of munitions on Egyptian positions. No civilian targets were deliberately attacked, but there were human errors which resulted in civilians being killed. On 13 February 1970 a Phantom bombed an Egyptian factory, killing 70 civilians, and on 9 April a hit on a primary school killed 46 Egyptian children. The pressure on the Egyptians was such that they were forced to reduce resources along the Canal in order to protect its interior, which in turn eased pressure on the Israelis along the Bar Lev line and reduced casualties. But Israel also suffered heavily, because the Egyptian anti-aircraft defence system, 30 times as powerful as it had been before the 1967 war, hit hard at the IAF. In August 1970 a ceasefire was agreed, and until the 1973 war the front was more or less calm.

## QUEEN OF THE BATHTUB

The War of Attrition – often termed 'the forgotten war' – rarely hit the international headlines, and there are only a few studies of this relatively long and bloody conflict. But it did make a major impact on Israeli society. The decision of Israel's leadership to construct the Bar Lev line, to send troops on raids across the Suez canal, to bomb along the Canal, and finally to dispatch fighter-jets between January and April 1970 to bomb deep into Egypt, were all desperate attempts to respond to public demand to put an end to an immensely unpopular war. After the euphoria of the 1967 victory there could be nothing as disappointing and frustrating for the Israelis as the War of Attrition. And although Prime

Minister Meir claimed 'Never before has our situation been better', this was not what ordinary Israelis felt. What Israelis saw was bloodshed on the bank of the Suez Canal – between March 1969 and August 1970 alone, 138 soldiers were killed and 375 wounded; and a total of 400 Israelis were killed and more than 2,000 wounded between the end of the 1967 war and August 1970, the day a ceasefire between Israel and Egypt came into force. The Israeli public reacted strongly to the costs both human and material. Hanoch Levin's *Queen of the Bathtub* offered perhaps the strongest condemnation, and it was an expression of the Israelis' fatigue with wars and sacrifice. A satirical show, it attacked the 'joy' over war and the 'cult of fatalities'. And although there were some interest groups which boycotted the show and called for it to be stopped, it nevertheless attracted thousands of Israelis and was a novelty in a society which until then had showed itself willing to sacrifice without protest. Worse still, young pupils, on the eve of being recruited into the IDF, sent a letter to the Prime Minister saying, 'We don't know if we will be able to do what we have to do in the army'. Such a protest would have been unthinkable before the 1967 war.

It was also a costly war, and defence spending had to rise – in 1965 defence consumption as percentage of GNP was 9.5; it went up in 1966 to 10.4, reached 17.7 in 1967, in 1968 it rose to 18.2, a year later it was 20.2, in 1970 it was 25.7 and in 1971 a staggering 26.3 per cent. While previously there had been hardly any protest against high spending on defence, this was not the case after the 1967 war and during the War of Attrition. Israelis, mainly of North African origin, a home grown black panther movement had rioted in Jerusalem and Haifa in March 1971, challenging the government's priorities that seemingly placed social services, housing and other social concerns on the back burner and clearly secondary to spending on defence. Thus, with the approach of a critical year, 1973, Israeli society was deeply divided on a range of issues, and was becoming much more critical of its leadership.

# 4

## WAR AND PEACE

### 1973–9

Anwar el-Sadat, who succeeded President Nasser in September 1970, was perhaps the most dynamic political leader in the Middle East between 1970 and 1979; he made war (1973) and peace (1979), forcing the Israelis to respond to his initiatives. With hindsight we can say that Sadat, more than any other Middle Eastern leader at that time, transformed the international relationships of the region, and also – though indirectly and unintentionally – altered the political scene in Israel itself. By taking Israel by surprise and successfully launching an attack across the Suez Canal on 6 October 1973, he managed to put in train events which eventually resulted in Israelis turning against their leadership and voting for a right-wing Likud government under Menachem Begin, with whom Sadat eventually signed a landmark peace accord on 26 March 1979.

Arab politics is not the subject of this book, but it is

undeniable that the initiative throughout these critical years was firmly on the Arab side – mainly Egypt – and it therefore makes sense to begin the discussion of the 1973 Yom Kippur War, the peace which followed it and the impact of these events on Israeli society, in Egypt.

## THE DARK DONKEY

When Sadat became President of Egypt upon the death of Nasser, he was not taken seriously by his colleagues, who had chosen him for the top job because they considered him to be a front man who would do as he was told and continue Nasser's Arab nationalism and pro-Soviet policies. Nor did Sadat impress the Israelis, who nicknamed him 'the dark donkey' and regarded him as a transitional leader and little more than a figurehead. The Americans regarded Sadat as 'a semi-comic figure'. Indeed, at the time of his appointment to the top job, there was little to indicate that Sadat would become the leading figure in making war and peace in the Middle East in the 1970s. But soon after his accession to power, Sadat began showing his true colours, purging his opponents – mainly the group around Ali Sabri, a pro-Soviet Vice President – and taking bold initiatives in foreign policy.

As early as 1971, Sadat announced that this year would be 'the year of decision' – surely, hardly anyone understood what a 'year of decision' meant – but in an interview with Arnaud de Borchgrave of *Newsweek*, he declared that he would be prepared to recognize Israel and live in peace with her. Soon afterwards, on 4 February, Sadat dropped a 'peace bombshell', announcing in the Egyptian parliament an entirely new initiative. 'If Israel withdrew her forces in Sinai to the [Mitla and Giddi] Passes' (about 48km east of the Suez Canal), he declared,

> I would be willing to reopen the Suez Canal; to have my forces cross to the East Bank [of the Suez Canal] . . . to make a

solemn, official declaration of a cease-fire by six, rather than three, months; to restore diplomatic relations with the United States; and sign a peace agreement with Israel through the efforts of Dr Jarring, the representative of the Secretary General of the UN.

As Sadat later remarked: 'None of my opponents had fore-knowledge of my initiative ... they were surprised, indeed dumbfounded, to hear me declare it to the world'. It is hard to say, even with hindsight, whether Sadat's initiative had any chance of succeeding and the prevailing view is still that no compromise could have been reached on the basis of what Sadat was willing to offer in exchange for Israel's withdrawal from the Suez Canal and that neither side was ready for hard decisions at the time. Sadat's insistence on an unequivocal Israeli undertaking to withdraw completely from Sinai was also not helpful in convincing the Israeli government to accept his proposals. Nonetheless, the fact remains that in the early 1970s and well before his decision to launch a war against Israel, Sadat was willing to open a dialogue with her, and he did offer a programme to achieve this aim. The problem, it seems, was more on the Israeli side, where Prime Minister Golda Meir – she had been recalled from retirement to succeed Eshkol, who died in February 1969 – failed to show any flexibility. As a former foreign minister in Ben Gurion's government, she presided, most reluctantly we should say, over the withdrawal of Israeli troops from the Sinai and Sharm el-Sheikh, the base commanding the entrance to the Gulf of Aqaba which Israel had occupied in 1956. Yet the return, under intense inter-national pressure, of this occupied land to Egypt in 1957 did not lead to peace, and in May 1967, as we have already shown, President Nasser dispatched forces to Sharm el-Sheikh and declared a maritime blockade on the Straits of Tiran, to be closed to Israeli shipping. With this in mind, Meir was adamant and firm in her opposition to the return of occupied land for less than what she considered to be a genuine peace and recognition by the Arabs of Israel's right to live peacefully in the Middle East.

It is important to note, however, that within Meir's cabinet there was a group of ministers which did favour a limited withdrawal from the Suez Canal. Notable among them was Defence Minister Moshe Dayan who, as we have shown in the previous chapter, had objected in 1967 to the occupation of the Suez Canal, and as early as August 1970 had made the suggestion to pull back a little way from Suez so that the Egyptians could then resume navigation and rehabilitate their canal zone cities. Dayan's proposal – he envisaged a retreat of some 35km – was a realistic policy based on the assumption that Israel would be in less danger of war if it pulled back from the Canal so that Nasser could operate it. For with ships sailing to and fro there would be little incentive for Nasser to resume war, since this would prevent international shipping from using the Canal and result in Egypt losing much-needed revenues. But as we have already seen, in spite of his pluck, prowess and originality, Dayan was no fighter for his ideas and was not someone to impose his will on colleagues, so that when Meir objected to his plan – she saw in it the beginning of an Israeli withdrawal to the old boundaries without the equivalent of a peace treaty – he simply gave way to the Prime Minister.

Meir's reply to President Sadat's offer came on 9 February 1971 in a speech to the Knesset in which, as Gideon Rafael, a senior foreign ministry official, put it, 'She extended him a finger – not a hand'. In retrospect, this was a colossal missed opportunity for, if Israel had only been willing to negotiate an unequivocal withdrawal from the bank of the Suez Canal, the Yom Kippur War might well have been averted. But Dayan's typical reluctance to fight for his realistic policies and Meir's uncompromising personality combined to pave the way for the immobilism which was a main feature of Israel's policies in the early 1970s, and was eventually to lead to the outbreak of hostilities more devastating than those of any previous war, except for that of 1948. We now know that, in fact, Meir had failed to comprehend the line of thought behind Dayan's proposal to withdraw, and as she frankly put it to a meeting of the central committee of the Labor party on 5 December 1973:

> I admit and confess that when defence minister [Dayan] proposed a few years ago that we agree to withdraw from the Suez Canal, in order that the Egyptians open it to shipping and rehabilitate their canal zone cities, I failed to understand what he was talking about. Just like that to suggest that we withdraw from the Canal [without the Egyptians giving us something in return]?

Sadat's offer to open a dialogue with the Israelis was taken much more seriously by American President Richard Nixon who, in the summer of 1971, sent Under-Secretary of State Joseph Sisco – a highly qualified professional and a skilful diplomat – to the Middle East to try and break the impasse by convincing Prime Minister Meir to agree to a withdrawal from the Suez Canal. What very much encouraged the President was that, privately, Israeli Defence Minister Dayan let Washington understand that he was in favour of a withdrawal from the Canal. Nevertheless, as Sisco later recalled, the President said to him: 'Press Golda but if she reacts negatively, don't press it to a confrontation . . . between Israel and the United States'. We should remember that at that time Israel was considered by the American administration to be a reliable strategic asset in the region, and Washington had no stomach to impose on Israel policies which might endanger the special relations between the two countries. So with a presidential mandate to talk but not to exercise too much pressure, Sisco travelled to Israel and met with Meir's cabinet. But soon he returned to Washington empty-handed and downhearted, and as he later recalled: 'After two days of in-depth discussion, it was clear we weren't making much progress . . . the reaction of the Prime Minister was a negative one'.[1]

In an attempt to persuade the United States that he was serious about opening a dialogue with Israel, and to hint that the key for such a dialogue lay in Washington rather than in Moscow, Sadat took a bold step, and on 18 July 1972 expelled from Egypt 15,000 Soviet advisers. These advisers, who had arrived in Egypt following Sadat's predecessor's visit to Moscow in January 1970, played a crucial role in the Egyptian army, and even took direct part in fighting against the Israelis. But if by taking this step Sadat had hoped that the American administration would react by pressurizing Israel to accept withdrawal he was due for a disappointment. As we have already said, Israel was at that time a strategic asset in the Middle East, and the US administration would not challenge Meir's insistence on not yielding an inch of occupied land for less than a full recognition and acceptance of Israel by the Arabs in the Middle East. Nonetheless, Sadat remained undeterred, and in a further attempt to persuade Washington to help him open a dialogue, he dispatched his national security adviser, Hafez Ismail, to meet President Nixon and his national security adviser Henry Kissinger. Ismail met the President in the White House on 23 February 1973, and he then had three secret meetings with Kissinger on 24–5 February, but it came to nothing, mainly because Washington would not believe Sadat, whose 'zig-zag' foreign policies confused both them and the Israelis. For, at the same time when he was hinting that Egypt was in the American camp, Sadat also signed a 15-year 'Treaty of Friendship and

Cooperation' with the Soviets, and when asked by the Americans about this he flatly replied that Egypt was free to make her own decisions.

Back in Cairo, Ismail reported to Sadat on his meetings in Washington and, according to then Chief of Staff of the Egyptian army Saad el-Shazli, declared that Kissinger had said to him: 'I cannot deal with your problem unless it becomes a crisis', which according to el-Shazli was regarded by Sadat as a sign that 'Kissinger was encouraging him to go to war. That war was the only option'.[2] It is interesting to note that at about this time, April 1973, Kissinger said in an interview to Arnaud de Borchgrave of Newsweek that he 'expects something to happen which can be very serious [in the Middle East]'.

Meanwhile, Sadat was also concerned about the improvement in US/USSR relations which meant, as he saw it, that the superpowers were unlikely to embark on a major initiative in the Middle East lest this put a strain on their improving relationship. Détente, in Sadat's eyes, was a new situation likely to reduce the Middle Eastern problem to a minor item on the international agenda and freeze the status quo, leaving Arab lands in Israeli hands.

Sadat was disappointed. His initiatives had run aground, his approaches to Washington had failed to produce practical results, he had failed to dislodge Israel from its entrenched positions, and he had become a laughing stock in the eyes of his own people to whom he had repeatedly promised that the 'year of decision' was around the corner.

## A MAJOR SHIFT IN POLICY

The record clearly shows that quite independently of his diplomatic initiatives, Sadat also gave orders to prepare a plan of campaign for operation against Israel. He summoned a meeting with the Army High Command on 24 October 1972. At this, he explained that 'it is clear that there is no hope of Egypt's liberating its land through political methods' and he went on to instruct his commanders to step up preparations and be ready to launch a *limited* war against Israel.[3] This was a startling turn-about, and a radical departure from previous policies, because until then Egypt had clung stubbornly to a policy of total, all-out war against Israel, aimed at freeing all the Sinai which Israel had occupied in 1967. Why did Sadat so dramatically change Egypt's policy from total to limited war, which he knew could only lead to the freeing of part of the Sinai? The reason is as follows:

When the 1967 war ended, Sadat's predecessor Nasser came to the conclusion that for Egypt to be able to embark on an all-out war to liberate all the land it had lost in the 1967 war, two preconditions must be fulfilled. The first was that Egypt obtain Scud missiles so that she could threaten Israel's population centres. The second precondition was that the Egyptian air force be equipped with advanced long-range fighter-bombers to enable it to penetrate deep into Israel and strike at airports, communications centres and other strategic installations. Indeed, during his visit to Moscow on 22 January 1970, Nasser, according to Chief of Staff Mohammed Fawzi who had accompanied him, 'Repeated his demand for [long-range] fighter-bombers because the range of our bombers does not enable us to reach deep into Israel'.[4] Sadat, like his predecessor, also recognized that without these weapons – long-range fighter-bombers and Scud missiles – Egypt would not be able to liberate its occupied lands; and therefore, in a secret letter, dated 30 August 1972, which he sent to Soviet President Leonid Brezhnev, he said:

> I mentioned in our frequent discussions that we needed a *retaliatory weapon* which would deter the enemy . . . because of his knowledge that we would then be able to retaliate in kind and attack his inland positions. *It was obvious, and still is, that,*

> *deprived of such a retaliatory weapon, we would remain incapable*
> *of taking any kind of military action.*[5]

The 'retaliatory weapon' to which Sadat referred was the Scud missile.

Moscow, however, consistently refused to supply Egypt with advanced fighter-bombers and with 'retaliatory weapons', presumably because it had realized that for Egypt to be in a position to strike at Israel was not in Moscow's interest at this time in the early 1970s, because of its improved relationships with Washington. That Moscow refused to supply offensive weapons to Egypt – it only provided it with arms for defence – we know from Sadat's own letter to Brezhnev, where he mentions the 'embargo you have imposed on us for the last five years, in regard to "retaliation weapons" '. That this embargo also included long-range fighter-bombers, which Egypt so desperately needed if it was to embark on a war to liberate the whole of the Sinai, we know from a recent testimony of Pavel Akopov, a Soviet diplomat who was present at meetings in which the supply of weapons to Egypt was discussed. According to Akopov:

> I was present at negotiations [regarding the supply of weapons to Egypt] with Nasser, and afterwards the same issues were raised by Sadat all the time . . . Sadat was always putting the question of supplying him with this sort of armament which we could not give them: say, aircraft that could fly from Cairo to Tel Aviv, and he was always asking for them so that he could bomb Tel Aviv.[6]

In this lies the reason for Sadat's decision to abandon the aim of embarking on a total, major war to liberate the Sinai and to concentrate instead on a more limited war. For his realization that Moscow was unlikely to provide him with the long-range fighter-bombers and Scud missiles which had been seen by his predecessor and himself as the preconditions for a total war against Israel, brought him to the conclusion that he should try to achieve a more limited objective and hope that this would break the political impasse and result in his regaining the Sinai through political negotiations. As Egyptian General Mohamed Abdel Ghani Gamassy put it: 'The idea of a limited war came from the fact that we did not have enough equipment to go into a general war; the Soviets would not give us enough arms'.[7]

As the meeting with his military command progressed, Sadat came to realize that there was strong opposition within the armed forces even to a limited war. General Abdel Kader Hassan, for instance, protested and expressed doubts about the possibility of winning a war against Israel, arguing that Egypt was not yet prepared for such a conflict and was not strong enough to challenge the Israelis, and that:

> We might succeed in the initial phase of our attack, but then we would undoubtedly be forced on to the defensive by the enemy. The upshot could be that the Israelis would be in a stronger position than they are now. And what of us? We have to consider that most of our interior has no proper defences against air attacks. . . . We do not want to find ourselves screaming once more for the help of the Soviet Union.[8]

A long and acrimonious debate followed, in which other commanders too expressed their reservations and opposition to launching a war, arguing that Egypt lacked basic equipment and was not yet ready to strike at Israel. But Sadat was adamant. He had already made up his mind, and because he was not proposing a full-blown major war but a limited one it did not matter that he was not equipped for a total war. He thus curtly told his military commanders that the decision whether or not to embark on war rested with him and not with them. He also said:

'We are confronted with a challenge. To be or not to be. We will simply have to use our talents and our planning to compensate for our lack of some kinds of equipment. God bless you'. On the basis of Sadat's instructions, the Egyptian High Command began drawing plans for a limited war against Israel, and also embarked on frequent false mobilizations to deceive the Israelis; 22 mobilizations would take place between 1972 and 1973, and not until the twenty-third would the attack on Israel be launched.

Sadat wished to attack Israel simultaneously from two directions in order to compel her to split forces and be weakened by having to fight on two fronts. To this end he invited President Assad of Syria to come to Egypt, and they met at Bourg el-Arab in the western desert in April 1973, where Sadat explained that he had 'decided to fight my battle this year and have issued the relevant instructions to [Minister of War] Marshal Ali'. Sadat then asked Assad 'What do you say to this?' Wishing to regain the Golan Heights which he had lost to Israel in 1967, Assad replied: 'I'll be with you. We're going to fight and are preparing for it'.[9] Proceeding with military preparations, the presidents decided to set up the 'Higher Council' of Egyptian and Syrian generals, which was tasked with cooperating and drawing up final plans for war against Israel, and with working out the detailed arrangements of a deception programme aimed at catching Israel off guard.

## A DOUBLE AGENT[10]

Much has been written about how Egypt, and to a lesser extent Syria, deceived the Israelis by constantly mobilizing forces, bringing the situation along the borders to the brink of war and then demobilizing in order to reduce Israel's alertness, until the moment came to strike on Yom Kippur, 6 October. That the Israelis were caught napping, off-guard and with no mobilized forces adequate to repel the invaders was often explained in terms of the failure of AMAN, Israeli Military Intelligence, to predict that hostilities would break out, and its insistence on a low probability of war in spite of a stream of information which was flowing in and showed that the enemy was already in jump-off points and strong enough to launch a massive attack. The view that the failure to predict the outbreak of hostilities and as a result to mobilize the reserves on time to repel the invaders was solely due to AMAN, was later supported by the Agranat Commission which investigated the failures of the IDF in the initial phases of the war, and whose brutal verdict, published in 1974, put the blame for the failure mainly – though not exclusively – on AMAN. But we now know that crucial information was concealed from the Agranat Commission, and what is now available clearly indicates that responsibility for the failure to see that war was on Israel's door step and that mobilization of reserves was urgently needed, rested not only with AMAN – it has been done less than justice – but also with the politicians and, in particular, the Mossad which, ironically, was praised by the commission.

To understand fully how and why Israel stumbled into the trap and was caught off-guard on Yom Kippur 1973, we should go back to the days after the 1967 war. In 1969, the Mossad recruited a top Egyptian official. In fact, he recruited himself, knocking on the door of the Israeli embassy in London and volunteering to work for the Mossad. This man, although only in his mid-twenties, was very close to President Nasser and later became the right-hand man of Nasser's successor Sadat. In *Israel's Secret Wars*, Ian Black and Benny Morris quote an Israeli intelligence officer who said of this Egyptian Mossad agent that he was: 'The best agent any country ever had . . . a miraculous source'. Indeed, the man was held in high esteem in Israel, and the documents he had turned over to the Mossad were read – as raw material – by the Prime Minister, Defence Minister, Chief of Staff and Director of Military Intelligence. The Agranat

Commission, which would later investigate Israel's failure in the Yom Kippur War, referred to the information provided by this agent as 'unique material from an especially important Mossad source'. In return, this agent received a generous fee – more than £100,000 for each meeting he held with his Israeli handler whose first name was Dubi.

Perhaps the most important document ever handed over by Mossad's Egyptian agent was the transcript of a conversation President Nasser had in Moscow on 22 January 1970, where he, as shown above, 'repeated his demand for [long-range] fighter-bombers because the range of our bombers does not enable to reach deep into Israel'. Another crucial document which this agent turned over to the Mossad was the secret message addressed by President Sadat to President Leonid Brezhnev, on 30 August 1972, in which Sadat, as we showed above, asked for 'a retaliatory weapon' (meaning Scud missiles) adding that 'It was obvious, and still is, that, deprived of such a retaliatory weapon, we would remain incapable of taking any kind of military action'.[11] The Egyptian Mossad agent not only handed over these two (and other) documents, but he also explained to his Mossad contact that for both Nasser and Sadat, having long-range fighter-bombers and Scud missiles was a precondition for embarking on war, and that without these weapons Egypt would not attack Israel.

On the basis of this dramatic written and verbal information, the entire Israeli pre-Yom Kippur War strategy was recast – it became known as the 'Conception' – and in a nutshell, it assumed that Egypt would make war on Israel only after it had obtained advanced fighter-bombers and Scuds. Israel began to monitor Egyptian airfields for evidence that these weapons had arrived in Egypt, for if they were to, and if the Sinai were still in Israeli hands, then after a period of training and assimilation, Egypt would be prepared for a military attack and would most likely strike.

However, what the Israeli leadership failed to realize was that the man they considered to be their top Mossad agent in Egypt was, in fact, a double agent also working for President Sadat. And while the information he supplied which suggested that Egypt would not attack without fighter-bombers and Scuds was indeed true at the time, this position was later abandoned by Sadat who, as shown, came to the conclusion that Moscow was unlikely to provide him with these crucial weapons, and that he had no other option but to embark on a limited rather than a total war against Israel. Clearly, the Mossad's Egyptian agent knew about Sadat's new policy, for he was the President's henchman, but he failed to notify the Israelis of the change in policy. For Israel, the unfortunate result of this was that she continued to believe that Egypt was holding to its previous policy.

Furthermore, parallel to providing the Israelis with critical information, this spy also embarked on a campaign of mis-information. He warned of an imminent war in 1972 which never happened, but when he did it again in the spring of 1973 he really did cause difficulties for the Israelis. That spring, he told his Mossad handler Dubi that Sadat was mobilizing forces and would attack Israel on 15 May. The arrival in Egypt on 7 April of a squadron of 16 Iraqi Hunters and 16 Mirage planes had strengthened the view in Israel that Egypt would indeed strike. To respond to this warning, the IDF High Command drew up a plan codenamed 'Blue-White' which was aimed at mobilizing and deploying reserve forces, speeding up military purchases and crystallizing preparations for war. But views differed within the Israeli military establishment regarding the way Israel should respond to the agent's warning. Director of military intelligence Eli Zeira insisted that the probability of war was remote, and he also argued that the Egyptians were resurfacing some of their airports (he mentioned Mansura) and would not embark on war while the work was in progress. But Zeira was overruled by Chief of Staff David Elazar and Defence Minister Dayan, who decided that what the Mossad's Egyptian agent had told them about an imminent attack was probably true and that, although it contradicted his previous written information, it should be taken seriously.

On 19 April, 'Blue-White' was implemented; but the Egyptian attack did not materialize, and on 12 August 1973 the forces were dispersed (this was just seven weeks before the Yom Kippur War). This futile mobilization cost Israel a fortune – $45 million – and irritated many, particularly the Minister of Finance, who complained that the country was needlessly wasting much money. We now know that Sadat did not intend to attack Israel in April–May 1973 and that the Mossad double agent's report was intended to cause a false alarm as part of his misinformation campaign. 'I had no intention of starting a war in May' Sadat wrote in his memoirs 'but as part of my strategic deception plan I launched a mass media campaign then and took various civil defence measures which led the Israelis to believe that war was imminent'.[12] General Gamassy, the Egyptian director of operations, also said, referring to the April–May Egyptian mobilization, that the actions were: 'Something we did . . . to deceive the Israeli intelligence'.[13] And General Fuad Awidi of the Egyptian army intelligence service said in an interview to an Israeli newspaper: 'The exercises and mobilizations in May 1973 were part of our deception plan'.[14] In fact, as we shall soon see, it was only in August 1973 that a final decision regarding the date of an attack on Israel was made in Alexandria, and that, therefore, 15 May could never have been a D-day for war, as reported by the Mossad's Egyptian double agent.

It is fairly clear, then, that the Egyptian Mossad agent – the double agent – played a crucial part in the Egyptian deception plan, and that what he reported was taken very seriously indeed by the decision-makers in Israel. Although AMAN did indeed fail to interpret Arab intentions, it was the Mossad and the politicians who were so hypnotized by Sadat's right-hand man, who was their top agent, that they failed to realize two crucial things. First, that the agent's information that Egypt would not attack before obtaining Scud missiles and advanced fighter-bombers ('The Conception') was no longer valid in the spring of 1973 and therefore the Israeli strategy based upon it was erroneous, and war was to be expected even without the fulfilment of the previous Egyptian preconditions. Second, that the man they considered to be their best agent in the Arab world was, in fact, hiding crucial information from them while simultaneously feeding them false information regarding Egyptian intentions, as he had explicitly done late in 1972 and, in particular, in April–May 1973, when his false warning caused a purposeless mobilization in Israel. This latter major call-up had adverse long-term implications for Israel; for it evoked such criticism that when later that year war was just around the corner and a mobilization of the reserves was urgently needed, the Israeli political-military leadership hesitated, fearing that it was yet again a false alarm.

## FINAL PREPARATIONS IN EGYPT AND SYRIA

As we have seen, a final decision by Egypt and Syria to embark on war was not made before the summer of 1973. At a meeting on 22–3 August, in what was once Ras el-Tin Palace in Alexandria, the 'Higher Council' of Egypt and Syria met, and as the Syrian chief of operations Abdel Razzak Al-Dardary later recalled: 'We agreed on the last points of cooperation between the two fronts. We put the final touches. We finalized the deception plan'.[15] After two days of secret talks, the military planners were ready to inform their political leadership – Presidents Sadat and Assad – that two time periods in the coming months, 7–11 September and 5–10 October, would be suitable for launching an attack on Israel, and all the military required was an advance warning of 15 days.[16]

On 28 August, Sadat flew to Saudi Arabia to inform King Feisal that he intended to strike at Israel and to ensure the King's financial support during and after the war. It should be mentioned here that Sadat was accompanied, among others, by the associate who had been providing misleading information to the Mossad. This man was present at a meeting between the President and the King in which Sadat confirmed that he was to embark on an all-out war against Israel. After this meeting, however, this Mossad agent would falsely report to the Israelis that Sadat had decided to postpone the war – a lie, and unequivocal proof that he was deliberately misleading the Israelis.

Sadat also visited Qatar and Syria, and discussed the final war plans with President Assad, after which Assad convened the regional leadership of the Ba'ath Party, to whom he said: 'It seems that our Egyptian brothers have decided that the political path is no longer getting them anywhere . . . if Egypt goes to war and we decided against war, that would be bad for our image before the Arab world'.[17] One of the participants, George Saddeqni, who became Minister of Information on 26 September, later recalled that 'This statement made us feel that the decision had already been made and that the president was consulting us as a formality'.[18]

In Cairo on 13 September, Presidents Sadat and Assad and King Hussein of Jordan convened for a summit meeting. In fact, neither Sadat nor Assad wished to meet the King, who had been ostracized by the Arab world because of his harsh treatment of the Palestinians during 'Black September' in 1970, and his expulsion of them in 1971 after continued fighting. Egypt had, in fact, severed diplomatic relations with Jordan in March 1972 because of Hussein's attempts to unite Jordan with the West Bank after an Israeli withdrawal which implied peace between Jordan and Israel. But now under pressure from King Feisal of Saudi Arabia, whose financial support was essential for the implementation of the campaign, Sadat agreed to mend fences with Hussein and invited him to join the summit in Cairo. Yet nothing was said to him about the possibility of war against Israel, and as Zeid Rifai, Jordanian Prime Minister, later testified: 'The discussions did touch on the Arab–Israeli conflict but neither one, Sadat or Assad, mentioned anything about the vague possibility of a war. Never, never was the topic mentioned'.[19] But through a spy in the Syrian army the Jordanians discovered that there was a joint Syrian–Egyptian plan to attack Israel, and as the King was against war – for he did not want Israeli or Syrian troops to cross his territory, nor to be forced to join the battle by domestic pressure as was the case in 1967 – he decided to warn the Israelis. A meeting was arranged for him with Israel's Prime Minister Meir – the strictest secrecy was kept – and on 25 September 1973 he flew his helicopter to Israel where he met the Prime Minister in the *Midrasha*, the Mossad's HQ in Herzliya just north of Tel Aviv. This is what he told Golda Meir (their exchange is presented here verbatim):

KING HUSSEIN From a very very sensitive source in Syria, that we have had information from in the past and passed it on, in terms of preparations and plans, actually all the units that were meant to be in training and were prepared to take part in this Syrian action are now, as of the last two days or so, in position of pre-attack. That were meant to be part of the plan, except for one minor modification – the 3rd division is meant also to cater for any possible Israeli movement through Jordan on their flank. That includes their aircraft, their missiles and everything else, that is out on the front at this stage. Now this had all come under the guise of training but in accordance with the information we had previously, these are the pre-jump positions and all the units are now in these positions. Whether it means anything or not, nobody knows. But I have my doubts. However, one cannot be sure. One must take those as facts.

GOLDA MEIR Is it conceivable that the Syrians would start something without full cooperation with the Egyptians?
KING HUSSEIN I don't think so. I think they would cooperate.[20]

This was an extraordinary event – King Hussein, whose country was officially at war with Israel, flew to the enemy to warn it
of an imminent invasion by his Arab brothers. We will never
know why Meir did not ask the King the crucial question: 'When
will they attack?', but she did call her Defence Minister Dayan,
notify him of her meeting with the King and tell him of the
warning. As the conversation between Meir and King Hussein
was secretly taped and filmed by the Mossad, Dayan also received
the transcript, which was in English, and which he passed over
to the Chief of Staff who, on the next day, 26 September,
discussed the matter with his colleagues. As extracts from this
discussion are now available, it is shocking to realize that the
Israeli High Command, and Defence Minister Dayan himself,
simply failed to understand what the King was saying to the
Prime Minister. For while, as the above extract shows, the King's
warning was that '[Egypt and Syria] would co-operate [in their
attack]', Chief of Staff Elazar said in the meeting that: 'It is not
known if [Syrian preparations to open fire] are in cooperation
with the Egyptians'. He also said – disregarding the fact that
according to the transcript the King's was a clear warning of a
joint Egyptian–Syrian attack – that 'There could be nothing more
idiotic for Syria than to attack on its own'. Dayan also failed to
understand what the King was saying, and commented that the
Syrians 'will find it difficult to go to war without Egypt'. Thus,
ironically, Prime Minister Meir, whose English was perfect –
she grew up in America – failed to grasp the importance of
Hussein's warning, while Dayan and the military command,
probably because of their poor command of the English language, simply failed to understand that the King was giving
warning of a joint Egyptian–Syrian attack. The end result was that

the crucial warning – just ten days before the war – was not heeded; no reserves were mobilized to deter the assembling Syrians and Egyptians or to block them when they started moving.

All this time the build-up of Egyptian and Syrian forces steadily continued. In Egypt mobilization was announced on 27 September, but to lull suspicion and to camouflage its intention the Egyptian High Command ordered, on 4 October, the demobilization of 20,000 men of the 27 September intake. Furthermore, instructions for officers desiring to leave during the course of the exercise to take part in the Umra, the small pilgrimage to Mecca, were announced in Al-Ahram. On 1 October the Egyptian 'strategic exercise' called 'Tharir 41', which included massive movements of troops and armour and was to last until 7 October, had started; on the 6th the exercise maps would be replaced with the genuine war maps. In Syria, in order to lull Israel's suspicion, the new Minister of Information George Saddeqni had announced that, in the week of 6 October, Assad would be visiting the faraway provinces of Deir Al-Zour and Hasaka.

On 3 October 1973, a three-man Egyptian delegation – Minister of War Ahmed Ismail, intelligence officer Hassan Gretly and Chief of Staff of the Federal Operation General Staff Bahey Edin Noufal – flew to Damascus on a secret special mission. Noufal later recalled:

> We went on a cargo plane and no one knew we were going. We had to deliver the final order of war to the Syrians by hand. Ahmed Ismail joked while we were sitting uncomfortably in the cargo plane, saying 'What happens if the Israelis catch us and they find us with the order of war?' I said: 'I will simply eat the piece of paper, it is small and easy to swallow'. We asked to see [Syrian Minister of Defence] Mustapha Tlas. When we arrived Tlas was very surprised because he didn't know we were coming. He quickly gathered all the top brass at headquarters. We

discussed the date again; the Syrians were unhappy because they wanted more time to empty their oil refineries [at Homs, which would be a certain target for Israel]. We couldn't agree on this.[21]

They fixed 6 October as the date of war, though there was an argument about the timing of the attack. The Egyptians wanted to start it in the late afternoon, so that the sun would be in the eyes of the Israelis and Egyptian engineers could build bridges over the Suez canal under cover of darkness. The Syrians, on the other hand, wanted a dawn attack so that the sun rising from the east would blind the Israelis; the two sides settled on 2 p.m.[22]

That day, President Sadat called in the Soviet Ambassador Vladimir Vinogradov, to whom he said: 'I'd like to inform you officially that I and Syria have decided to start military operations against Israel so as to break the present deadlock'.[23] In spite of the July 1972 expulsion of the Soviets, there were still a few hundred in Egypt (and also in Syria) whom the Soviet authorities now decided to evacuate. The next day five giant Antonov-22s landed to pick up Russian families from Syria, and six arrived in Egypt. Additionally, Soviet ships began steaming out of Alexandria to the open sea, and a Soviet ship carrying supplies wandered around in the Mediterranean, not entering the port of Alexandria. All this traffic was picked up by AMAN, Israel's military intelligence.

On Friday at 11.30 a.m., Prime Minister Golda Meir convened her cabinet – there were five ministers in addition to herself – to discuss the situation. The Chief of Staff and Director of Military Intelligence described the situation at the fronts. The Syrians and Egyptians, they reported, were ready at jump-off points, which served well for defence and equally well for launching an attack. The evaluation of the Director of Military Intelligence, which was accepted by the Chief of Staff, was that an attack was not likely and the assumption was that if war was imminent, there would be further indications and intelligence reports to this effect. The cabinet decided to entrust the Prime Minister with the authority to mobilize the reserves if this should be necessary the next day (the next meeting of the cabinet was scheduled for Sunday).

Had mobilization been ordered on Friday – for according to Israeli doctrine of warfare such a concentration of enemy troops along the borders did indeed merit a mobilization – history might have taken a different turning, but this was not to be the case. It seems that those present at this crucial Friday meeting – just a day before war broke out – believed, wrongly as we shall soon see, that even if attacked, Israel's regular forces and the IAF could check the invaders and at least impose a delay on their advance until the arrival of the reserves; at the same time they grossly underestimated the enemy's strength. What also deterred them from authorizing all-out mobilization was a fear that an increase in the fighting forces might be seen as a threat and so accelerate the danger of war and even spark a clash of arms. Of course, the false mobilization of April–May 1973 which had cost Israel a fortune and led to heavy criticism was still fresh in their minds, and they hesitated to call up the reserves lest this should turn out to be yet another false alarm.

Let us now turn to the forces concentrated on both sides of the borders and examine their military aims.

## THE OPPOSING FORCES AND THEIR AIMS

### Sinai

Egypt's combat force on the eve of the war comprised 19 infantry brigades, eight mechanized brigades, ten armoured brigades, three airborne brigades, an amphibious brigade and an R-17E SSM brigade. In terms of weaponry these forces had about 1,700 tanks, 2,000 armoured vehicles, 2,500 artillery pieces, 1,500 anti-tank guns, 700 anti-tank guided weapons, several thousand RPG-7 portable anti-tank projectiles and more than a thousand RPG-43 anti-tank grenades. The equipping of Egyptian troops with a massive number of anti-tank guns was an important development missed by the Israelis, and was to cause them great damage, particularly in the initial phases of the war. The Egyptian air force had 400 fighter-bombers, 70 transport aircraft and 140 helicopters, and in the air defence 150 SAM battalions and 2,500 anti-aircraft guns. The SAM missile umbrella, which the Egyptians had advanced closer to the Suez Canal bank after and in breach of the Israeli–Egyptian ceasefire agreements of 7 August 1970, would totally neutralize the IAF in the initial phase of the war and would prevent it from striking at Egyptian troops and supporting Israeli ground forces. In their navy the Egyptians had 12 submarines, five destroyers, three frigates, 12 submarine chasers, 17 CSA and Komar class missile patrol boats, 30 Shershaen and P-6 motor-torpedo boats, 14 minesweepers and 14 landing craft. This substantial force was reinforced by other Arab contingency forces: from Algeria a MiG-21 squadron, an SU-7 squadron, a MiG-17 squadron and an armoured brigade; from Libya two Mirage III squadrons and an armoured brigade; from Iraq a Hawker Hunter squadron; from Morocco and Sudan each an infantry brigade; from Kuwait and Tunisia each an infantry battalion.

The Egyptian military plan named 'Operation Badr' was straightforward, incorporating a thrust by five infantry divisions – the three northern divisions constituted the 2nd army and the two southern divisions the 3rd – across the Suez Canal on the widest possible front, virtually the entire length of the Canal. Such a wide invasion would not give the Israelis any clue as to the main thrust of the attack, and thus confuse and prevent them from concentrating forces for a counter-attack. To enable the

Egyptian troops to hold their bridgeheads, they were each reinforced with an armoured brigade, a battalion of self-propelled SU-100 anti-tank guns and an anti-tank guided weapon battalion. The Israelis knew the finest details of the Egyptian military plan; a document of some 40 pages setting out the plan and including detailed maps had been supplied to them by the CIA on 16 April 1972.

As already explained, the essential feature of the Egyptian military plan was that it was intended as a limited operation: after crossing the Suez Canal and gaining a foothold on its eastern bank, forces were to penetrate no more than 10–15km into the desert and then dig in. This was a logical way to proceed, because a limited move across the Canal and into the desert would enable the Egyptian forces to remain under the protection of the SAM missile umbrella, thus deterring the IAF from harassing them.

However, during the planning phase, the Syrians insisted that the Egyptians move deeper into the Sinai in order to pin down Israeli forces and ease potential pressure on Syria. To please the Syrians and in order not to lose them as crucial partners in the war, the Egyptians tricked them by drawing a false attack plan which indicated deeper penetration into the desert in the direction of the Sinai passes, some 48km east of the Canal. Chief of Staff of the Egyptian army el-Shazli later said of this bluff: 'We made this other plan extending our advance all the way to the passes only in order to show it to the Syrians'.[24] The latter, in turn, swallowed the bait, and as Syrian Minister of Defence Mustapha Tlas later recalled: 'So it was agreed that the Egyptians would advance to the [passes] ... and meanwhile we would occupy the Golan Heights'.[25]

The Israeli defence plan against any potential Egyptian offensive was basic and unimaginative. Called *Shovach Yonim* ('Operation Dovecote'), it was drawn up by the IDF in August 1970. Under it, the 180km front – 160km along the Suez Canal and

20km along the Mediterranean – was divided into three sectors: northern, central and southern. The northern sector was to resist any potential attack in the direction of Kantara-El Arish; the central sector opposed a potential offensive from Ismailia in the direction of Abu Ageila, and the southern sector was to repel any potential thrust from Suez in the direction of the Mitla and Giddi passes. Within each sector there were three lines of defence: the front line comprised the Bar Lev line, which together with the Suez Canal formed a formidable barrier 180m wide, on the eastern side of which and rising to a height of 20m stood a gigantic sand dune, sloping in places at 45–65 degrees, which ran so close to the Canal that its face merged with the steeper gradient of the concrete banking. The second Israeli defence line was 5–8km behind the Suez Canal and comprised three battalions, 40 tanks to a battalion, with a battalion assigned to each sector. The third line of defence, between 19km and 32km behind the Canal, was based on reserve forces and comprised three armoured brigades, 120 tanks to a brigade, less the battalions forward in the second line. The Israeli plan was that, if attacked, the second line of defence should move up to its firing position at the water's edge or to the ramps just behind it, and the third line move up to the second line in order to create a front line of defence made up of a brigade of infantry in the Bar Lev line plus 120 tanks in three tank battalions.

On the eve of the Yom Kippur War the entire Israeli line of defence was held by a mere ten infantry platoons, 12 artillery batteries (fifty-two cannons), 290 tanks, two ground-to-air missiles (Hawks), and six anti-aircraft batteries. This very thin shield of 450 troops was deployed in 16 strongholds and four observation points. The reason why there were so few troops along the Suez Canal and why only about half of the Bar Lev line positions were manned, was that Ariel Sharon, OC Southern Command until a few weeks before the war, did not believe in the concept of the Bar Lev line, but failing to persuade his superiors that a line of defence would crumble in war and therefore Israel's strategy should be mobile – in which he was to be proved right – he retained the line but shut down 16 out of its thirty strongholds.[26] The result was that the fortifications were too far apart to give each other effective fire support and, when war broke out, the Egyptian troops after crossing the Canal were able to move into the desert mainly through the wide gaps between these fortifications.

## The Golan Heights

On the Golan Heights, a Syrian force of three infantry divisions and a strength of 45,000 men was deployed, with each division made up of two infantry brigades, a tank brigade and a mechanized brigade. The 7th division with its 68th and 85th infantry brigades was in jump-off positions in the northern sector; the 9th division with its 52nd and 33rd infantry brigades was deployed and in jump-off points in the central sector; and the 5th division, which included the 112th and 61st infantry brigades, also in jump-off places and deployed along a line stretching from Rafid to the Yarmouk. In addition to 540 tanks which were with the front-line forces, the Syrians had an extra 460 tanks in reserve just behind the first line. Additional Syrian forces included the Republican Guard, a brigade in strength which was equipped with T-62 tanks and whose mission was to protect the regime in Damascus, and two armoured brigades and some 200 static tanks in the line, making a total of approximately 1,500 Syrian tanks ready for battle; this formidable force was supported by 942 pieces of artillery. Other Arab countries sent forces to help the war effort; Iraq sent to Syria three MiG-21 squadrons, a MiG-17 squadron, its 3rd armoured division and an infantry division. Morocco sent to Syria a tank regiment, and Jordan sent its 40th and 3rd armoured brigades; the latter, however, did not arrive until 22 October and so did not take part in fighting. The Syrian forces were concentrated under an umbrella of thirty-six ground-to-air missiles which were deployed on the Golan Heights and close to the capital Damascus. This missile system covered an area stretching 8km into Israel's territory and was capable of detecting anything flying under 500ft. This was an immense problem to the Israelis, for it denied the IAF freedom of movement even on its own land. This threat seemed so formidable that in the summer of 1973, Deputy Chief of Staff Yisrael Tal proposed that it be destroyed. However, his proposal was rejected and, as we shall see, later in the war the IAF would pay a heavy price for this.

The Syrian war plan was called Mashrua 110 ('Operation 110') and it envisaged the occupation of the Golan Heights, the establishment of bridgeheads west of the Jordan river, and then movement towards Nazareth in Israel's Galilee. Syrian troops were also to seize the Israeli Hermon foothold, which at a height of 2,100m above sea level had provided the Israelis with an ideal observation point into the adjacent territories of Syria. As with the Egyptian war plan, AMAN knew the Syrian war plan down to its finest operational details.

The Israeli forces facing the Syrians comprised ten infantry platoons, 178 tanks, and 11 artillery batteries with a total of 44 pieces. This force was much bigger than the standard force deployed on the Heights, the reason being the rising tensions between Israel and Syria following a major air battle on 13 September 1973. That day, two Israeli Phantoms and four Mirages had flown over Syrian territory on a photo-reconnaissance mission, and when the Syrians dispatched MiGs to deflect them an aerial battle ensued in which the Israelis shot down eight MiGs, losing one Mirage of their own. An attempt by the Israelis to rescue their Mirage pilot, who had ejected, led to a second dogfight and ended in the shooting down of another four MiGs, bringing the total Syrian losses to 12 and so causing them a major humiliation. In the past, the Syrians had reacted massively to incidents of such gravity, but on this occasion days had passed without a reaction, which caused suspicion and uneasiness on the Israeli side, and apprehension that the Syrians were planning a large retaliatory action. At a General Staff meeting on 24 September, Defence Minister Dayan agreed to demands made by Yitzhak Hofi – he had taken over as GOC Northern Command in 1972 – to reinforce his forces on the Golan Heights and strengthen the front line.[27] This reinforcement was backed up by a visit made by Dayan on 26 September, which was the eve of *Rosh Hashana*, the Jewish New Year, to the Golan Heights, where he also issued a firm warning to the Syrians. It is interesting to note that Dayan's tour of the Golan Heights came a day after King Hussein's visit to Israel when he had warned that Egypt and Syria intended to launch an attack on Israel. It might be that Dayan's trip to the north was partially a result of Hussein's warning. As we shall see, this reinforcement was crucial, and when war broke out a few days later, Israeli forces on the Golan Heights performed better than those in the Sinai.

The Israeli military plan to meet any potential challenge from Syria was called 'Operation Chalk' and its sole aim was 'to destroy [any] enemy forces' attempting to retake the Golan Heights.

## WAR

Saturday 6 October: in Israel Yom Kippur, the most sacred day in the Jewish calendar, and in the Arab world the tenth day of the month-long fast of Ramadan. This is what happened in Egypt, Syria and Israel between 1 and 2 p.m. of this day.

*In Egypt* President Sadat arrived in Centre no. 10, the headquarters from where he would direct the war; he was wearing his uniform, as the President of Egypt is also the supreme commander of the armed forces. Just before 2 p.m., 222 Egyptian bombers took off from seven airfields and flew low on bombing missions against Israeli military targets in the Sinai. The opening gambit of the Egyptians in 1973 was similar to that of the Israelis in 1967 – a massive air strike. Soon after, Egyptian guns began a tremendous bombardment and in the first minute of the attack 10,500 shells landed on Israeli positions at the rate of 175 shells per second.

*In Syria*   In the operations room, a bunker two floors underground, President Assad arrived wearing his military uniform. Then, according to the testimony of former Minister of Information George Saddeqni:

> A few minutes before 2 o'clock there was silence. There was this big white clock on the wall and everyone was staring at it in complete silence. At 2 sharp, the telephone rang and Assad picked it up. The war had started. Then the telephones started going wild and there was a lot of commotion in the operations room.[28]

Sixty Syrian aircraft – part of the combined Egyptian–Syrian air attack which was called *Awasef* ('Storms') – flew to bomb Israeli targets, and Syrian guns opened a fierce and intense barrage to soften up Israeli positions.

*In Israel*   Ministers and military personnel were at an emergency meeting at the office of Prime Minister Meir in Tel Aviv. A final confirmation that war would break out was given in person to head of the Mossad Zvika Zamir by Sadat's henchman who, as we have already mentioned, was an agent of Mossad. This top Egyptian spy had travelled to what is often described in Israeli literature as a 'European capital'; it was, in fact, London. How did he slip out of Egypt on the eve of the war? His boss Sadat must have known about it. Was it with the consent of Sadat who was using him to mislead the Israelis? We will probably never know for certain the answers to these questions, but at that late-night meeting between 5 and 6 October, in a flat in London, he told Zamir that war would break out at 6 p.m. on 6 October. This warning, he must have known, was too short a notice for the Israelis, whose main reserve force had to be called up. But even now he was clearly misleading the Israelis, for the war did not start at 6 p.m., as he told Zamir, but four hours before, at 2 p.m.

Mobilization of reserves started at around 10 a.m. on 6 October, but this only got under way after an acrimonious argument between Defence Minister Dayan and Chief of Staff Elazar. Dayan favoured a limited mobilization of the air force and two divisions, one to the north and the other to the south, which could, he mistakenly believed, together with the IAF hold up the attackers. Elazar, on the other hand, insisted on full mobilization so he could undertake an immediate counter-attack; Elazar was attack-minded but for this he urgently needed considerable force. As the two failed to agree, the matter was brought to the Prime Minister to decide. 'My god', she later confided to her memoirs 'I had to decide which of them is right?'[29] In the end, Meir opted for Elazar's proposal and full mobilization was ordered. But much time was lost; from the final confirmation given to the head of the Mossad by Sadat's henchmen in London that war would break out – it was passed by Zamir to Israel at 4 a.m. on 6 October – to the actual start of war at 2 p.m. there remained ten hours, of which about five had been spent on endless arguments between Dayan and Elazar regarding how many troops to mobilize. In the meantime none were mobilized until Prime Minister Meir took the final decision. It is ironic that in the Six Day War of June 1967, stunning Israeli success was partly due to the recklessness of the Egyptian High Command, whereas now it was the other way round and the initial success of Egypt and Syria was partly due to the foolishness and ineptitude of Israel's leadership.

At 2.05 p.m., while the meeting at Meir's office was still underway, the aide-de-camp of the Defence Minister walked in and passed a note to Dayan. It said: 'The Syrians and Egyptians have opened fire, the Syrian air force dispatched aeroplanes, Egyptian dinghies cross the [Suez] Canal, Sharm [el-Sheikh] and military bases in west Sinai are under bombardment'.[30] The Egyptian and Syrian offensive was now in full swing. The following is an extract from the diary of Egyptian Chief of Staff General Shazli describing the crossing of the Suez Canal:

> At 1420 hours, they (the Egyptian divisions) opened direct fire against the Bar Lev strongpoints. And the 4,000 men of Wave One poured over our ramparts and slithered in disciplined lines down to the water's edge. The dinghies were readied, 720 of them, and a few minutes after 1420 hours, as the canisters began to belch clouds of covering smoke, our first assault wave was paddling furiously across the canal, their strokes falling into the rhythm of their chants 'Allahu Akbar . . . Allahu Akbar . . .'[31]

And head of operations Abdel Ghani Gamassy recalls: 'Our troops crossed the [Suez] Canal. They were shouting "God is great, God is great" and they planted the Egyptian flag on the Sinai itself'.[32] Each of the five Egyptian divisions crossed the Canal and built a bridgehead which connected with each other to create a continuity along the front. Every 15 minutes a wave of troops crossed, and by 3.15 p.m. the Egyptian army had already put 20 infantry battalions − 800 officers and 13,500 men complete with portable and hand-dragged support weapons − into the desert. At 5.30 p.m. the Egyptians began landing commando forces carrying portable anti-tank weapons deep in the Sinai in an attempt to prevent the Israeli reserve forces from reaching the front line at the Suez Canal. Forty-eight helicopters carrying commandos flew into the desert; 20 of them were shot down, but those which did get through did much damage to Israeli reserves arriving on the scene. In the meantime the crossing had continued in earnest. This is an extract from General Shazli's diary of war, dated Sunday, 7 October:

> By 0800 hours the battle of the crossing had been won. . . . In 18 hours we had put across the canal 90,000 men, 850 tanks and 11,000 vehicles. . . . Over the whole 24 hours, the total grew to 100,000 men, 1,000 tanks and 13,500 vehicles.[33]

The 505 Israeli troops in the Bar Lev line (when war broke out, 55 soldiers whose tanks had been hit joined the 450 in the strongholds) were mostly ill trained low-grade troops of the Jerusalemite brigade; they found themselves in desperate straits and could do little to stem the Egyptian troops who surged across the Canal like a tidal wave and had immense numerical superiority. The Bar Lev line crumbled quickly and the strongpoints fell. Worse still, because Shmuel Gonen – he was made OC Southern Command on 15 July 1973, succeeding Ariel Sharon – was told that war would start at 6 p.m., he had decided to deploy his forces at the last minute so that the Egyptians could not gain a clear picture of the layout of his forces, and could not alter their plans accordingly. But when the war started earlier than expected this proved to be a colossal error. General Gonen also made a further tactical error which proved very damaging; instead of deploying two thirds of his forces in advance positions and one third behind, he did it the other way round, and when the Egyptians opened fire the Israeli front line of defence was extremely weak. Of the 290 Israeli tanks which were in the Sinai when war broke out, 153 were soon hit and put out of action. The principal cause of the heavy loss of tanks was the way the Egyptian anti-tank guns, comparatively small and handy, were pushed out ahead of their own tanks to positions from where they could get close to the Israeli tanks and hit them.

The arrival of Israeli reserves at the front was crucial. Before the war it had been assumed that no more than 36 per cent of tanks and other vehicles would have to reach the front on treads, with the rest being carried on transporters. But so desperate was the situation and so urgent the need for more forces on the scene, that 82 per cent of the vehicles reached the front on treads. Worse still, the IAF was unable to provide support to these forces and check the enemy, having suffered horrific damage thanks to the efficiency of the Egyptian and Syrian missile system – 35 Israeli planes were shot down in the first 24 hours of the war. Given that 52 per cent of the defence budget in 1973 was devoted to the air force, this was a most disappointing performance, for whereas in the 1967 war the most decisive factor of the Israeli success was air power, now the IAF totally failed in its mission. In the first hours of war not only did the Bar Lev line crumble, but with it the entire Israeli theory – that the regular army supported by the IAF could hold up any Arab invasion – which proved to be wishful thinking.

## FIGHTING BACK – THE GOLAN HEIGHTS

Priority had to be given to the Golan Heights, where the Israelis could not afford to yield ground because settlements were close to the border and there were no physical obstacles to hinder the advancing Syrians. Following their successful air strike, Syrian armoured forces – a first wave of 500 tanks and a later addition of 300 – crashed through the Israeli lines along the entire front and penetrated into the Golan Heights. They had concentrated their main breakthrough at two points – one north and the other south of Kuneitra. So overwhelming and massive was the Syrian assault, that although Israeli forces on the Heights had been reinforced following the air battle of 13 September, they still failed in the opening phase to stem the Syrian southern thrust, where the attackers had managed to advance towards the descent of the Jordan river and at 1 p.m. on 7 October were only some 6km from it.

On the night of 6–7 October, the Israeli General Staff had decided to send a further division to reinforce the two now on the Golan Heights; but the situation was still critical and all the Israelis were interested in was to end the war on almost any terms. As Yisrael Tal, Deputy Chief of Staff explains:

> The aim . . . contrary to popular belief, was to put an end to the war . . . to create a situation where the Syrians think that we are moving on Damascus and call for Russian support . . . and we even decided [among ourselves] that [we will even accept that] the Egyptians remain in the [places they had already occupied in the] Sinai. [We] only [wanted] to put an end to the war . . . this is the truth.[34]

To achieve this aim, Chief of Staff Elazar asked for political permission to strike at the morale of the Syrian civilian population by bombing its cities and thus pressurizing the Syrian leadership into stopping the war. According to Tal: '[Chief of Staff Elazar] had insisted on bombing the population in Damascus and Haled so that the Syrians would shout *gevalt* ["help"]'.[35] Indeed, upon receiving political permission, the IAF, on 9 October, struck at the Syrian Defence Ministry and the Air Force Headquarters in Damascus, as well as at targets in Homs. What provided an almost miraculous reprieve to the Israelis was the fact that on that day the Syrians ran out of ground-to-air missiles and the IAF made the most of this situation. This was a successful day on the Golan Heights; as Dayan later remarked in his memoirs:

> That night, 9 October, I found the mood had changed . . . there was a feeling that on that day they had passed the rock-bottom

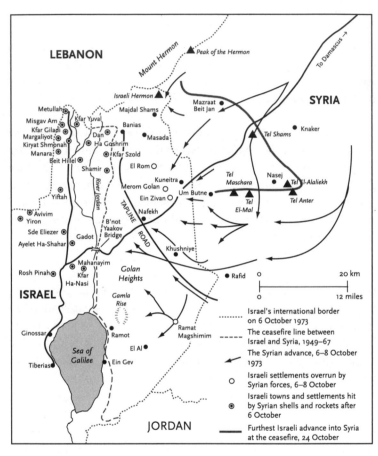

*Map 4* The 1973 Yom Kippur War: the Syrian front

point and that the momentum of the Syrian attack had been broken. The enemy forces had begun to retreat.[36]

On 11 October the Israelis struck at the 40th Jordanian tank brigade – it lost 27 killed and 50 wounded, and 14 of its tanks were disabled beyond repair. The Israelis then turned on the Iraqis, hit them hard and drove back the entire Syrian–Jordanian–Iraqi assault and retook the Golan Heights. 'At the end of the first week of war', noted Defence Minister Dayan in his memoirs, 'it was the Syrians who were on the defensive, and the campaign was being fought on their soil, east of the lines through which they had broken six days earlier'.[37]

## THE TIDE TURNS IN THE DESERT

In the Sinai, with the arrival of the reserves, the Israelis had on the scene a total of eight armoured brigades with 960 tanks (mainly Centurion M-48s and M-60s), compared with about 1,000 on the Egyptian side (200 T-62s, 500 T-54s and the rest T-55s). On 8 October, without waiting to concentrate, the Israelis opened a major offensive which was aimed at disrupting the Egyptian military machine and wiping out the forces that had crossed the Suez Canal before they could be properly established on its eastern bank. But the outcome was a disastrous failure and the Israelis paid a heavy price in men and material for the abortive effort. This stroke has often been criticized, after the event, as a rushed job, and so in a sense it was. But then the history of war shows that a stroke of this kind has very often been successful, especially because of its demoralizing effect on the opposing troops and their commanders. But in the event, this failure turned 8 October into one of the darkest moments of the war for the Israelis, and correspondingly one of the brightest for the Egyptians. Defence Minister Dayan later wrote: 'The day [8 October] was a total failure',[38] while the

Egyptian Chief of Staff el-Shazli noted with satisfaction in his war diary that

> The enemy persists in throwing away the lives of their tank crews. They assault in 'penny packet' groupings . . . in the latest manifestation, two brigades have driven against the 16th [Egyptian] division. Once again, the attack had been stopped with heavy losses. . . . Our strategy always has been to force the enemy to fight on our terms; but we never expected them to collaborate.[39]

But soon the scales tilted against the Egyptians. At the beginning of the war they had enjoyed the advantage of surprise and preponderant superiority of forces, but now the Israelis were nearly fully mobilized, they had recovered their balance, were regrouping, switching forces from the Golan Heights – where hostilities had more or less ceased on 11 October – and were ready to hit back. The coming Israeli success, however, was not so much a result of superior insight or strategy rather than the result of miscalculations and shortsightedness on the Egyptian side. We should recall that the original Egyptian plan was limited – to cross the Suez Canal, move only a few kilometres into the desert, obtain a lodgement and defend it while remaining under the safe cover of the SAM missile system. But aiming at following up their initial success, and under intense pressure from Damascus to keep on fighting in order to pin down the Israelis and relieve pressure on Syria, the Egyptians decided to alter their original war plans and push deeper into the Sinai in the direction of the passes. Their Chief of Staff el-Shazli was vehemently against the sudden change of plan, since he knew that moving away from the missile umbrella would expose the troops as targets for the IAF, which still had overwhelming superiority in the air. El-Shazli pleaded as persuasively as he could with Sadat to adhere to the original limited plan, but he was overruled by Minister of War Ismail and the President himself.

At first light on 14 October, four Egyptian armoured brigades and a mechanized infantry brigade opened an offensive with four independent thrusts in the direction of the passes of Refidim, Giddi and Mitla. But as Mohamed Heikal rightly observed, 'What had been open for Egypt to accomplish on 7 October was no longer there to be achieved on 14 October'.[40] Indeed, as el-Shazli predicted, the move deeper into the desert made the Egyptian troops easy prey for the IAF which, away from the missile umbrella, had command of the sky and was able to harass the advancing troops and tanks with impunity. Additionally, the Egyptian T-62 and T-54 tanks were no match for the much more advanced Israeli Centurion M-48 and M-60.

For the Israeli political-military leadership, the Egyptian offensive came just in time, for they were sharply divided and could not agree how to proceed. The practical question was one of timing and revolved around the question of when to move ahead and cross the Suez Canal. Chief of Staff Elazar wanted to wait, former Chief of Staff Bar Lev wanted to cross as soon as possible, and Deputy Chief of Staff Tal insisted that Israel should wait for the Egyptians to attack first, hit them from dug-in positions and only then move to the offensive and cross to the west bank of the Canal. And it was while this heated discussion was still under way that information came in that the Egyptians would soon open their offensive; in practice this meant that Tal's view was accepted by default.[41] This critical information was given to the Israelis by one of their spies – a top Egyptian general.

In the desert, Ariel Sharon, a divisional commander, had witnessed the Egyptian offensive and its collapse, and recalling it later he wrote 'On Sunday October 14 at 06:20 massed Egyptian tank forces moved towards our lines. By early afternoon, 100–120 tanks of the Egyptian 21st armoured division were either

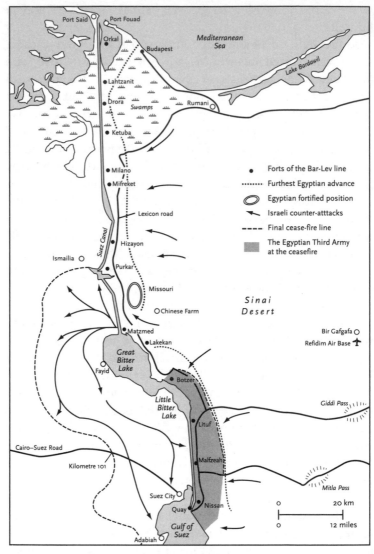

*Map 5* The 1973 Yom Kippur War: the Egyptian front

flaming like torches or lying dead on the sand'. Indeed, the Egyptian offensive was a costly error and as disastrous as Israel's offensive on 8 October. By midday the attacking forces, which had managed to advance only a few kilometres into the desert, were brought to a complete halt and – suffering heavy losses of 250 tanks, which more than doubled their losses in the whole war to date – they began to fall back to the line from which they had started. Now the tables were turned and the Israelis took the offensive. Divisional commander Sharon recalls: 'That night approval came to cross the Canal. My division would break through the Egyptian lines, secure a corridor to the Canal and establish a crossing point at Deversoir on the east bank'.[42] Late on the night of 15 October, Sharon's forces approached the Suez Canal through the open seam between the Egyptian 2nd and 3rd armies and began crossing it just north of the Great Bitter Lake at Deversoir. By 18 October, Israel had on the west bank of the Canal a substantial force of three armoured brigades and an infantry brigade. By midday another armoured brigade had crossed, swelling the Israeli force to four armoured brigades and an infantry brigade. By 20 October the Israelis had secured three bridges across the Suez Canal, which enabled them to transfer more troops and tanks to the west bank.

On Monday 22 October, a ceasefire was announced, and it came into force at 6.52 p.m. But on 23 October, determined to improve their bargaining position, the Israelis breached the ceasefire and launched a concerted assault by four armoured brigades. They encircled the Egyptian 3rd army in the southern part of the Suez Canal and the town of Suez, and continued south to reach Adabiah, on the coast some ten miles below Suez. By 24 October, the 3rd army – two reinforced divisions, about 45,000 men and 250 tanks – was completely cut off, and that evening, after Soviet threats and growing American pressure, Israel agreed to a second ceasefire. It refused, however, to return to the lines of

22 October, and by now Israeli forces were within 101km of Cairo and 45km from Damascus.

In January 1974 Israel and Egypt signed disengagement agreements, and the terms of the disengagement between Israeli and Syrian troops were drafted on 31 May 1974. As Defence Minister Dayan noted in his memoirs: 'It marked the formal end to the Yom Kippur war. The fire at the front died down. The last of the prisoners came home. The Israel Defence Forces could release the reserves'.[43] It is estimated that the Arabs had lost 15,600 men in the war, with 35,000 wounded and 8,700 captured. The IDF lost 2,569 men, with 7,251 wounded and 314 taken prisoner. The Arabs lost 440 aeroplanes; Israel lost 102. The Arabs lost 2,250 tanks compared with 400 Israeli tanks which were totally destroyed by enemy gunfire and 600 which were hit but were repaired and returned to full service. The Arabs lost 770 cannons; Israel lost 25. Twelve Arab missile boats were sunk; the Israelis lost none.

## WAR, PEACE AND SOCIETY

The 1967 Six Day War, the 1968–70 War of Attrition and the 1973 Yom Kippur War all took place within a short period of time – six years or so. But there was a huge difference in the way the Israeli public reacted to each of these wars, and in the way each of these confrontations affected Israeli society. In 1967, the Israelis had a period of three weeks – the so-called 'waiting period' – in which they could assess the situation and express their views regarding the leadership and the way they were handling the crisis. When the people of Israel thought that their political leaders were not performing satisfactorily, they demanded a political change and the politicians were forced to accept it, as was the case when Dayan was made Defence Minister instead of Eshkol. Public reaction to the War of Attrition along the Suez Canal had its own characteristics. The war was

*Plate 1* *(Above)* On the march: Jewish troops file past a ruined building in the northern port city of Haifa after its capture during the 1948 war. © Bettmann/CORBIS *(Below)* Large bundles of personal possessions are carried on the heads of Arab women as they flee from their village near Haifa. They became refugees never allowed to return to their homes. © Bettmann/CORBIS

Plate 2  *(Above)* Tired but victorious: Israel's Chief of Staff Yitzhak Rabin
(left) and Defence Minister Moshe Dayan (right) flying home from
the battlefield on the day after the 1967 Six Day War. © David
Rubinger/CORBIS *(Below)* Israeli troops at the Wailing Wall, East
Jerusalem in June 1967. Capturing this part of Jerusalem was a
dream come true, but it made a solution of the Arab-Israeli conflict
harder. © David Rubinger/CORBIS

Plate 3 *(Above)* Egyptian troops plant their flag on the east bank of the Suez Canal. Crossing the Canal during the early stages of the October 1973 war restored Egyptian pride and dignity. Photo by Bride Lane Library/ Popperfoto/Getty Images *(Below)* General Ariel Sharon (right) and Defence Minister Moshe Dayan (left) on the West Bank of the Suez Canal, 18 October 1973. They are smiling after Sharon successfully counter-attacked and managed to cross the Suez Canal into Egypt. © Bettmann/Corbis

*Plate 4 (Above)* Defence Minister Ariel Sharon (centre) pointing at a map with General Amos Yaron (right), commander of the Beirut area during the 1982 Lebanon war. Sharon was the architect of Israel's disastrous invasion of Lebanon which led to thousands of casualties and eventually cost him his post. © David Rubinger/CORBIS

*(Below)* Between 800 and 1500 Palestinian refugees were massacred at the Sabra and Shatilla Refugee Camps in Lebanon by Israel's allies, the Christian Lebanese Forces, in September 1982. © Michel Philippot/Sygma/Corbis

Plate 5 *(Above)* A Palestinian boy throws stones at an Israeli tank during clashes in the West Bank city of Nablus. Stones were the main weapons used by Palestinian insurgents during the first *intifada* from 1987 to 1993. © Alaa Badarneh/epa/Corbis *(Below)* A photo of a Palestinian baby dressed like a suicide bomber, explosives strapped around its waist. During the second *intifada* from 2000, suicide bombers played a leading role in Palestinian resistance against the Israeli occupation. © Reuters/CORBIS

*Plate 6 (Above)* A poster of Yasser Arafat behind an Israeli tank in Ramallah during Operation Defensive Shield, March-April 2002. In a sweeping invasion, Israeli forces reoccupied every major Palestinian town and city. © Reuters/CORBIS *(Below)* A Palestinian woman, a resident of the Jenin refugee camp, praises *Allah* after salvage workers found a cache of money on the site of her ruined home. Much of the Jenin refugee camp was destroyed by Israeli forces as they fought a hard battle with entrenched militants during Defensive Shield. Photo by Chris Hondros/Getty Images

*Plate 7 (Above)* Spiritual leader and founder of the Islamic movement
Hamas, the paraplegic cleric Sheikh Ahmed Yassin, is pushed in a
wheelchair to a mosque for Friday prayers in Gaza.
© MOHAMMED SALEM/Reuters/Corbis *(Below)* Palestinians
inspect the site where Sheikh Yassin was assassinated by Israeli
helicopters as he left a mosque on 22 March 2004. Photo courtesy
Press Association Images.

*Plate 8 (Above)* Israeli girls write messages to Hezbollah on 155mm artillery shells to be fired against targets in Lebanon during the second Lebanon war in 2006. © Pavel Wolberg/epa/Corbis *(Below)* Lebanese walk through the rubble in Beirut's southern suburbs on the first day of a ceasefire between Israel and Lebanon, 14 August 2006. © Lynsey Addario/Corbis

relatively long and, as in 1967, the public had plenty of time to assess the situation and express its views regarding the way its political-military leadership was handling the crisis. Mounting public pressure forced the leadership to look for quick solutions to reduce the growing number of casualties, and this led to the construction of the Bar Lev line, and the attempt to de-escalate the war by initially intensifying it with bombing missions deep into Egypt. The Yom Kippur War of 1973 was different – it surprised the Israelis and caught them completely off their guard, and there was no time for the public to assess the situation and express its feelings. All Israelis could do was to join their units and be mobilized to the front to repel the attackers. The aftermath of the Yom Kippur War found Israeli society in a state of deep collective shock, but as soon as the guns fell silent there came a strong public reaction which put enormous pressure on the leadership to investigate the failures which had led to Israel being caught unprepared. The Agranat Commission, which investigated the events before and during the initial phases of the war, put much of the blame on the military commanders, and although it seemed at first that the politicians would emerge unscathed, this was not to be the case. The government had misjudged the Arab threat and this, in the postwar period, led to a general re-evaluation by society of the Labor government's ability to be trusted with the state's security. Indeed, about four years after the war the Israelis voted Labor out of office and elected a Likud government headed by Menachem Begin. This, after almost 30 years of Labor rule, was more than a change of government – it was a revolution Israeli-style, and it was mainly, though not exclusively, the result of the poor performance of the Labor leadership in the period leading up to the Yom Kippur War.

If we turn to Egypt we see that the general feeling was that although in the end Egypt had lost the war, it had nevertheless won an important battle in the opening phase of hostilities, inflicting setbacks on the hitherto invincible Israelis, proving Egypt their match and regaining the nation's pride, self-respect and honour. This was good enough for President Sadat to embark on his next bold initiative and invite himself to Jerusalem to face the Israelis and offer to open a dialogue. Two years later, Sadat and Prime Minister Begin signed the first-ever peace agreement between Israel and an Arab state. Although the price for this peace was the return of the Sinai Desert to Egypt, Israel accepted this without much protest. Ironically, however, the peace accord with Egypt, the implication of which was that the danger of Israel's being destroyed by a successful Arab invasion became remote, further removed the very cement – that is, an acute external threat – which had kept the turbulent Israeli society together for many years and made its people willing and determined fighters. Now, with the external danger diminished, Israelis, as we shall see in the following chapter, were less willing than before to take up arms.

# 5

## WAR IN LEBANON

### 1982

## THE PARTIES INVOLVED

Israel's invasion of Lebanon in the summer of 1982 was a traumatic experience for its armed forces and for its people as a whole. To understand fully how Israel plunged into the Lebanese quagmire and became involved in such a disastrous adventure, we should first identify the main players on the Lebanese scene.

Since 1 January 1944, the day all remaining political power was transferred from the French to the Lebanese people, politics in this country had been a matter of a fragile and precarious balance between more than 12 officially recognized religious communities and sectarian groups, in particular Maronite Christians, Sunni Moslem and Shiia Moslem. Stability in Lebanon was dependent on a constitutional compromise by which a succession of Maronite Christians held the presidency, the prime minister was a Sunni Moslem and the speaker of Parliament was a deviationist Shiia Moslem. The arrival in Lebanon, from September 1970, of waves of Palestinians, mostly Moslems, had accentuated the traditional rivalry between left-leaning Moslems and rightist, mainly Maronite, Christians. These Palestinians, had, in fact, been pushed out of Jordan following failed attempts by some of its leftist groups to take over the country, which they wished to turn into a hinterland from which to attack Israel. A few of these Palestinian groups went even further by attempting to topple King Hussein, whom they considered to be a reactionary leader and the pawn of western powers in the region. In the process of trying to take over Jordan and bring down the King, the Palestinian guerrillas had turned Jordan, particularly its capital Amman, into a chaotic place; they manned road blocks, even levied taxes on thousands of Palestinian refugees, and provoked the King's loyal armed forces. 'It was a nightmarish scenario', the King later recalled, 'a breakdown of law and order; a situation where people were not able to go around without being stopped and searched by Palestinians, where vehicles were confiscated, people shot, people disappeared'.[1] The last straw came when Palestinians of George Habash's left-wing guerrilla group hijacked western aeroplanes, and after a stand-off in the Jordan desert blew them up. This humiliated the King, who, seeing power slipping out of his hands, turned on the Palestinian guerrillas, overcame them and expelled them from his kingdom. This is how they came to Lebanon.

There, Yasser Arafat – by now Chairman of the Palestinian Liberation Organization (PLO) – and his guerrillas settled in the south of the country, close to the border with Israel, and established their headquarters in the capital, Beirut. They also formed an alliance with the Lebanese National Movement, the LNM, which was led by the Druze leader Kamal Jumblat, and was a loose confederation of various nationalist and progressive Moslem-dominated parties, including the Arab Ba'ath Socialist

Party, the Progressive Socialist Party, the Syrian Social Nationalist Party, the Communist Party, the Communist Action Organization, the Popular Nasserist Organization and the Independent Nasserites. One of the demands of the LNM–PLO alliance was reform of the political system to make it equitable to Moslems, who now – largely because of the arrival of so many of them from Jordan – formed a majority in Lebanon. The LNM–PLO alliance was in competition with the Lebanese Front. This was a confederation of Maronite Christian political parties, including the Phalange Party, the National Liberal Party, the Guardians of the Cedars and the Maronite League. It was officially headed by Camille Chamoun, but the Gemayel clan had considerable influence and, as we shall see, Bashir Gemayel later became the strongman of this group, and in the summer of 1982 was elected President of Lebanon. While the LNM–PLO alliance demanded reform of the political system so this would better reflect its numbers within the Lebanese population, the Lebanese Front insisted that the Maronites be entitled to a special position, irrespective of them being a minority in Lebanon. However divided against itself, the Front remained united in its enmity against the LNM–PLO group.

Relationships between the two alliances were fragile, but had deteriorated dramatically following an Israeli raid on the heart of Beirut on 10 April 1973, where a commando squad led by Ehud Barak, a future prime minister of Israel, assassinated three Palestinian leaders – Kamal Nasser, Yusif Najar and Kamal Edwan – whom the Israelis held responsible for the killing of 11 of their athletes at the Olympic Games in Munich in September 1972. The Lebanese army – composed mostly of Maronite troops – which was located in the area where the Israelis were operating, did not intervene, and this reinforced Palestinian suspicions that the Maronite leadership had tacitly approved the Israeli raid in order to weaken the Palestinians in Lebanon. With such tensions, only a spark was needed to ignite the Lebanese powder keg, and what eventually set it off was the killing, on 13 April 1975, of four Christians by a Palestinian gunman at a church in East Beirut, which was followed, on the next day, by the killing of 27 Palestinians at the Tel Zatar refugee camp by the Maronites. This train of events, which heralded the so-called Lebanese civil war, soon sucked in two regional powers – Syria and Israel.

Syrian forces were invited into Lebanon by the Maronite President Suleiman Franjieh, in order to stop the raging civil war, keep the peace and save the Lebanese Front from total defeat at the hands of the LNM–PLO alliance, which by then controlled two thirds of the country. President Assad of Syria had welcomed the invitation, for he regarded Lebanon as Syria's own back yard; he also understood that, should a war with the traditional enemy, Israel, break out, control of Lebanon could enable him to prevent Israeli troops from approaching and threatening Damascus from the rear, namely from the direction of Lebanon. On 1 June 1976, Syrian troops marched into Lebanon, deployed along the road linking Beirut and Damascus, and took positions in Beirut itself and in the Beka'a valley in eastern Lebanon. Israel, which was then led by Prime Minister Yitzhak Rabin, did not object to Syrian intervention in Lebanon, but made it clear that Syrian troops must not move down beyond a line running south of Sidon to the east and 25km north of the Litani river.

Israel's involvement in the Lebanese civil war can be traced back – grotesque as it may seen – to a crucial meeting on the steps of the Magdalene Church in Paris. There, back in the early 1970s, an Israeli agent of the Mossad promised, albeit unofficially, to a Christian leader by the strange name Mugagbag, that, if asked, Israel would assist the Christians in Lebanon. This led to a meeting in 1975 between Israel's Prime Minister Rabin and the Maronite Christian leader Camille Chamoun, on board an Israeli destroyer in the Mediterranean, to discuss Israeli aid to the Maronites in Lebanon. A year later, with the civil war in Lebanon raging and the Maronite Christian forces under growing pressure and in serious military straits, a Maronite Christian leader, Joseph Abu Khalil, approached Mugagbag, and on 12 March 1976 they set sail from Kaslik in Lebanon to the port of Haifa. Their ship was stopped at sea by an Israeli patrol boat, and after identifying themselves and explaining the purpose of their trip they were taken to Tel Aviv, where they met Israel's Defence Minister Shimon Peres. Peres asked Abu Khalil: 'Why have you come and what do you want?', to which Abu Khalil replied 'I have come to ask you for weapons. We need ammunition'.[2] Peres discussed the matter with Prime Minister Rabin, and they decided to help the Maronites in Lebanon.

It is often alleged that Israel's principal motive in offering support to the Maronites in Lebanon was sympathy and compassion. This, however, is utterly untrue; the truth of the matter is that in providing weapons and some other assistance to the Maronites Israel was perfectly serving her own national interests. First, the Maronites were fighting the PLO and other traditional enemies of Israel, and by assisting them Israel was using a proxy to do the 'dirty work' for her. Second, supporting the Maronites provided the Israelis, Mossad in particular, with a 'window' to the Arab world, which was crucial for the purposes of gathering intelligence. We should also remember that the Maronite approach came before Israel had signed the Camp David accords with Egypt, and that to be approached for help by people of an Arab state – albeit Maronite Christians – was a novel experience, and a request which the Israelis found difficult to decline. With political endorsement given, Israeli boats began sailing back and forth delivering arms to the Maronites. A boat would sail into Lebanese waters towing craft heaped with weapons and ammunition, and off the coast the craft would be released for the Maronites to tow away. Arming the Maronites was a major logistical operation and, although contacts with the Maronites in Lebanon were usually maintained by the Mossad, in this case the huge supply operation was supervised by the Israeli defence ministry. It is estimated that between 1975 and 1977 the Rabin government spent $150 million on arming the Maronites.

## THE LITANI CAMPAIGN: A REHEARSAL FOR THE 1982 INVASION

While supplying weapons to the Maronites was no more than an indirect involvement in Lebanese affairs, a major direct intervention, which has often been regarded as a rehearsal for Israel's invasion of 1982, came in March 1978. This followed a terrorist attack at the heart of Israel, when on 11 March 1978 nine Palestinians landed on a beach in Israel, walked to the Haifa–Tel Aviv coastal road, stopped two passing buses, crammed the passengers into one bus, and at gunpoint ordered the driver to go to Tel Aviv. In an exchange of fire between the kidnappers and Israeli security forces, just north of Tel Aviv, 28 Israeli passengers were killed, 78 wounded, and all nine terrorists killed. The government – now headed by Menachem Begin of Likud – decided to hit back, dispatching the IDF into Lebanon to carry out 'Operation Litani'. It was launched on the night of 14 March 1978, went on for seven days, and was the biggest military operation the IDF had undertaken since the 1973 Yom Kippur War. Israeli troops, 7,000 in all, with armour and artillery and the close air support of the IAF, occupied the entire area north of the Israeli border up to the Litani river, destroying PLO infrastructure. The operation was directed against the PLO, and the Israelis kept their distance from Syrian forces in order to avoid clashing with them.

What is so significant about this operation is the way it affected the thinking of Menachem Begin in 1982. Indeed, the success of the limited 'Operation Litani', and in particular the fact that Israeli troops managed to operate without clashing with the Syrians, led Begin to believe, on the eve of the 1982 invasion, that it was possible to act in Lebanon against the PLO without having to fight the Syrians. As we shall see, however, whereas in 1978 Defence Minister Ezer Weizman and his Chief of Staff Mordechai Gur took all possible measures to avoid a clash with the Syrians, the opposite happened in 1982, when Defence Minister Ariel Sharon, with the tacit agreement of his Chief of Staff Rafael Eitan, took direct action to provoke the Syrians and clash with them.

On 19 March, the UN Security Council adopted resolution 425 (by a vote of 12 to 0) calling on Israel to withdraw from Lebanon, and on 20 March the Council adopted resolution 426, entrusting a United Nations force, called UNIFIL, to deploy in south Lebanon and monitor the activities of the Palestinian guerrillas; on 30 June 1978, Israel agreed to pull its forces out of Lebanon (except for her 'security zone').

In the years that followed, UNIFIL failed to prevent the PLO from re-establishing itself in southern Lebanon, and there were many incidents in which the PLO and the Israelis exchanged fire. It seems, however, that in most cases it was Israel rather than the PLO which sparked the border clashes, for it was the policy of the Begin administration to keep the pressure on the PLO as a preventive measure. Prime Minister Begin clearly stated the aims of such an active policy, saying:

> Our strategy [against the PLO in Lebanon] is not a retaliatory action [which comes] after [the other side has already] struck [at us], but the prevention of [the ability of the PLO] to hit [us] by inflicting blows on . . . the murderers in their own bases.[3]

Or as he once put it in a speech in Tel Aviv: 'We go out to meet [the terrorists], we penetrate into their bases . . . we no longer wait for them to come to [attack] us and spill our blood'.

With the resignation of Ezer Weizman from the defence ministry on 26 May 1980, Israel's policy in Lebanon became even tougher, for it was now designed by Begin, who was not only Prime Minister but also Defence Minister, and had as his chief adviser the no-nonsense, hawkish Chief of Staff Eitan. In the summer of 1981 in particular, Israel put enormous pressure on the PLO in southern Lebanon. On 28 May, for instance, although unprovoked, the IAF embarked on a massive bombing campaign against PLO bases in southern Lebanon; the PLO reaction was cautious and restrained. On 10 July 1981, the IAF struck again, this time in and around Beirut, killing 100 − 30 of them guerrillas − and wounding 600. Now the PLO lashed back, massively shelling Israeli settlements in Galilee, killing six Israelis and wounding 38. Israel then hit back by launching a massive bombardment and causing Palestinians and Shiite civilians to flee northwards, and 70 per cent of the population of the Israeli town of Kiryat Shmona to flee southward. To stop the vicious circle, American President Ronald Reagan dispatched his special emissary Philip Habib, who with the help of the Saudi government, managed to broker a ceasefire between Israel and the PLO. Begin refused to call the Habib agreement a 'ceasefire' because it implied that Israel was apparently negotiating with the PLO. He called it 'An agreement to stop terrorist acts from Lebanon to Israel'. But a ceasefire it indeed was and this came into effect on 24 July 1981 and led to comparative peace along the border between Israel and Lebanon.

## ARIEL SHARON AND THE 'LEBANESE PROBLEM'

After Menachem Begin was re-elected Prime Minister for a second term, on 30 June 1981, he admitted Ariel ('Arik') Sharon, a man of great physical bulk and tremendous energy and toughness, into his cabinet as Defence Minister. It is often alleged that Begin's invitation to Sharon was due to the Prime Minister's admiration for generals − and Sharon was definitely one of the best soldiers Israel ever had. But there is, perhaps, a more convincing reason why Begin wanted Sharon in his cabinet, and this relates to Israel's relations with Egypt.

We should remember that according to the Camp David accords, signed between Israel and Egypt back in 1978, Israel had to return the Sinai to Egypt – a final withdrawal was due by 25 April 1982. Begin, so it seems, could not bear the thought that he, of all people, would have to clash with Jewish settlers in Sinai over the dismantling of their villages and townships and the return of the land to Egypt. Instead, he preferred to leave this unpleasant task to Sharon who, he believed, could carry out the evacuation smoothly because he was regarded as the champion of the settlers' cause, and was also deeply involved in the building of many of the settlements in Sinai. But ironically, while Begin brought Sharon into his cabinet because of Egypt, Sharon – who lobbied hard for the job of Defence Minister – wished to join the cabinet mainly because of Lebanon, where he recognized two principal problems which he was determined to tackle and resolve. One was the presence of the Syrians and their ground-to-air missile system in the Beka'a valley; the other was the presence of the PLO in Lebanon.

In the entry of Syrian troops into Lebanon, which was approved by Prime Minister Rabin against the advice of Sharon, who at the time served as Rabin's adviser, Sharon saw 'the root of the [Lebanese] problem'.[4] He felt that Rabin's tacit agreement to the Syrian march into Lebanon of June 1976 was a grave error of judgement because it had allowed the Syrians to strengthen their grip – politically and militarily – on Lebanon. Sharon saw a great danger in the Syrian missile system in eastern Lebanon, which had been established – due to Israel's short-sighted policies – in the Beka'a valley in 1981. This is how it came about: on 28 April of that year, the Maronites attempted to take Zahle, mostly Christian, by force. But the Syrians would not allow this because they regarded the Maronites' attempt as an effort to extend their influence to eastern Lebanon. When the Syrians intervened to stop the Maronites, the latter called for help, and Israel dispatched aircraft which promptly shot down two Syrian helicopters, killing all the troops on board. It is often alleged that the principal motive of the Maronites in their attempt to take Zahle, was to provoke the Syrians and thus draw Israel deeper into Lebanese affairs. This is hard to prove, although Prime Minister Begin did promise Camille Chamoun and Bashir Gemayel, when they visited him at his house in Jerusalem, that if the Syrians attacked from the air the IAF would come to their rescue.[5] In any case, if what the Maronites really wished to do was bring in the Israelis, then they succeeded, and indeed managed to complicate matters for Israel. For soon after the shooting-down of the Syrian helicopters, Damascus introduced SAM-6 batteries into the Beka'a valley to ensure that never again would the Israelis be able to intervene so aggressively in eastern Lebanon. The Syrian move was regarded in Israel as a serious development, for it reduced the freedom of action of the IAF over Lebanese land. Acting on the advice of Chief of Staff Eitan, who was supported by the commander of the IAF, the Israeli cabinet authorized the IAF to destroy the Syrian missile system. But this did not take place, for a strike which was planned for 30 April was called off because of poor weather conditions, and later the operation was put off again because the IAF was preparing to strike at Iraq's Osirak nuclear reactor south of Baghdad, which happened on 7 June 1981. Thus, when Sharon became Defence Minister, and on the eve of the 1982 war in Lebanon, the Syrian missile system was still in place.

Sharon believed that the PLO was attempting to turn the land of Lebanon – as it had tried to do in Jordan – into a base to strike at Israel. He was not impressed with the ceasefire brokered by Habib – it was holding well – and he argued that the PLO was taking advantage of the ceasefire to rearm and organize itself. Furthermore, Sharon, like others in Likud, strongly believed that the destruction of the PLO in Lebanon would shatter Arafat's influence among the inhabitants of the West Bank. He said: 'Quiet on the West Bank requires the destruction of the PLO in Lebanon',[6] and one of his colleagues, the then Foreign Minister Yitzhak Shamir, said: 'The defence of the West Bank starts in West Beirut'.[7]

These two problems – the Syrian and the PLO presence in Lebanon – were so interconnected that it was impossible, in Sharon's view, to deal with each of them separately, and this led him to the conclusion that

> Even if [Israel] wanted only to remove the terrorists (namely the PLO, from Lebanon), it had to take into consideration that the response of the Syrians would compel [it] to deal also with them – and this meant first of all [destroying] their missile [system].[8]

This is a most significant statement, for it shows that Sharon was well aware that if he were to order the IDF into Lebanon to root out the PLO – as thoroughly as he thought would be necessary – then the chances were high that Israeli troops would clash with Syrian troops stationed there. As we shall see, when he attempted to persuade the cabinet to endorse military action in Lebanon, Sharon would neglect to tell ministers that the implication of such an invasion was a high likelihood of a clash with the Syrians.

## SHARON AND THE ROAD TO WAR

On 20 December 1981, about four months after being appointed Defence Minister, Sharon presented to ministers his plans for a military operation – it was not yet called a war – against the PLO. This was the first time ministers had been told of an intention to operate in Lebanon, and it took them completely by surprise. The cabinet's overriding concern was that an attempt to destroy the PLO in Lebanon might lead to a clash with Syrian troops stationed there, which might, in turn, get out of hand and turn into a full-blown war between Israel and Syria on the Golan Heights. However, at this stage there was no vote on Sharon's proposal, and the cabinet did not have to commit itself to anything definitive; even if ministers were facing a dilemma they could delay any decision until the issue became imminent.

Sharon also began a campaign designed to prepare the American administration for the possibility of an Israeli invasion of Lebanon. Washington was, after all, Israel's most reliable ally, and it must not be faced with a fait accompli. In December, at more or less the same time as he presented the operational plans to the Israeli cabinet, Sharon also presented it, though in broad terms only, to the Americans. He invited US Special Ambassador Morris Draper, together with Philip Habib, President Reagan's envoy to the Middle East, to a meeting in Tel Aviv, and explained to them that Israel could not tolerate the shelling of its settlements from south Lebanon. He warned that 'if the terrorists continue to attack us we will wipe them out completely in Lebanon'. Habib reacted furiously to this statement, telling Sharon: 'This is madness. . . . The PLO isn't carrying out many raids. There is no need for such an Israeli reaction. We are living in the twentieth century . . . you can't just invade a country like this'.[9] The evidence shows that Habib was right; the ceasefire he had brokered in Lebanon was more or less holding, and the PLO was keeping a low profile, perhaps because it knew that Sharon was looking for a pretext to strike at them. But to Sharon this seemed irrelevant and in a further meeting, this time in Washington on 25 May 1982, he repeated the same line of thought to the upper echelons of the State Department. In an eyeball-to-eyeball meeting at the State Department, US Secretary of Defence Alexander Haig warned Sharon: 'This is unsatisfactory . . . nothing should be done in Lebanon without an internationally recognized provocation, and the Israeli reaction should be proportionate to that provocation'.[10] It is hard to say whether Haig meant to warn Sharon not to strike, or whether, in fact, he was hinting that under certain conditions Washington would accept an Israeli invasion of Lebanon. For how does one define an 'internationally recognized provocation'? And the same applies to Haig's warning that the Israeli response should be 'proportionate' – for how does one judge what 'proportionate' is? The possible interpretations are simply endless. It seems that Haig did realize that his remark to Sharon was too open-ended, for after the meeting he found it necessary to send a personal letter to Prime Minister Begin (dated 28 May) where he said that he 'hoped there was no ambiguity on the extent of [Washington's] concern about possible future Israeli military actions in Lebanon . . . [which] regardless of size, could have consequences none of us could foresee'. To this Begin replied: 'Mr Secretary, my dear friend, the man has not yet been born who will ever obtain from me consent to let Jews be killed by a bloodthirsty enemy'.[11]

## SEARCHING FOR A PRETEXT

With Washington effectively allowing Israel to act in Lebanon, given an 'internationally recognized provocation', the Israelis were now looking for one. On 3 April an agent of the Mossad, Ya'akov Bar-Siman-Tov, was shot dead in Paris, and a proposal to invade Lebanon in order to strike at the PLO was made at a meeting of the cabinet on 11 April 1982; five ministers opposed such an operation and Prime Minister Begin decided to put it on hold. Then, on 21 April, an artillery officer was killed in Lebanon and two others were injured when their vehicle hit a mine. In retaliation, the IAF struck at the PLO in Lebanon, killing 23, and the PLO hit back (on 9 May) with rockets and projectiles. But what was so significant about the PLO response was that not one Israeli village, kibbutz or settlement was hit, which seems to indicate that the PLO was signalling: We're avoiding hitting Israeli civilian centres, but we are capable of doing so and if provoked sufficiently, we shall do so. Yet this signal was either misunderstood by the Israelis, or they preferred not to see it this way, and the next day (10 May) Begin asked his cabinet to authorize the invasion of Lebanon by the IDF. This time 11 out of Begin's 18 ministers were in favour, and 17 May was fixed as the provisional date; but then, with seven of his minsters still resisting, Begin called the operation off just one day before it was due to start. It is interesting to note here that a day before his decision to call off the operation, Begin had received a message from Yasser Arafat via Brian Urquhart, Assistant Under-Secretary General of the UN, in which Arafat told Begin:

> I have learnt more from you as a resistance leader than from anyone else about how to combine politics and military tactics . . . you of all people must understand that it is not necessary to face me on the battlefield. Do not send a military force against me. Do not try to break me in Lebanon. You will not succeed.[12]

Incongruously enough, the incident that eventually brought war took place neither in Lebanon nor in Israel, but in London. On 3 June 1982, Palestinian gunmen of the Abu Nidal group shot the Israeli Ambassador to London, Shlomo Argov, and seriously injured him. There was no reason intrinsically why such an incident should turn into a *casus belli* and necessitate a massive Israeli invasion to wipe out the PLO in Lebanon, especially given that Abu Nidal was a sworn enemy of the PLO and its leader Arafat, whom he often dubbed 'the Jewess' son' and had even sent his people to assassinate him. But such was the mood in Israel following the attempt on the life of the Ambassador, that hardly any minister seemed to care that the assassins were from the Abu Nidal dissident group, and they were willing to accept the view expressed by the Chief of Staff and the Prime Minister that it did not matter which group had attempted to assassinate the Ambassador, and that Israel needed to strike at the PLO.

Thus, at its meeting on 4 June, which was a Friday, the cabinet instructed the IAF to strike at PLO targets in Lebanon. It is conceivable that those ministers and military advisers who favoured an all-out invasion assumed – rightly as we shall see – that the PLO would retaliate, and that this, in conjunction with the attempt on the life of the Ambassador, would provide Israel with the long-awaited pretext to invade.

That day at 3.15 p.m., Israeli aircraft took off from bases in Israel and a few minutes later struck at nine PLO targets – the sports centre in Beirut, which was a training camp and a military school, and another seven targets in south Beirut – this was a massive air bombardment on sensitive targets. When this happened Yasser Arafat was not in Lebanon, but in Jeddah, on a mediating mission to end the Iran–Iraq war, which demonstrates how much the Israeli invasion came as a total surprise to him in spite of evidence that the Israelis were planning a major attack. In the absence of Arafat, his deputy Abu Jihad – the Israelis would later assassinate him – took the decision to hit back, and for 24 hours the PLO shelled Israeli settlements in Galilee. With the situation in Lebanon deteriorating by the hour, the Israeli cabinet convened on Saturday 5 June at Begin's residence in Jerusalem, and with almost universal support authorized a military invasion of Lebanon, to which it gave the innocent-sounding name 'Operation Peace for Galilee'; it would later be called 'The War of Lebanon'. The following is resolution no. 676 of the cabinet, authorizing the invasion:

> (a) The IDF is entrusted with the mission of freeing all the Galilee settlements from the range of fire of terrorists, their Headquarters and bases concentrated in Lebanon. (b) The

operation is called 'Peace for Galilee'. (c) During the implementation of the decision the Syrian army should not be
attacked unless it attacks our forces. (d) The State of Israel
continues to strive to sign a peace treaty with independent
Lebanon, while maintaining its territorial integrity.

In this resolution the depth of penetration into Lebanon is not
specified, but during the cabinet discussion, Defence Minister
Sharon made it clear that the operation's objective was to
remove the 'terrorists' from firing range of Israel's northern
border, 'approximately 45 kilometres'. Beirut, the Lebanese capital, also seemed not to be included in the invasion. Indeed,
replying to a query raised by minister Simcha Ehrlich, Sharon
said that Beirut was 'out of the picture'. The evidence clearly
shows that what the cabinet ministers had in mind was a Litani-
type operation, namely a short and small-scale invasion directed
against the PLO only. As Foreign Minister Shamir later wrote in
his memoirs: 'Operation Peace for Galilee . . . was intended
to last no more than 48 hours, to penetrate Lebanon to a
maximum depth of some 40 kilometres and to destroy the
PLO'.[13]

## THE ISRAELI MILITARY PLAN AND THE OPPOSING FORCES ON THE EVE OF THE INVASION

### The IDF

There is much confusion in the literature regarding Israel's military aims and operational plans in Lebanon. This is understandable, for it is a confusion which springs from the gap between
the real operational plans as prepared and known to the military,
and the false impression given by Defence Minister Sharon to the
Israeli cabinet. There was, contrary to popular belief, only one
operational plan for invasion, and this was called 'Operation Big

Pines'. It envisaged a deep penetration of troops into Lebanon up to the Beirut–Damascus road – certainly beyond Sharon's '45 kilometres' – destroying the PLO infrastructure, linking up with Maronite Christian troops in the outskirts of Beirut and expelling the PLO from Lebanon, including Beirut. This plan had two versions, one which was known as 'Operation Little Pines' and the other 'Operation Rolling Pines', both of which envisaged a temporary limited movement into Lebanon.[14] The reason why these operational plans were drawn up is that it was not clear to the military planners whether, when a decision to invade had been made by the cabinet, there would be sufficient forces at jump-off points to execute 'Operation Big Pines'. Therefore, it was planned that if and when political authorization to invade was given, the invasion would start immediately with the available forces implementing either 'Little Pines' or 'Rolling Pines' (the difference between the two was marginal) and then, with the arrival and accumulation of more forces, the operation would expand to complete the implementation of 'Operation Big Pines'. In other words, the idea of the military planners was that even without all forces in jump-off positions, a small invasion would start and then develop into a broader operation which would bring the Israelis to Beirut. Sharon confirmed, after the war, that this was indeed the case, explaining that 'the two versions of Pines [Little and Rolling]' were to lead up to the 'big operational plan in stages' and the 'intention of Pines in all the versions [was to bring about] the destruction of the terrorism infrastructure and the occupation of Beirut'.[15]

Unlike the Israeli ministers, who thought in terms of a limited Litani-style campaign in which troops would only penetrate to a depth of 40–45km into Lebanon, the military planners always knew the way in which Sharon's mind was working and that he intended to get to Beirut. This they had learnt from Sharon himself, who told them, on a visit to Lebanon in February 1982, that there was no point in any action in Lebanon unless it was a thorough one, and no action against the PLO would be thorough unless it drove the PLO out of Beirut.[16] Later in this visit Sharon met Maronite leaders, to whom he said that when Israeli troops arrived in Beirut, 'we are asking you for two things. One to participate militarily in the Beirut battle, and second to sign a peace treaty with Israel'.[17] This suggestion was rejected out of hand by the older Maronite leaders attending, Pierre Gemayel and Camille Chamoun, but not by the young Bashir Gemayel. But, as we shall see, when Bashir Gemayel was in a position to take part in operations in Beirut, he did sit around letting the Israelis do the job alone. That Sharon's hidden agenda was intended from the very start to go all the way to Beirut also became apparent in a crucial meeting with military commanders on 4 May 1982, when he explained that the solution to the problems caused by the PLO 'lies only in an action that will bring about the actual destruction [of the PLO], destruction of [its] military power, [its] military command posts, and [its] political command centres in Beirut'. At the end of the day, Sharon told his commanders, 'we will get [to Beirut]'.[18]

So, ironically, the Israeli operational plan to move deep into Lebanon and reach Beirut was known to the military commanders and to the Maronite leadership, but not to the Israeli ministers, to whom Sharon said that 'Beirut is out of the picture' and that the intention was to penetrate no more than 45km north of the Israeli border. Furthermore, even the Syrians knew more about Israel's real intentions in Lebanon than most Israeli ministers did, for after the February meeting with Sharon, and through the mediation of Colonel Jonny Abdo, the Lebanese Chief of Military Intelligence, Bashir Gemayel, contacted the Syrian intelligence chief Mohammed Rahnim, telling him that the Israelis 'are preparing to invade Lebanon'. He then gave Rahnim full details of his talks with Sharon. And like the Syrians and the Maronites, the PLO in Lebanon also knew well before the Israeli ministers did that Sharon was planning a massive operation, invading well beyond 45km into Lebanon. For again, after the February meeting with Sharon, Gemayel, through the offices of Jonny Abdo, met Hani Hassan, a leading Palestinian and one of Arafat's closest colleagues, to whom he said 'I have information about a possible Israeli invasion that could reach as far as Beirut'. When Hassan said 'Our information is that the invasion will stop at Sidon', Gemayel replied, 'Don't bet on a limited invasion – expect a bigger one. The aim is to get you out of Lebanon'.[19]

The Israeli invasion was planned as a four-pronged attack of armour, mobile infantry and supporting units. Lebanon, because of its winding, undulating terrain and narrow mountain roads, is a very difficult country to invade as forces can hardly support each other. That is why Israeli planners envisaged an invasion in which forces operated in widely separated areas rather than in combination, namely a western theatre of war (along the coast and up to Beirut), an eastern sector (along the Beka'a and confronting the Syrians) and a central sector (forces 'sandwiched' between the western and eastern sectors).

The spearhead of the western force was to be the 211th armoured brigade, commanded by Colonel Eli Geva. Its task was to sweep along the coastal road, bypass highly populated areas and head on to Beirut. It was to be followed by the 91st division under the command of Brigadier-General Yitzhak Mordechai, which was to mop up towns and camps and keep the narrow road to the north open; and by other forces coming from east and west, namely Brigadier-General Avigdor Kahalani's 36th division coming from the central sector, and Brigadier-General Amos Yaron's 96th division and elements of the 35th parachute brigade landing from sea. In the central sector, Brigadier-General Menachem Einan's 162nd division was to advance northwards through the Shouf mountains in the direction of the Beirut–Damascus road in an attempt to cut off Syrian forces in Beirut from those in the east.

In the eastern sector of Lebanon, two divisions under the

overall command of Major-General Avigdor 'Yanoush' Ben Gal and his deputy Ehud Barak were charged with facing the main Syrian body in the Beka'a valley. It was envisaged that upon orders, forces in this sector would move northeast along the slopes of the Hermon Mountain in the direction of the Beka'a Valley and compel, as Sharon put it, 'a certain Syrian withdrawal'. All Israeli forces in Lebanon were subordinated to the Northern Command, which was headed by Major-General Amir Drori. On the eve of the invasion, a substantial force of about 57,000 men and more than 1,000 tanks was assembled in jump-off positions ready to implement 'Big Pines Operation'; of these 22,000 men and 220 tanks were to carry out operations in the western sector (forces heading to Beirut), and about 35,000 men and 800 tanks to face the Syrians and fight them if attacked or if so ordered. Additionally, the entire IAF was ready to provide air cover and support to the forces operating in Lebanon.

## The Syrians and the PLO

On the eve of the Israeli invasion, the Syrian force in Lebanon comprised some 30,000 men, 612 tanks, 150 armoured personnel carriers (APCs), and 300 pieces of artillery and anti-tank guns; additional forces were to join when the Israeli invasion began. Syrian forces were deployed in the Beka'a valley under the protection of a missile system, along the Beirut–Damascus road, and in Beirut itself, where they were organized in the independent 85th brigade. The Syrians had no offensive intentions in Lebanon, and did not wish to clash with the Israelis unless attacked.

PLO forces on the eve of the Israeli invasion comprised some 15,000 combatants and an additional militia which was recruited from among Palestinian refugees. These forces were organized in brigades and divisions, although they seldom operated in large units and preferred small guerrilla-style units. Of these, the Kastel brigade comprised 6,000 combatants, deployed in the area of Sidon (Ein el-Hilwe camp), Tyre (Rachidya and el-Bass camps) and Nabatiya. The Yarmuk brigade comprised approximately 6,000 combatants and was deployed in the area south of the Lebanon Mountain, and the Karameh brigade of some 1,500 combatants was deployed within the Syrian positions in the area of Hasbaiya and Rachaiya. Most of the head-quarters of the various Palestinian organizations were situated in Beirut, where there were also some 6,000 combatants. The PLO forces were equipped with 100 tanks (T-34s, T-54s and T-55s), 350 pieces of artillery, 150 half tracks, more than 200 anti-tank guns and more than 200 anti-aircraft guns.

## THE WAR

### The race for Beirut

The Israeli cabinet's decision to authorize the IDF to invade Lebanon put an end to the long waiting, and on the morning of 6 June the race for Beirut was under way. The Israeli attack started promisingly. Armoured columns led by the 211th brigade crossed the Israeli–Lebanese border at Rosh Hanikra, bypassed Tyre (at 2 p.m.) and crossed the Litani river over the Kasmia bridge (at 4 p.m.). Early that day, an amphibious force of the 96th division sailed from the ports of Ashdod and Haifa northward to land and join forces on their way to Beirut. Since the landing location was not yet fixed, commanders were kept together on board the cruiser *Geula*, and when the order came (at 9 p.m.) to land at the mouth of the Aouali river, they were sent back by small boats to join their forces at sea. The landing, which brought ashore a mixed force of tanks, APCs and four self-propelled 155mm guns, began at 11 p.m., with a marine commando unit taking positions and securing the beach against any hostile reception. After the landing, the force dug in, prepared to stay overnight, and continued to absorb reinforcements which arrived during the night; it then started moving towards Damour on the way to Beirut. On the morning of 7 June, Kahalani's 36th division, coming cross-country from the central sector, linked up with the coastal column, encircled Sidon and besieged the Ein el-Hilwe camp outside the town. On 9 June the advance to Beirut continued, and on 10 June the 211th armoured brigade reached Kefar Sil, just south of the capital. There it was checked and met stiff resistance from a PLO force. This was overcome after an infantry force had been brought up to clear the way. After capturing Kefar Sil, the column resumed its advance until it reached the southern tip of Beirut's international airport.

While the advance along the coast continued, the 35th paratroop brigade, which had been landed at the Aouali river on the first night of the invasion, was advancing through the mountains in an attempt to link up, as planned, with the Maronites just outside Beirut in Baabda; the link-up was achieved on 13 June. For the next two weeks Israeli forces continued to push north and encircle Beirut, and by 1 July the capital, which Sharon had told the cabinet was 'out of the picture', was very much in the picture and under siege. PLO guerrillas, 500,000 Palestinians, Moslem Lebanese civilians and the 85th Syrian brigade, were all encircled. The siege would last 70 days.

## Fighting the Syrians

In the 1978 Litani campaign, as has been shown, Israeli troops operating in the Lebanon did not clash with Syrian forces. This was mainly because special precautions were taken by the Israelis not to provoke the Syrians in any way. Thus troop movements were always away from the Syrians, neither in their direction nor under their noses, and messages were transmitted to Damascus that the operation was limited and aimed only against the PLO.

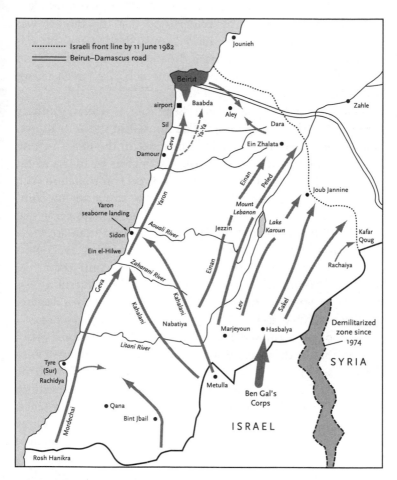

*Map 6* Lebanon, 'Operation Peace for Galilee' 6–11 June 1982

But now it was all different. Sharon, as we have already explained, considered the Syrian presence in Lebanon and its missile system in the Beka'a valley to be an immense problem for Israel, and although he understood that the cabinet was unlikely to approve an operation against the Syrians, he was nevertheless determined to make the most of the situation and provoke the Syrians to shoot first, in which case Israeli troops would be free to hit back – and hard.

General Avigdor ('Yanoush') Ben Gal, a veteran military commander who had distinguished himself in the Yom Kippur War and was now the overall commander of the eastern front, later explained to the author that it was clear to him and his colleagues that they were heading for a direct confrontation with the Syrians in Lebanon. 'If one looks at the structure and composition of the force', Ben Gal explained, 'one realizes *a priori* that [Israel had intended] to fight against a regular Syrian army . . . there was a force with a lot of artillery . . . combat helicopters . . . and hundreds of tanks'.[20] And as General Amir Drori, OC Northern Command, later testified: 'the big question was whether or not the Syrians would intervene . . . *and it was clear to us that they would [intervene]*'.[21] A war game called *Shoshanim* ('Roses'), which took place on 8 March 1982 to test the operational plans, showed that, without any doubt, Israeli forces would clash with the Syrians in Lebanon. Such high probability of a battle with the Syrians in Lebanon was frequently discussed in meetings between Defence Minister Sharon and the military. For instance, on 4 May 1982 at the HQ of Northern Command, military commanders warned Sharon – who was perhaps the ablest strategist among them and certainly understood what they meant – that the present composition of Israeli forces and their operational plans was sure to lead to a clash with the Syrians. The commanders' comments were professional in character, namely that the advance of substantial Israeli forces near the Syrian–Lebanese border in the direction of the Beirut–Damascus road

and just under the noses of Syrian guns, as well as the concentration of a large number of Israeli troops close to the town of
Jezzin, where Syrian forces were stationed, would certainly
result in military contact with the Syrians. Sharon, however, does
not seem to have sought guidance from his generals – he had
already decided his policy and thus rejected any alteration of the
plans. For his overriding, though hidden, aim, as we have already
explained, was to clash with the Syrians, and he was determined
to provoke them. For Sharon, the war which cabinet ministers
regarded as aimed at breaking the back of the PLO was also an
opportunity to confront the Syrians in Lebanon.

As his military commanders had predicted – and as Sharon
probably hoped – between 8 and 11 June Israeli and Syrian
forces clashed in Lebanon. This confrontation had four crucial
and significant turning points. First was the battle in Jezzin,
which signalled the beginning of the Israeli–Syrian engagement;
second was the battle in Ein Zhalata, which signalled the failure
of the Israeli attempt to 'push' the Syrians – to use Sharon's
jargon – out of the Beka'a without confronting them head-on;
third was the head-on offensive against the Syrians; and fourth,
finally, was the destruction of their missile system in the Beka'a.

After crossing into Lebanon on the first day of the war, the
advancing Israeli forces in the eastern sector moved towards the
Hasbaiya area where, at around noon, the Syrians opened fire.
When this happened Sharon issued instructions to Chief of Staff
Eitan to prepare forces for the central sector to move north and
outflank the Syrians; he gave this order without consulting the
cabinet, but it seems he was confident that he could get its
backing. At a late-night meeting of the cabinet in Jerusalem,
Sharon reported: 'At noon the Syrians opened artillery fire without being fired at, from [their] heavy D-30 cannons from their
emplacements, on our . . . forces and we sustained several casualties'.[22] To overcome this resistance, Sharon – his mind always
teemed with original ideas, and he could sustain these with

technical arguments – proposed that ministers choose between two options: either a frontal assault against the Syrian forces, which he knew the cabinet would not want to approve and probably preferred them not to, or 'An advance [of Israeli forces] to the north in an attempt [to outflank] and confront the rear of the Syrians', which he rightly assumed would be seen as the lesser of two evils and as a result would be the ministers' preferred option.[23] A third option, which was simply not to take any action, for after all the cabinet did not wish any confrontation with the Syrians in Lebanon, was never put forward. As for the second option, namely the outflanking move, this was favoured by the Prime Minister, who swung his weight in support of it and praised it as 'Hannibal's manoeuvre', so leading his cabinet to endorse it (resolution 690). The cabinet was not, however, aware of two crucial facts which Sharon had failed to mention; first, that in order to implement the proposed plan forces would have to pass through the emplacement of Jezzin, a critical strategic point which was held by a Syrian infantry battalion and an armoured force of T-55s and which, on the night of 6 June, was reinforced by another infantry battalion and commandos. Second, that an outflanking manouevre would not necessarily induce the Syrians to withdraw, rather it might compel them to dig in and fight in an attempt to prevent the advancing Israelis from reaching the Beirut–Damascus road, thus cutting off the bulk of Syrian troops in Beirut from those in Damascus and the Beka'a valley. The decision of the cabinet was executed by the 162nd division, and led to a fierce battle with Syrian forces in Jezzin on 8 June. Calling up reinforcements, the Syrians fought back in fury and inflicted serious casualties on the Israelis. In the end, however, they gave way and the Israelis took Jezzin.

But soon the battle took a turn for the worse, and the whole outlook in the eastern section of Lebanon changed dramatically when a force of the 162nd Israeli division ran into a Syrian trap and was checked at a place called Ein Zhalata. This was significant, because it meant that the force whose task was to outflank the Syrians could no longer proceed with its mission. Sharon, his 'Hannibal manoeuvre' bogged down, decided to recast his plan and ordered, at a meeting with commanders on the morning of 9 June, that Ben Gal's forces move northwards, as soon and as fast as possible, and destroy the Syrian 1st division which was just coming down from Syria as a reinforcement. This, in military terms, meant giving up the attempt to 'push' the Syrians by an outflanking manoeuvre, and instead confronting them head-on. The commanders who had attended the meeting with Sharon and understood that the implications of the Defence Minister's instruction were an all-out head-on offensive against the Syrians, resisted. Yekutiel Adam, a former deputy chief of staff – he would later be killed in a PLO ambush – stood up and bluntly asked Sharon whether his order did not contradict the objectives set by the cabinet not to attack the Syrians. Sharon disregarded this challenge, overruled Adam, who gave way in face of Sharon's force of personality and position, and went on to instruct General Ben Gal to go ahead with the mission.

With the 162nd division bogged down in Ein Zhalata and Ben Gal's forces moving straight towards the Syrians, a new problem emerged: the Syrian missile 'umbrella' which hindered the IAF from providing air support to the ground forces. It is often alleged that Sharon now saw an opportunity to strike at the missile system under the pretext of aiding the troops on the ground. Indeed, in a cabinet meeting on Wednesday 9 June, Sharon proposed destroying the missile system, marshalling all his arguments for taking this step. The Prime Minister was in favour – this Sharon already knew for he had discussed it with him previously – but other ministers had qualms about the proposed operation, fearing that it might escalate the war even further. When ministers expressed tentative reservations Sharon forced their hand by arguing that bombing the missile system was essential to 'minimize Israeli casualties', for devoid of air support they would be exposed to enemy fire. This argument had its effect, and when the old, wise and experienced Minister of the Interior Dr Yosef Burg agreed to support the operation, Sharon knew that he had won over the cabinet. He passed a note to Amos Amir, Deputy Commander of the IAF, who was present at the meeting. 'Amos', it went, 'I ride horses [and I know that] when you jump over obstacles the highest obstacle is the most difficult. [Minister] Burg has been the highest obstacle and we have overcome it . . . Arik'.[24]

This major operation against the Syrian missile system in the Beka'a was delivered that day at 2 p.m. by 96 F-15 and F-16 aircraft which, in a most efficient strike and within two and a half hours, knocked out 17 of 19 Syrian batteries and severely damaged the remaining two, which were also knocked out in a renewed attack on the next day. In the course of this assault, the Syrian air force intervened and lost 96 MiGs without any cost to the Israelis. This was a sensational triumph for the IAF, one which can be compared only with its successes on the morning of 5 June 1967, when it had destroyed almost the entire Egyptian air force on the ground, or its successful bombing of the Iraqi nuclear reactor on 7 June 1981. Following this massive air strike, Israeli forces on the ground embarked on an all-out assault against the 1st and 3rd Syrian armoured divisions, attacking them along the entire line, particularly east and west of Lake Karoun.

On 11 June, a ceasefire between Israel and Syria in the eastern sector of Lebanon came into effect; at this stage the Syrians still held the Beirut–Damascus road, but later, on Sharon's instructions, Israeli troops crept forwards and captured it. Thus, with the fight against the Syrians in Lebanon over, Sharon could congratulate himself on having achieved his hidden agenda. Although his colleagues had opposed any clash with the Syrians in Lebanon, he had managed to provoke the Syrians, and when they opened fire his forces had hit back and dislodged them from their positions. Moreover, by capturing the Beirut–Damascus road Sharon had effectively cut off the Syrians in Beirut from the bulk of their forces in the eastern part of Lebanon, a move which was crucial in order to tighten the noose on Beirut. And perhaps most important of all, he had managed to persuade the cabinet to approve a major air strike against the Syrian missile system and subsequently succeeded in destroying it.

## Beirut under siege

The battle with the Syrians was short and decisive, but this was not to be the case in Beirut, where Arafat and his men dug in and became inextricably mingled with the civilian population, rather than leaving Beirut as the Israelis wished them to do. Bashir Gemayel – by now the undisputed Maronite Christian leader in Lebanon – was adamant in refusing to send his men into Beirut to clear it of the PLO. Even the daring Sharon would not send troops into an Arab capital to conduct bitter street-fighting with the PLO. And thus with few options left, Sharon ordered his military command to tighten the siege on Beirut, to bomb areas where the PLO was hiding, and to take other measures such as cutting off water and electricity supplies and stopping food from reaching the population. The line of thought behind this brutal policy was that, if pressed hard enough, the people and government of Beirut would eventually demand Arafat's departure in order to save themselves from further hardships. So while the IAF bombed relentlessly, and guns poured salvo upon salvo into West Beirut, Israeli troops were tightening the noose around the Palestinian areas. On 3 July they seized the green line separating East and West Beirut, and took control of the Museum checkpoint in Gallery Samaan. This meant that West Beirut was totally sealed off from its eastern counterpart. On 4 July the

Israelis cut off all food, water and fuel supplies and took over Beirut's international airport. At a meeting in Tel Aviv on 11 July, Sharon instructed the air force to hit 'terrorist camps' in the south of Beirut which, as Sharon put it, 'must be destroyed, razed to the ground'. More than 500 buildings were targeted, and destroyed from the air or by artillery, with naval vessels offshore joining the battle by launching missiles into West Beirut.

But not all went well, for as the war dragged on, the number of casualties mounted and plans to enter Beirut were being drawn up, opposition to Sharon began to grow within the ranks of the IDF. Around mid-July, the commander of the 211st armoured brigade, who had led the Israeli column along the coastal axis up to Beirut, told Sharon 'this is not our fight . . . we must not let ourselves be dragged into Lebanon's internal affairs'.[25] He then took the unusual step of leaving his brigade while the war was still in progress, and was later relieved of his command. This was a significant event, for never before in Israel's military history had a commander of this rank abandoned his troops and, more than anything, it came to reflect a growing uneasiness among the rank and file. It was indeed bad news for Sharon (officially Defence Minister but effectively super-chief of staff of the IDF in all but name), who, like many great military commanders, had a clear picture of the battle and how he would win it, but failed to carry his subordinates with him.

But growing uneasiness within the IDF, and even among ministers, was still not strong enough to put an end to Israeli activities in Lebanon, and under Sharon's instructions pressure on the PLO and the Syrians in Beirut grew. On 4–5 August IDF troops entered the Hippodrome, thus increasing the pressure on the besieged forces, and on 9 August an intense artillery barrage on Beirut was accompanied by IAF attacks on the Palestinian refugee camps of Sabra, Shatilla and Bourj el Barajne. Three days later, on 12 August, the IAF conducted yet another heavy air bombardment, which lasted for more than 12 hours; unofficial reports put the number of people killed in what became known as 'Black Thursday' at 300.

With Beirut in ruins and the Israelis intensifying the pressure, the siege became unendurable and the Lebanese government sent Chief of Intelligence Jonny Abdo to Arafat as a special emissary, with the demand that Arafat leave Beirut with his men in order to end Israeli harassment of the Lebanese.[26] Without the support of the government of Lebanon, and with the Israeli noose tightening about him, Arafat – with his shrewd sense of reality – came to realize that this was the end of the game. So he acquiesced to the Lebanese government's demand, and deposited a letter to this effect in the hands of Lebanese Prime Minister Shafiq al-Wazzan.[27] On 22 August the first PLO contingent of 379 men left Beirut, and over the course of the next 12 days 14,398 Palestinians were evacuated; Arafat left on 30 August 1982, and 5,200 Syrian troops also departed.

On 23 August, Bashir Gemayel was elected President of Lebanon, and should have taken office on 23 September, but – as things go in Lebanon – he was assassinated on 14 September in Ashrafiya. This was a mortal blow to Sharon's plan in Lebanon, for he had invested enormously in Gemayel and hoped he would sign a peace treaty with Israel. The bomb that killed Gemayel destroyed every reasonable chance that Israel and Lebanon could sign a workable peace treaty. To 'restore order', Israeli troops, on 16 September at 5.00 p.m., marched into Beirut and took up positions there ('Operation Iron Brain'). This was the first time Israel had ever occupied an Arab capital. Yet there was still more to come. Between 16 and 18 September, with the approval of the Israelis, the Maronite Phalangist militia entered the refugee camps of Sabra and Shatilla to 'clean out' the 2,000 PLO guerillas who, according to reports, were still hiding there.[28] But, again, as things go in Lebanon, they massacred hundreds of Palestinians – children, women and men. The Israelis did not take part in the killing, although they did provide artillery support and also – contrary to Israeli official statements – Israeli paratroopers of the 35th brigade were present in the camps while the killing was still under way or immediately after it. The assassination of Gemayel and the massacre which followed it symbolizes, perhaps more than anything else, the total collapse of Israel's disastrous adventure in Lebanon in 1982. It had cost her more than 700 lives, and led to world condemnation.

## THE LEBANON WAR AND ISRAELI SOCIETY

The Lebanon invasion marked a new era in the attitude of the Israelis to war. If between 1948 and 1967 Israelis had shown an unconditional willingness to serve and to sacrifice and had hardly ever expressed criticism of their leadership, and if after 1967, in spite of growing criticism and dissent, Israelis were still willing to take up arms and rally behind their leadership in war, then in 1982, for the first time in Israel's history, Israelis criticized and also took a stand by refusing to cooperate and fight.

The Lebanon War was perhaps the most controversial of all of Israel's wars, and it broke the former national consensus on defence and encouraged the previously little known phenomenon of conscientious objection. While the war was still in progress, 86 reservists, including 15 officers, had sent a letter to the government which became known as the 'Letter of the 100', stating their opposition to the war and requesting to do their reserve duty not in Lebanon but within Israeli territory. A movement called 'Soldiers against Silence' was formed, calling for the removal from office of the Defence Minister and for an immediate end to the war. By September 1982, over 500 Israelis had enrolled as supporters of a new organization called *Yesh Gvul* (in English 'Enough is Enough'), which became the spearhead of opposition to the war. After the massacres in Sabra and

Shatilla, opposition to the war grew dramatically, and the number of men expressing their unwillingness to serve in Lebanon soared. In an attempt to keep the phenomenon of refusal to serve under the carpet, the authorities often came to 'private arrangements' with soldiers. According to a report in the *New York Times* (2 May 1983), citing an Israeli source, hundreds of refusers had been spared jail by the government to avoid publicity. But there were still people who were sent to jail. By March 1983, 28 Israelis were known to have served time in prison rather than in Lebanon, and by September 86 jail sentences are known to have been given to reservists; by January 1985, 30 months after the invasion, 143 reservists had been jailed for refusal to serve in Lebanon. These may be insignificant numbers for a state whose population at the time exceeded four million but, given that refusal to serve and fight was virtually unknown before this war, the figures are indeed significant and represent an important attack on what had been taboo in Israeli society.

The war also prompted some of the biggest demonstrations in the history of the state. On 26 July, while war was still raging in Lebanon, 10,000 civilians gathered in Tel Aviv to protest, and as one minister in Begin's cabinet put it: 'It was the first time in the history of Israel that such an event had taken place during the course of a war'.[29] Public agitation over the continuing war, its accompanying casualty list, and such horrors as were manifested at Sabra and Shatilla, brought to Tel Aviv in September more than 400,000 protesters, whose pressure led to the establishment of a Commission of Inquiry, whose findings when published led to the removal from office of the architect of the war, Ariel Sharon. The war in Lebanon was also Israel's first ever war in which a senior military commander, Colonel Eli Geva, resigned while war was still in progress, and it was the first time ever that a whole brigade let it be known that if called to serve in Lebanon it would refuse to obey orders.

That Israelis were reluctant to take part in the war is often explained in terms of this being a 'war of choice', namely a fight which was not forced on Israel but rather one which it had forced on one of its neighbours. But this explanation is flawed, for the 1982 war was not the first 'war of choice' Israel had experienced. In 1956, for example, Israel forced a war on Egypt, and 11 years later, in June 1967, it repeated this exercise, forcing a war on Egypt and then on Syria. Yet the difference between then and now was that in 1956 and 1967 the Israelis had fully cooperated and supported the government in its war policy and were willing to take up arms, whereas now large segments of society, as we have shown, were strongly against the war, some even refusing to take part in it. The explanation for this change of attitude, so it seems, has to do more with a change of perception by the Israelis with regard to the level of the external danger to their state and existence. For both in 1956 and again in 1967, they had felt – rightly or wrongly – that a great external threat still existed and that they were being asked to take up arms in order to remove an acute danger. But in 1982 things looked different. For the peace with Egypt (which was holding well despite Israel's invading Lebanon) seemed to remove the danger to Israel's existence, while in the north and east the Golan Heights and the West Bank seemed to provide a buffer zone against any attempt to invade the country. With this in mind, Israelis felt less threatened than before and were thus more reluctant to take up arms and fight in wars.

# 6

## *INTIFADA*

### 1987–93

The *intifada* – the Palestinian uprising in the Gaza Strip, the West Bank and Jerusalem from 1987 to 1993 – imposed on the IDF and on Israeli society as a whole a new sort of warfare, one which Israel found difficult to cope with. Very different from Israel's previous wars, the Palestinian uprising, nevertheless, had one common feature with the Six Day War of June 1967, and particularly with the Yom Kippur War of October 1973, and that is the way it surprised the Israelis, catching them off-guard and completely unprepared both mentally and physically for this new challenge. How did the *intifada* come about? Who were the rebels and what were their motives? What effect did the uprising have on the Israelis?

## THE SURPRISE

It is natural to cling to the last in a train of incidents as being the actual cause of great events. We often say such things as: 'The killing of four Christians by a Palestinian gunman at a church in East Beirut on 13 April 1975 caused the civil war in Lebanon', or 'The attempt on the life of Israel's Ambassador to London, Shlomo Argov, on 3 June 1982, caused the Israeli invasion of Lebanon'. But rather than being the causes, these incidents should be regarded as the triggers, the sparks, the last straw in an accumulation of incidents which leads to the big event. This is how we should regard the traffic accident, on Tuesday 8 December 1987, between an Israeli vehicle and a car carrying Palestinian labourers returning from a day's work in Israel, which touched off the intifada; it was the spark rather than the real cause of the uprising. Indeed, there have been traffic accidents like this before, and there was nothing to suggest that this particular one, in which four Palestinians were killed and several others injured, should lead to an all-out revolt which would last almost six years and result in hundreds of casualties on both the Israeli and Palestinian sides. But such was the tension, and so charged the atmosphere in the occupied territories at that time, that even a traffic accident was sufficient to trigger a big explosion, particularly since rumours persisted that this was not a straightforward accident but an act of vengeance by an Israeli, whose relative, Shlomo Sekle, had been stabbed to death in the market of Gaza two days earlier. The view that this was not an innocent accident was reinforced by a statement issued by PLO leader Yasser Arafat in Tunis on 13 December 1987, saying that the killing of the four was a 'premeditated Israeli attack'.

Big gatherings are notorious for having the potential to turn into ugly demonstrations, and this is precisely what happened when hundreds of mourners in Jabalya, Gaza's largest and poorest camp where more than 60,000 refugees dwell, returned

from the funerals of the four victims of the accident and turned
on Israeli troops stationed in the area, hurling stones and bottles
at them. These, we now know, were the first events of what soon
became known as the *intifada*, which is literally the shivering that
grips a person suffering from fever and is often used to refer to
brief upheavals.

At first, the Israeli military and political establishment failed to
acknowledge the real nature of the disturbances which were still
confined to the Gaza Strip. They thought – and on the face of
it there was no reason for them to think otherwise – that this
was no more than a flare-up of unrest not radically different
from previous periods of disorder.[1] So much so that even Yitzhak
Rabin, an experienced soldier and by then Defence Minister in
Yitzhak Shamir's Likud–Labor government, did not cancel his
previously scheduled trip to Washington (10 December), where
he was due, among other things, to agree the final price for
70 F-16 fighter planes that Israel was intending to purchase
from the US. With hindsight, it is ironic that Israel was about to
buy perhaps the most sophisticated weapons on the market,
without realizing that in the war which had already started in the
occupied territories these weapons would be useless. What is
more puzzling is that, even after ten days of disturbances in the
occupied territories, the Israeli government was still unaware of
the real nature of the events. Rabin demonstrated this when,
upon his return home from the US on 21 December, he convened an airport press conference where he stated that 'Iran and
Syria were behind the unrest in the territories'. And Prime
Minister Shamir, who in the absence of Rabin was also the acting
Defence Minister, put the blame for inflaming the situation on
the leadership of the PLO. These, we now know, were totally
unfounded statements, for the reality is that neither Iran nor
Syria was involved in inciting the Palestinians, and they were as
surprised as both the PLO and indeed the Israelis by the outburst
of violence. The statements of both Rabin and Shamir also

contradicted IDF's own figures of the time, which showed that about 80 per cent of violent incidents in the occupied territories were initiated locally.

With the benefit of hindsight, which should not, however, be seen as wisdom after the event, we can categorically state that the intifada was not, as is sometimes alleged, a wholly unexpected phenomenon. Indeed, there had been plenty of indications that a major transformation was underway in the occupied territories, that forces were bubbling under the surface and that there was considerable unrest in the Gaza Strip and the West Bank. Figures for the West Bank, which were available to the Israelis on the eve of the uprising, show that between April 1986 and May 1987 there was a weekly average of 56 violent demonstrations, involving stone throwing, blocking of roads, raising of the banned Palestinian flag, distributing of leaflets, burning tyres and daubing walls with nationalist graffiti. There was also an average of four incidents a week involving the use of firearms, knives, explosives and petrol bombs, in addition to a weekly arrest of an average of 81 West Bankers accused of taking part in demonstrations or engaging in what the Israelis had defined as 'acts of terrorism'. Compared with the previous year these figures indicate a stunning rise of 133 per cent in the number of demonstrations, 183 per cent in the burning of tyres (487 incidents up from 172), 140 per cent in the throwing of stones, and 68 per cent in the blocking of roads. In October 1987, just before the intifada broke out, one correspondent had reported:

> You can feel the tension. Worshippers – Jew and Moslem alike – scurry rather than walk. Tourists cluster together and are protected by armed soldiers. . . . In Gaza, you drive a car with Israeli plates at peril. . . . The marketplaces are empty of Israeli shoppers and thousands of Gazans have stayed away from jobs in Israel – some in protest, others out of fear. . . . Fear,

suspicion and growing hatred have replaced any hope of
dialogue.[2]

There was also a remarkable change in the quality of Palestinian
operations directed against the Israelis, which had become
bolder and more daring than in the past, as was manifested in
the killing of an Israeli soldier who was shot in broad daylight in
the main street of Gaza, in August 1987.

Israeli troops on the ground realized that methods which had
been used in the past to dispel demonstrations (which as we
have already shown were rife in the pre-uprising period) were
not, on the eve of the *intifada*, as effective as they had previously
been. Firing into the air, for instance, which had in the past
caused Palestinian demonstrators to scatter, was no longer effective; neither was the method commonly used to disperse college
girls, which was for an Israeli soldier to open his fly and begin
tugging down his pants. But then, as the saying goes, 'Eyes have
they but they see not', and the Israeli political-military leadership had failed, in spite of available information (as in October
1973), to read the writing on the wall and see that what they
were facing was a much more serious event than a bout of
violence.

## A SOCIAL UPRISING

### The rebels: their motives and aims

Who were the rebels? Schiff and Ya'ari say they were first and
foremost 'the poor . . . the forsaken and forgotten at the bottom
of the social heap'.[3] These were desperate people, mostly refugees from previous wars between Israel and the Arabs, who had
been living in appalling, disgraceful, harsh and insanitary conditions in the occupied territories, mainly in Gaza's eight refugee
camps, where unemployment was running at 50–60 per cent

and large families, often two or three generations, were crammed into small tumbledown dwellings. Their conditions and standards of living were better than they had been when Israel had occupied these areas 20 years before – telephone subscribers multiplied sixfold, and the number of private cars grew tenfold – but standards were still appalling. In 1973 the Israelis embarked on a programme aimed at rehabilitating the refugees by constructing apartments and providing money to inhabitants to build their own houses. But this was done at a snail's pace and fell short of Palestinians' expectations. On the eve of the intifada only 8,600 families had been moved to new housing, and at this rate it was apparent that the camps would never be dismantled, for it would take about 50 years to build new homes for the other 33,000 families, while natural increase proceeded at more than double the pace of construction. This was frustrating, especially for the younger generation of Palestinians, many of whom were working in Israel, where high standards of living demonstrated to them how appalling was their own situation.

Indeed, most of the demonstrators, at least on the eve of the uprising, were labourers who worked from dawn to dusk in 'dirty jobs' of the sort Israelis shunned; they knew the Israelis well and spoke their language. But when questioned, after being arrested by the Israelis, regarding their motives in joining the intifada, they often complained of injustice done to them by Israeli employers. They talked of the harsh way they were treated by a country which demanded they pay social security – which they knew would never be repaid to them – but also banned them from joining labour unions and establishing workers' committees. They were humiliated and often delayed for hours with no explanation at the Erez Checkpoint, which is the main gate from the Gaza Strip to Israel, and they were occasionally forced to imitate barking, bleating, or other animal sounds before being allowed to cross into Israel. They were not allowed to stay overnight in Israel and, while many of them did make the long daily journey back home, some preferred to break the law and hide overnight in Israel to spare themselves the humiliation at the Erez crossing just to emerge the next morning at their working place. These people, who became the spearhead of the *intifada*, had no wish to cultivate Palestinian national consciousness, and in fact many of them knew little about the Palestinian National Covenant or about such concepts as 'the right to self-determination'. What they were looking for when joining the demonstrations was simply a better life.

Another group to join the *intifada* were graduates. In the 1970s graduates could easily find jobs, especially in the Gulf, but the crisis in the oil economies and fewer opportunities in Jordan meant that some 15,000 Palestinian college graduates were unemployed on the eve of the *intifada*; they were desperate and bored and they directed their anger and frustration at the Israelis. The Israelis, in turn, were aghast, for after all it was during the 20 years of occupation that they had allowed the building of seven new universities on the West Bank, and when graduates of these institutions now joined the uprising, the Israelis felt betrayed; they felt that the graduates were biting the hand which had fed them.

Islamic militants, such as a group calling itself 'Islamic Jihad', also involved themselves the moment the first attacks on the Israelis started. Established in 1981, after splitting from the Moslem Brotherhood in the occupied territories, Islamic Jihad first became widely known in February 1986, when some of its members tossed a grenade at a group of Israeli soldiers and Jewish settlers. This was followed by more attacks, notably in October 1986, when Islamic Jihad activists threw hand grenades at an Israeli military graduation ceremony at the Western Wall. At a later stage another fundamentalist group, Hamas, would join and play a leading part in the revolt.

The rebels of all groups represented a new generation of Palestinians, who after 20 years of Israeli occupation were far more militant and radical than previous generations, and whose role models were not Yasser Arafat, George Habash and others of the PLO old guard, but rather such young daring activists as the six Palestinians who escaped from the Gaza Central Prison in May 1987 and later in October were shot dead in a shoot-out with Shin Bet, Israel's internal security police. Another role model to catch the imagination of these young Palestinians was the young member of Ahmed Jibril's Syrian-backed PFLP, who on 25 November 1987 – just before the outbreak of the *intifada* – flew across the Lebanese border in an ultra-light hang-glider, landed in a field, entered a nearby Israeli army camp and mowed down six soldiers and wounded 13 before being shot. In the occupied territories this attack which became known in Israel as 'The night of the hang-gliders' caused widespread satisfaction, and it was seen as a heroic operation which destroyed the myth of Israeli defences. Indeed, what these daring operations did was to help puncture Israel's image of invincibility among young Palestinians in the occupied territories, and prepare them, above all mentally, for the *intifada*.

## THE EXPLOSION

### Palestinian action – Israeli reaction

The day after the funerals at Jabalya, Palestinians in the Gaza Strip blocked roads with rocks, tyres, broken furniture and steel sewage pipes; they also stoned Israeli soldiers. Unlike the events of the previous day, which had been spontaneous, these were pre-planned by local leaders. When met by a hail of stones, Israeli troops resorted to live ammunition, and this resulted in the killing of 17-year-old Hatem Abu Sisi, who was shot by a bullet through the heart and became the first 'martyr' of the *intifada*. From Jabalya the demonstrations and riots spread like a wildfire to other refugee camps – to Khan Yunis, al Bourej, Nuseirat and Ma'azi, and then to Rafah. They then spread to the more secular and affluent West Bank – to Balata, Kalandia and other villages and towns. This opening wave of riots lasted 12 consecutive days and was particularly intense in the Gaza Strip, where it seemed as if all ages and classes were out on the streets confronting the Israelis.

It was clear from the start that the IDF was ill prepared and had no ready made answer to the problem of civil resistance on this scale, in which the weapons used by the rebels were so primitive that Israel's tanks, aeroplanes, rockets and artillery lost all significance. It was an odd situation, in which the Israelis were so powerful that they could not apply their might and, ironically, if they were to be able to deal effectively with the problem without shooting the demonstrators – for Israel could not afford this due to public opinion at home and abroad – they had to downgrade their weapons. It is important to note here that the Palestinians' policy was not to resort to arms, as they knew that if they did use guns the Israelis would then have a pretext to use their might and crush the uprising by using their more sophisticated arms. What the Israeli troops needed was the most basic and elementary riot gear such as shields, helmets, clubs and tear gas, but these were all in short supply, and as then Deputy Chief of Staff Ehud Barak later admitted to the author, 'We were not technically prepared to deal with a violent popular riot on this scale'.[4]

Why the Israelis were not 'technically' prepared for the out-break of an uprising is hard to explain, but the fact remains that although officials at the defence ministry did contemplate, in the years before the *intifada*, the idea of purchasing vehicles equipped with water cannon for dispersing demonstrations, as well as other anti-riot devices such as stunt guns, slippery dust to coat the streets, nets for trapping demonstrators, and sneeze bombs, no action had followed. Special dogs were trained to disperse demonstrators, but were never throughout the 20 years of occupation put on the streets lest Israel be accused of resorting to methods used in South Africa or Nazi Germany. What was also evident from the start was that the Israelis lacked any experience in dealing with large-scale riots. In the past it had been suggested that special units be trained to deal with potential riots, but the army High Command objected to this, preferring to have army units serve occasionally in the occupied territories so they could gain some experience in dealing with civil unrest and get to know the terrain.

During the opening days and weeks of the *intifada* the Israeli High Command was in a state of disarray; it was simply at a loss and did not know how to deal with the new warfare which had been imposed on it. Its first move, however, was to react to calls for reinforcement, and within three days the number of troops patrolling the occupied territories had increased threefold in comparison to normal times. Although renowned for its flexibility and ability to alter and adapt itself to changing situations, the Israeli High Command was, in the opening phases of the uprising, no match for the Palestinians, whose ability to devise quick new methods to adapt to changes in the IDF's tactics had made the latter obsolete even before they were fully implemented. Thus, when the Israelis decided that foot patrols were ineffective in dealing with the riots, and that they should turn to motorized patrols in jeeps and command cars, the Palestinians immediately reacted by sprinkling the roads with nails to puncture the tyres of the Israeli vehicles.

Israel's worst fear was that the riots might spread to Jerusalem, where the international media had a strong presence and could broadcast the disturbances and Israeli reaction to the world. This nightmare came true when, on 19 December 1987, riots started simultaneously in a number of locations in the capital, with no fewer than 5,000 Palestinians taking part in them. East Jerusalem now experienced the worst violence since the Six

Day War of June 1967, and the scenes previously seen on the streets of the Gaza Strip and West Bank of barricades, burning tyres, Palestinian flags and stone-throwing were evident in Jerusalem. Demonstrators set fire to municipal vehicles and stoned Israeli-owned restaurants in East Jerusalem, and cars carrying Israeli plates passing through the Arab districts of Jerusalem – Abu Dis, Shuafat, Jebel Mukaber and Azariah.

Israeli strategy in Jerusalem was a systematic campaign of harassment aimed at putting indirect but intense pressure on the Palestinians: they stopped and searched Arab cars, checked the condition of windscreen wipers and seat belts or made sure that the driver and passengers had paid their taxes. Furthermore, a new rule forbade Moslems from outside the city to pray at the Haram al-Sharif, the noble sanctuary, where the Dome of the Rock and the Al-Aqsa Mosque had stood for over 1,500 years; everyone entering a mosque in Jerusalem was checked. In addition, neighbourhoods where violence recurred were placed under curfew. But still the disturbances continued.

The local Palestinian leadership in the Gaza Strip and West Bank was quick to organize itself and give a clear direction to what seemed to be, at first sight, utter chaos. Representatives of Fatah (Yasser Arafat), the Popular Front (George Habash), the Democratic Front (Naif Hawatmeh), the Palestine Communist Party and Islamic Jihad all joined forces against the common enemy, Israel, and established the 'Unified National Leadership of the Uprising' (UNLU) which became the coordinating body of the *intifada* on the West Bank. The names of the UNLU's leaders remained anonymous, partly because of the fear that revealing their identity might lead to a situation where fellow Palestinians refused to obey their instructions, for after all they were petty, often unknown, local leaders. There was also the fear that coming out into the open might invite pressure from the PLO, which was alarmed from the start in case the local leadership took over and marginalized it. And obviously, if UNLU leaders were to identify themselves it would become much easier for Israeli security services to arrest or even kill them.

The UNLU leaders communicated to and led the Palestinians by issuing leaflets and communiqués in which they encouraged their followers to take direct action against the Israelis. The 60,000 copies of the first communiqué were issued on 10 January 1988. It called on 'the heroes of the stone and firebomb war to redouble the revolutionary content . . . shake the oppressive regime down to its foundations [and create] . . . inviolable unity'. More practically it called on the Palestinians to take the following measures:

> All roads must be closed to the occupation forces . . . its cowardly soldiers must be prevented from entering refugee camps and large population centres by barricades and burning tyres. . . . Stones must land on the heads of the occupying soldiers and those who collaborate with them. Palestinian flags are to be flown from minarets, churches, rooftops, and electricity poles everywhere. . . . We must set the ground burning under the feet of the occupiers. Let the whole world know that the volcanic uprising that has ignited the Palestinian people will not cease until the achievement of independence in a Palestinian state whose capital is Jerusalem.[5]

In this and other communiqués the aims of the uprising were further crystallized, and included among others: forcing the withdrawal of the IDF from cities, towns and refugee camps; evacuating Ariel Sharon from his house in the Old City of Jerusalem where he settled in the Moslem quarter in a move which outraged the Arabs and was aimed to show that Jerusalem belonged to the Jewish people; repealing the Emergency Regulations (such as administrative detention, deportation, the demolition of houses and other collective punishments implemented by the army); releasing detainees; halting the expropriation of land and the establishment of new Jewish settlements on Arab land; abolishing value-added tax; dispersing all the municipal, village and refugee camp councils, and the holding of democratic elections in the West Bank and Gaza Strip.

Most communiqués were drafted by a certain Mohamad Labadi, who became a leading figure during the period of the *intifada*, and were then sent to his colleagues, who represented all factions of the PLO, for final approval. Occasionally, however, the entire command would meet, each time in a different location in East Jerusalem to escape Israeli interference, to decide its policy and work on its leaflets, which were then distributed by young boys and girls who placed them in the entrance of mosques, or plastered them on telephone poles alongside Palestinian flags. Later, the texts of the communiqués would be also broadcast by the Voice of the PLO radio station in Bagdhad and the Al Quds Palestinian Arab Radio based in Damascus.

It is notable that the PLO leadership in Tunis was not at all involved in organizing the *intifada* during its initial stages, but was indeed very worried that local leaders would gain influence at its expense. This is why it put strong pressure on the local leadership and, beginning with communiqué no. 3 of 18 January 1988, all leaflets were signed also by the PLO and read 'Palestine Liberation Organization – Unified National Leadership of the Palestinian Uprising in the Occupied Territories'. This, so PLO-Tunis believed, would make it clear that the UNLU leadership was no more that an 'arm' of the PLO acting on its behalf in the occupied territories. While the UNLU was functioning on the West Bank, a similar body was established in the Gaza Strip. It was, however, not as influential as its West Bank counterpart, mainly because the Islamic fundamentalists held themselves aloof and refused to take part in this committee of leaders.

The first few weeks of the *intifada*, that is from 9 to 31 December 1987, were chaotic and violent. Figures show that in this short period 22 Palestinians were killed by Israeli gunfire; five of them were youths aged between 13 and 16. In addition, some 320 were injured, two thirds of them aged between 17 and 21. The high toll amongst youths was the direct result of them taking an active part in the uprising, but it was also because the practice of Israeli troops was to shoot at the legs of the demonstrators in order not to kill them – which for children was lethal. On the Israeli side, 56 soldiers and 30 civilians were injured by stones and bottles. In this single month there were 1,412 separate incidents of demonstrations, stoning, tyre-burning, blocking roads and raising barricades. At least 109 firebombs were thrown, in addition to 12 instances of arson and three grenade attacks; some 270 Palestinians were arrested.

In the meantime, after recovering from its initial shock, the IDF, in mid-January 1988, deployed two divisional commands on the West Bank and a third in the Gaza Strip; the number of men patrolling Palestinian areas rose to the point where there was a shortage of equipment, and it was necessary to open up emergency stores and distribute equipment usually reserved for all-out wars with Arab regular armies.

In spite of growing pressure, the riots did not cease: the UNLU continued to function, and its prestige among the Palestinians steadily grew. In fact, it became so influential that under its pressure four municipal council members appointed by the Israelis resigned in February 1988, and on 11 March there was a mass resignation of Palestinian policemen. The Palestinians also organized communal support, with 'Popular Committees' springing up in almost every city and village of the Gaza Strip and the West Bank, and covering every sphere of life from education and security to business activity and sanitation, as well as youth, student, women's and workers' affairs. It is estimated that during the years of the intifada there were around 45,000 local committees of various kinds in the territories.

## ENTER HAMAS

A nasty surprise awaited Israelis when a new militant fundamentalist group which was an offshoot of the Moslem Brotherhood joined the *intifada*. It was called the 'Islamic Resistance
Movement' (*Harakat al-Muqawama al Islami*), that is 'Hamas' from
the Arabic acronym whose literal meaning is 'courage' or 'zeal'.
Hamas was set up by Sheikh Ahmad Yassin and six other
leaders of the Moslem Brotherhood in the occupied territories,
and it was financed mainly by its supporters worldwide, who
made contributions as part of the *zakat* – the Islamic tax. It was
well organized, especially in the Gaza Strip. Three of its Islamic
activists were appointed to serve as commanders: one was put
in charge of political affairs, the second in charge of propaganda and the printing and distributing of handbills, and the
third, Salah Shehadeh, whose code name was '101', was put in
charge of military matters and led the armed wing of
Hamas, which was named after Izz al Din Qassam, leader of the
Arab *intifada* against the British from 1936 to 1939. It had about
200 volunteers, who received the title *Mujahedu Falastin* ('holy
fighters of Palestine'). Hamas divided the Gaza Strip into five
districts, each headed by an operations officer and a liaison
officer whose job was to maintain regular contact with Islamic
activists on the West Bank. Hamas swiftly rose to prominence,
and by the second month of the *intifada* it was playing a leading
role.

It should be mentioned that the emergence of the fundamentalists, both Islamic Jihad and Hamas, to power and influence on the West Bank and particularly in the Gaza Strip, was
partly the result of Israel's folly and short-sighted policy which
attempted, in the years before the uprising, to play the fundamentalists off against the PLO in order to counterbalance and
weaken the latter. Ironically, however, while the PLO had avoided
any hint of anti-Semitism, the fundamentalists gloried in it, and

Jew hatred was a common feature of their publications, as shown in the following extracts from *The Covenant of the Islamic Resistance Movement*:

> There is no solution to the Palestinian problem except by Jihad.... The Nazism of the Jews does not skip women and children, it scares everyone.... This wealth [of the Jews] permitted them to take over control of the world media such as news agencies, the press, publication houses, broadcasting and the like. [They also have used this] wealth to stir revolutions in various parts of the globe.... They stood behind the French and the Communist Revolutions.... They also used the money to establish clandestine organizations which are spreading around the world in order to destroy societies and carry out Zionist interests. Such organizations are: the Free Masons, Rotary Clubs, Lions Clubs, B'nai B'rith and the like. All of them are destructive spying organizations. They also used the money to take over control of the Imperialist states and made them colonize many countries in order to exploit the wealth of those countries.... [the Jews] stood behind World War I, so as to wipe out the Islamic Caliphate.... [The Jews] ... established the League of Nations in order to rule the world by means of that organization. They also stood behind World War II, where they collected immense benefits from trading with war materials.... They inspired the establishment of the United Nations and the Security Council ... in order to rule the world.... There was no war that broke out anywhere without their fingerprints on it.... The Zionist invasion is a mischievous one.... [The Jews] stand behind the diffusion of drugs and toxic of all kinds in order to facilitate its control and expansion.... After Palestine [the Jews] will covet expansion from the Nile to the Euphrates. Only when they have completed digesting the area on which they will have laid their hand, they will look forward to more expansion.... Their scheme has

been laid out in the Protocols of the Elders of Zion. . . . We have no escape from pooling together all the forces and energies to face this despicable Nazi-Tatar invasion.[6]

Given this approach, it is indeed puzzling that the Israelis came to regard Hamas as less wicked than the PLO and opted for the fundamentalists, allowing them to blossom. Indeed, for a time before the *intifada*, fundamentalist Moslems could move, with tacit Israeli agreement, into positions of power in the Gaza Strip and the West Bank; some were even allowed to take jobs in the Israeli Civil Administration, the body in daily contact with the Palestinian population at all levels of life. The strengthening position and growing influence of the fundamentalists in Gaza is manifested in figures showing that in the mid-1980s there was a rise in prayer attendance and a return to the traditional Moslem way of life, with Gaza's 77 mosques at the end of the 1967 war multiplying to 160 in the following two decades. On the West Bank new mosques were being built at a rate of 40 per year. Although less influential on the West Bank, the Islamic fundamentalists nevertheless held key positions in the small Islamic College in Hebron, and in Nablus they controlled the allocation of welfare to 10,000 needy families, granting loans and scholarships, and running orphanages, homes for the aged and even an independent high school.

It was only in the second year of the uprising that the Israelis came to realize that activists of Hamas were at the forefront of the *intifada* and, unlike other Palestinian groups which made it their policy to refrain from the use of arms, were preparing caches of arms and explosives. In July and September 1988 the Israelis struck at Hamas, arresting 120 activists and liquidating its command. But this did not spell the end for this group, since it took the movement's middle echelon only a few weeks to recover from the blow and re-embark on anti-Israeli activities.

## RECOVERING THE INITIATIVE BUT FAILING TO SUPPRESS THE UPRISING

To quell the growing resistance and put an end to the uprising, the army resorted to various methods ranging from cutting off telephone lines and electricity to placing extended curfews on villages, towns and whole cities. On the West Bank localized curfews were imposed, while in Gaza more broad curfews were used. During 1988, no fewer than 1,600 curfew orders were issued in the occupied territories, 118 of them for five days or more; all in all some 60 per cent of the Palestinian population experienced life under curfew. The army also uprooted trees and occasionally entire orchards to deny the Palestinians the hiding places from where they could strike at Israeli troops; according to Palestinian figures, during 1988 the Israelis uprooted more than 25,000 olive and fruit trees. Furthermore, the demolishing of houses, which before the outbreak of the intifada was considered an extraordinary measure used only against Palestinians who had committed serious offences, became, as from December 1987, a common means of administrative punishment. Thus, whereas before the outbreak of the intifada demolishing a house had required the special approval of the Defence Minister, now with the intifada underway, it was left to the discretion of an area commander. Figures show that it was used frequently: in 1987 the number of houses demolished was 103, and in 1988 it rose to a staggering 423. Deportations, another draconian measure, were also used to quell the disturbances, as well as the closure of schools and universities which had been shut down for most of the first 18 months of the intifada.

The use of live ammunition against stone-throwers who were mostly children was disastrous for the Israelis from a public relations point of view. The Israelis thus looked for ammunition which would enable them to hit Palestinians from a distance but not kill them. In 1989 rubber bullets were introduced. But these proved to be ineffective and so were replaced by plastic bullets, which proved to be more lethal than expected and so were replaced by rubber bullets with steel centres. Troops were also provided with light, easy-to-handle clubs, strong enough not to break even when inflicting the heaviest of blows – ironically, the firms that manufactured these clubs employed mostly Arab workers from the Gaza Strip. At a meeting with troops in Ramallah, Defence Minister Rabin told them: 'Gentlemen, start using your hands, or clubs and simply beat the demonstrators in order to restore order'.[7] This became known as Rabin's 'break their bones' policy, and it is a testimony to the troops' frustration that they took Rabin's advice literally; the blows they inflicted on Palestinians left many of these people handicapped. So, ironically, as Schiff and Ya'ari have observed:

> Rather than being hailed as a symbol of sanity, or at least the lesser of two evils, and rather than being used with discretion to subdue rioters resisting arrest, the club reverted to being an emblem of barbarity and was employed with abandon by men who had simply let the uprising get their goat.[8]

In the face of worldwide condemnation, the Israeli authorities were forced to modify Rabin's instructions, which subsequently stated: 'Force is not to be used against sensitive parts of the body', and later,

> Force may be used against violence and those resisting arrest while the violence is being committed, up to the point of capture. [But] the exercise of force against anyone who has been stopped, is under arrest, or is already in custody and is not behaving violently is absolutely forbidden.

The Israelis also revised and amended legal procedures to

facilitate mass arrests of rioters, and the establishment of new detention facilities in March 1988 in Ketziot, which had a capacity of 7,000 prisoners, and at Daharieh, near Hebron, made it possible to hold thousands of detainees for extended periods. About 50,000 Palestinians were arrested during the first 18 months of the intifada, with more than 12,000 of them held in administrative detention for periods of varying length. One in every 80 Palestinian adults in the occupied territories was imprisoned by administrative order, while one in 40 had spent more than 24 hours in detention for taking part in the uprising. But jails, as the Israelis later learnt, only produced more militants; for while the Israelis could ensure that their prisoners did not run away, they could not really control lives inside the jails. Thus the jails had effectively turned into political schools, where a new generation of Palestinian leaders was formed and a strong bond created among the Palestinians.

Economic measures were also used by the Israelis to put down the rebellion. For example, a systematic campaign was launched to break the Palestinian tax strike, which had been introduced by the Palestinian population following UNLU's instructions. The campaign was carried out during curfews, with the security forces' full cooperation, and proved to be highly effective from the Israeli point of view; in the Gaza Strip, for example, the income from taxes actually rose at the end of 1988. Furthermore, individualized types of economic punishment were imposed, such as the banning of Palestinian villages in the Jordan Valley from bringing their harvest to market in Jericho, which was a devastating blow for them for they relied heavily on selling their crops in Jericho. Economic measures hit the Palestinians hard. In 1988 their standard of living, which was already low, fell by as much as 30–40 per cent, and by the beginning of 1989 the unemployment figure had risen sharply, with the number of people working in Israel, a critical source of income for the Palestinian economy, declining by more than 25 per cent. Israel also paid heavily for this war of attrition. As a consequence of the *intifada*, its commercial turnover fell 25 per cent below the original forecast for 1988, which translated into a loss of almost $1 billion. In the building and textile trades, the decline reached as much as 10–15 per cent; tourism dropped by 14 per cent and total exports from Israel to the occupied territories diminished by no less than 34 per cent.

But even these measures failed to stop the rioting – the Palestinians continued to throw stones, to raise the Palestinian flag, and to spray walls with political graffiti, often in one of the four colours of the Palestinian standard. Red in the flag signified the blood of the martyrs, green the fertility of the Palestinian plains, white, peace, and black the oppression of occupation to be removed when Palestine was liberated. A revolt, which at its opening stage was carried out by the impoverished classes who only wished to improve their standards of living, now turned into a statement of political import.

A year of uprising, from December 1987 to December 1988, proved to be very violent and produced a high death toll. Three hundred and eleven Palestinians were killed, 44 of them aged 13–16, and nine under the age of nine lost their lives. In addition, 15 Palestinian civilians were killed by Israeli civilians, six Israeli civilians were killed by Palestinians, and four Israeli security force personnel were killed by Palestinians. The number of houses demolished during this period had reached a staggering 526.

There were times when it seemed as if the revolt was spreading from the occupied territories to Israel itself. In July 1989, for instance, a Palestinian refugee from Gaza wrested the steering wheel of a passenger bus from its driver and sent it over a cliff, killing 15 people. In May 1990, a former Israeli soldier opened fire on unarmed Arab workers south of Tel Aviv, killing seven. Hamas was also causing Israel great problems, and in May 1989 the Israelis inflicted a second blow on the organization, arresting its spiritual leader Sheikh Yassin along with his aides and some 260 activists. But fundamentalism remained, especially in the Gaza Strip, a mass movement resolved to destroy Israel and change the face of Palestinian society. When in the early 1990s Israelis and Palestinians embarked on the road to peace, Hamas was to inflict apalling acts of terrorism which would often halt and reverse the entire peace process.

Officially, the intifada continued until Israel and the Palestinians had signed the Oslo Agreement on 13 September 1993. In the period between 9 December 1987 and 13 September 1993, 1,070 Palestinian civilians were killed by Israeli security forces in the occupied territories and 17 more in Israel. Of those killed, 64 were children under the age of 12, and 173 were aged 13–16. In addition, 54 Palestinian civilians were killed by Israeli civilians (mostly settlers) in the territories, and a further 21 in Israel. In the same period, 48 Israeli civilians were killed by Palestinians in the occupied territories, and 53 within Israel itself. Forty-two Israelis of the security forces were killed by Palestinians in the occupied territories, and 17 were killed in Israel. Thousands of Palestinians and hundreds of Israelis were injured, and 1,473 Palestinian houses were demolished. Deportation of activists was also rife; 413 Hamas and Islamic Jihad activists were deported to southern Lebanon in December 1992.

## INTIFADA AND ISRAELI SOCIETY

The Israelis were shocked to the core by the magnitude and ferocity of the Palestinian uprising, for as Schiff and Ya'ari correctly observed:

> There seemed to be a collective mental block in Israel [with regard to the Palestinians and occupied territories]. . . . The Jewish public tended to repress the Palestinian issue entirely, relating to the territories as though they were a distant land. In

a sense the Israelis discovered the territories twice: at the end of the Six Day War, when attention was riveted on their historical landscape with all its biblical landmarks, and again some twenty years later, in December 1987, when the Palestinian population made it impossible for them to cling to the blinders that had made the million and a half Arabs under Israeli military rule so conveniently invisible.[9]

And as the Israeli novelist David Grossman observed in *The Yellow Wind*, just before the *intifada* erupted: 'We [Israelis] have lived for 20 years in a false and artificial situation based on illusions, on a teetering centre of gravity between hate and fear, in a desert void of emotion and consciousness'. Someday, Grossman warned, 'it will exact a deadly price'.[10] Indeed, Israelis by no means ignored the occupied territories, and when the *intifada* came it sent a sharp jolt through the whole of society, forcing it to re-examine propositions that had long been taken for granted. As the uprising dragged on from week to week, month to month and year to year, and with a high death toll on both sides, Israelis came increasingly to realize that their country was slipping back to the starting line in its conflict with the Palestinians. Through this shocking experience, the Israelis came to realize that their leaders had deceived them in pronouncing that the Palestinian people did not exist, or, as Prime Minister Golda Meir used to put it, 'there is no Palestinian nation'. Israelis now saw how they had all been dragged down to the level of brute violence, and they ceased to believe that 'benevolent occupation' was possible.

What the *intifada* did to Israeli society was to divide it and sharpen its polarization, with the first division drawn between Israelis and the 700,000 Arab Israelis living within the Green Line. We should remember that although most Arabs left Palestine during 1947–8 and also during the 1967 war, there was still in Israel, on the eve of the *intifada*, a community of Arabs making up about 17 per cent of Israel's total population.

Throughout the years these Arab Israelis had become an integral part of Israeli society; they held Israeli identity cards, spoke Hebrew, studied and worked in Israel. But with their fellow Palestinians revolting in the occupied territories, the Arabs of Israel found it increasingly difficult to remain aloof. On 17 December, just a week after the outbreak of the *intifada*, they held a general strike and rallies in support of Palestinians in the occupied territories, and on 21 December embarked on a general strike. They also sent food and medicine to the territories, and donated blood; a few even made their bank accounts available to the PLO for transferring funds to the territories. In taking these actions, the Arabs of Israel showed themselves to be more Palestinian than Israeli, and for the Jewish Israelis this was a shocking realization.

But the *intifada* also sharply divided the Jewish population itself, and although there was a general move to the political right and a wave of extremism in Israel, there was also a sharp move to the left, where a growing number of Israelis emerged to declare themselves unwilling to serve in the occupied territories and put down the uprising. From this point of view, the trend which had begun in the Lebanon war, of Israelis refusing to take up arms, was continuing. In fact, as far back as October 1987, that is just before the outbreak of the *intifada*, a group of 50 high school students about to become eligible for military service had signed a letter to Defence Minister Rabin expressing their intention to refuse to serve beyond the Green line; at the time they claimed they had 'hundreds of supporters'. With the *intifada* rearing its ugly head, the number of Israelis refusing to serve in the territories increased rapidly, with the protest movement *Yesh Gvul* – which had played a leading role during the Lebanon war – encouraging this stand. At the end of December 1987, 16 more students joined the group which had sent the October letter to the Defence Minister. Also that December, 160 reservists, including one woman, one Jerusalem city councillor and several officers, followed suit by declaring that they refused to participate in putting down the *intifada*. In mid-February 1988, *Yesh Gvul* announced that 260 reservists had proclaimed that they would not carry out any orders to beat Palestinians. With the number of Israelis refusing to serve in the occupied territories growing by the day, the military authorities attempted to keep the phenomenon under the carpet, as it had done during the Lebanon war, and it came to arrangements with many of those refusing to serve, promising not to send them to fulfil missions in the occupied territories. Nevertheless, as was the case during the Lebanon war, there were those who were sent to jail: on 18 July 1989, it was reported in the *Jerusalem Post* that 77 Israeli soldiers had been imprisoned for refusing to serve in the occupied territories. Although these numbers are small, they are not insignificant, especially if we remember that from the immediate pre-state period until 1970, only a little over 100 Jewish Israelis publicly refused to serve. Also, as was the case during the 1982 war in Lebanon, big demonstrations took place in Israel while troops in the territories were still grappling with the uprising. Thus, on 23 January 1988, between 80,000 and 100,000 Israelis took part in a demonstration in Tel Aviv to denounce Israeli policies in the occupied territories, and in Nazareth Jews and Arabs held a rally, carrying banners with names of Palestinians killed by Israelis.

It was the signing of the 1993 Oslo Agreement which ended the *intifada* and enabled a return to some sort of normality in Israeli–Palestinian relationships and Jewish–Arab relationships within Israel proper. But not for long.

# 7

## THE *AL-AQSA INTIFADA*

### 2000–5

Seven years after the end of the first *intifada*, a new uprising erupted, which soon came to be known as the *Al-Aqsa intifada*, named after the mosque in Jerusalem's Old City where riots first erupted. The perspective of history will probably identify this insurgency in the occupied territories, from 2000 to present, as the continuation of the first *intifada*, though there are significant differences between the two events. While the stone and the bottle were the symbols and indeed the main weapons of the Palestinians during the first *intifada*, in the second uprising they were superseded by rifles, pistols, hand grenades, mortars and suicide bombs. And while in the first *intifada* clashes between Palestinian insurgents and Israeli security forces took place in the centre of Palestinian towns and cities, by the time of the second *intifada* these urban areas were no longer routinely patrolled by Israeli forces – the Israelis having withdrawn from them as part of the 1993 Oslo agreements – and as a result clashes now took place on the edges of towns and cities, usually close to Israeli military checkpoints. Also, unlike the 1987–93 uprising when Palestinians had mainly targeted Israeli security forces, during the *Al-Aqsa intifada* they struck at Jewish settlers with drive-by shootings, ambushes, sniper fire, mortar attacks and machine-gun fire on Jewish settlements; perhaps most notably, Palestinians now attacked Israeli civilians with suicide bombs in cafés, shops, markets and on buses in Jerusalem and Tel Aviv.

The second *intifada* was sparked by a visit of the right-wing opposition leader Ariel Sharon on 28 September 2000 to Temple Mount, the holiest site in Judaism, located in Jerusalem. Sharon's visit was aimed at boosting his support, particularly within his own Likud Party, where a political rival, Benjamin Netanyahu, was enjoying growing popularity. But on the ruins of the Jewish Temple stands a compound the Muslims call Haram Al-Sharif ('the Noble Sanctuary', or 'The Haram'), which Sharon planned to tour, and which contains a number of mosques, including Al-Aqsa, holy to Muslims as the place from where the prophet Muhammad ascended to heaven. Palestinians therefore regarded Sharon's visit as a deliberately provocative move, and it upset them even more that his visit was due to take place around the time of the anniversary of the massacre of Palestinian refugees at the Sabra and Shatilla camps in Lebanon in 1982, an event for which Sharon, Defence Minister at the time, was found to be indirectly responsible by an Israeli commission.

On the day of Sharon's visit, the Muslim morning prayers on Haram Al-Sharif took place at around 5.54 a.m. and passed without incident. However, from around 7.00 in the morning, in anticipation of Sharon's visit, political figures began arriving at the scene, including both Israeli and Palestinian supporters and detractors of the visit. Palestinian youth, eventually number-ing around 1,500, also gathered, and were confronted by 1,500 Israeli police, who were present in order to forestall any violence. Sharon arrived at Temple Mount at 7.57 a.m., had his tour of the compound, refrained from entering the mosques and left at 8.31 a.m. There were only limited disturbances during the visit, but for the remainder of the day there were sporadic outbreaks of Palestinian stone throwing at Israeli police on Temple Mount and its vicinity. These incidents, we know in hindsight, were the opening of the *Al-Aqsa intifada*.

Sharon's visit was just the catalyst for the second *intifada* and not its deep cause.[1] This is to be found elsewhere, namely in what was perceived at that time as the collapse of the Israeli–Palestinian Oslo peace process as symbolized, perhaps more than anything else, by the failed Camp David Summit of July 2000.

## A FAILED SUMMIT

Convened by President Bill Clinton, the Camp David Summit was the initiative of the Israeli Prime Minister Ehud Barak. The Prime Minister pressured Clinton to summon a summit in which Barak and Arafat would take personal charge of negotiations over the last remaining points of disagreement before signing a final peace deal that would put an end to decades of Palestinian–Jewish strife. Arafat, however, was reluctant. First, because he suspected that given the close relations between Israel and the US, he would be cornered and confronted by a Clinton–Barak front and be held responsible should the summit collapse. Second, and perhaps more importantly, his interpretation of previous agreements with Israel led him to believe that 90 per cent of occupied land was already due to be under his control and he wanted this done *before* any endgame summit with Barak. However, with Barak insisting on a summit and President Clinton determined to sort out the Palestinian–Israeli conflict before he left office, invitations were issued by the White House which, of

JERUSALEM

OLD CITY

Dome of
the Rock

TEMPLE MOUNT/
HARAM AL-SHARIF

Al-Aqsa
Mosque

Site of
clashes

750 ft. (225 m)

*Map 7* The *Al-Aqsa* Compound (based on Corbis aerial photo)

course, Barak was happy to accept and which Arafat could not be seen to decline, however much he may have wanted to.

The summit, at the Presidential retreat of Camp David, opened on 11 July, and during its 14-day course Barak presented to Arafat an extraordinary array of offers which went far beyond what previous Israeli governments had ever offered the Palestinians. These included a proposed transfer to Palestinians of the entire Gaza Strip, as well as 92 per cent of West Bank land for the purpose of establishing a Palestinian state. The remaining 8 per cent of West Bank land, where 80 per cent of Israeli settlers lived, would, under the terms of Barak's offer, be annexed to Israel and the Palestinians would be compensated by getting land elsewhere. Although nothing was officially signed at the Camp David Summit, we know that Arafat accepted Barak's offer regarding the above land division.[2]

A heated debate took place at the summit regarding Palestinian refugees of previous wars. Arafat insisted that Israel should take responsibility for all those Palestinians who fled the area when the state of Israel was created in 1948 and in subsequent conflicts, claiming a 'Right of Return' to Israel for every Palestinian refugee who desired it. Did Arafat really believe Israel could accept millions of, mostly Muslim, refugees and their children and grandchildren, the return of whom would transform the Jewish nature of the state? Probably not, but he insisted on the *principle* that every refugee should have the right to return. Prime Minister Barak, however, rejected this request, even refusing to use the expression 'Right of Return', opting instead for Palestinian 'Claims of Return'. What Barak offered Arafat at Camp David was a 'satisfactory solution' (these were the exact words he used) to the problem, by which he meant that between 10,000 and 12,000 Palestinian refugees would be allowed to return to Israel proper to reunite with their families, and a mechanism would be devised by which the international community would contribute $20–25 billion to settle all the refugees' claims. The funds – it was thought – would be given as compensation to refugee households and as an aid grant to countries willing to rehabilitate Palestinian refugees. The refugees, according to plans discussed at the summit, would be offered three options: to settle in the future Palestinian state; to remain where they were; or to emigrate to countries that would voluntarily open their gates to them, such as Canada, Australia and Norway. While a formal agreement on this matter was not achieved at the Camp David Summit, some progress had nonetheless been made.

The issue that bogged down the summit and eventually led to its collapse was, however, the fate of Jerusalem, notably who would have sovereignty over the Jewish Temple Mount or the Muslim Haram Al-Sharif. Physical separation of the sites is impractical given that the Haram is built on top of the Jewish Temple Mount ruins. Departing from Israel's traditional demand to keep all of Jerusalem under its control, Barak at Camp David was quite generous in agreeing to divide it with the Palestinians. Thus, he proposed a partition whereby, generally speaking, Arab areas of Jerusalem would go to the Palestinians, and Jewish neighbourhoods remain under Israel's control. Barak also agreed to partition the Old City, by transferring the Muslim and Christian quarters to Arafat and keeping the Jewish and the Armenian quarters. But at the same time the Prime Minister insisted that the heart of Jerusalem, namely Temple Mount/Haram would not be divided and that Israel would maintain sovereignty over the area, and the Palestinians would only be given custodianship.

For Arafat, however, who regarded himself as the guardian of the Haram not just for Palestinians but for all Muslims, this was a tricky situation. True, Barak presented him with a generous offer, but refrained from giving him what he felt he *really* needed, namely sovereignty over the holy area. Arafat thus rejected Barak's offer, the summit collapsed and the road was open for a war of words. The two leaders, after returning home, blamed each other for the summit's collapse and President Clinton, who

was personally involved in the nitty-gritty of negotiations, publicly sided with Barak, lavishing praise on the Prime Minister for
his flexibility and chiding Arafat for his lack of it. 'The Prime
Minister', Clinton said, 'moved forward from his initial position
more than Chairman Arafat.'³ Barak, after returning home, made
it clear that 'there was no partner to peace'. This was a dangerous
accusation, for if indeed this was the case then it signalled the
end, at least for the time being, of the peace process, and thus
increasing the likelihood of war. It was also quite inaccurate
because there *was* indeed a partner to peace – Arafat; true, he was
stubborn and was not liked much by Israelis, but he was the
partner nonetheless.

The effect of the failure at Camp David on the situation in the
occupied territories was devastating. It added to the frustration
of Palestinians with a lengthy peace process that had so far won
them only the shards of an independent state and had not, as
they had hoped, improved the reality of their daily lives. It also
disappointed Israelis, who concluded that nothing could satisfy
the Palestinian appetite. And after all, if the two leaders, after
being locked together for two weeks in Camp David, could not
reach a deal, then what else could be done to salvage the peace
process? While Arafat and Barak were entangled in a war of
words and exchange of insults, tensions on the ground mounted
and the occupied territories turned into a powder keg. Sharon's
visit to Temple Mount/Haram Al-Sharif – the main stumbling
block that led to the collapse of the Camp David Summit – at this
most sensitive time, provided the spark which ignited the
powder.

## CONFRONTATION

On Friday 29 September, the day following Sharon's tour,
Sheikh Hian Al-Adrisi gave the oration at the Al-Aqsa Mosque to
a congregation of 22,000. When this and the prayers ended,

Palestinians began hurling stones from the Haram compound towards the Wailing Wall, which stands at the foot of the Haram and where Jews were gathered to pray as it was the eve of the Jewish New Year. At 1.22 p.m., Palestinians attacked a police station adjacent to Temple Mount and the police forcibly entered the area causing many casualties. On this day, five Palestinians were killed, and more than 200 injured; the Israelis suffered 60 injured.

Prime Minister Barak summoned an emergency meeting with IDF Chief of Staff Shaul Mofaz and others to review the situation. It was reported to him that far from being a spontaneous wave of violence, Palestinian riots were pre-organized and led by local Palestinian leaders, men such as Marwan Bargouti. This violent campaign, the Israelis concluded, was aimed at diverting attention from the failings of Arafat at the Camp David Summit. The Prime Minister gave his instructions:

> To reinforce forces [in sensitive locations] . . . increase alert in potentially friction areas with Israeli Arabs [who might join the riots] . . . to communicate with the Palestinian Authority at all levels and [ask them to] instil calm and prevent deterioration . . . to decrease [Israeli] presence on Temple Mount [in order to reduce friction] . . . to contact the Americans and French and ask for [their] support in calming down the situation . . . [Foreign Minister] Shlomo Ben Ami to talk to Arafat and appear on CNN to call on the Palestinian Authority to stop incitement . . . if needed we'll gather again during Rosh Ha'shanah [the Jewish New Year].[4]

Next day, 30 September, the Prime Minister received intelligence reports saying that while the Palestinian leadership had issued instructions to field leaders to calm the situation down, the language of the message was far from decisive and their call for a general strike to mourn the victims of the previous day's riots guaranteed that there would be more bloody clashes with the police and army. Indeed, on that day, Palestinian demonstrators scuffled with Israeli security forces and riots spread as far as the northern West Bank town of Nablus and Hebron in the south. Palestinian demonstrators threw stones and bottles, blocked main roads, set tyres on fire and damaged IDF vehicles; Palestinian police often joined the demonstrators using the guns given to them by Israel as part of the Oslo Agreement. From the West Bank the riots then spread to the Gaza Strip where a 12-year-old Palestinian boy, Mohammed al-Dura, was pinned down with his father in crossfire between Palestinian snipers and Israeli troops and was shot dead. The scene was captured by a cameraman working for a French news agency, and footage of the boy's death was shown over and over again on Palestinian television, fuelling the rapidly escalating war. On that day, 13 Palestinians were killed and 400 injured.

A Palestinian mob attacked Joseph's Tomb, a Jewish holy site in Nablus, on 1 October. This was a serious breach of Israeli–Palestinian agreements, as Joseph's Tomb – like other sites such as the Shalom al Israel synagogue in Jericho – had a special status. Situated within areas under full Palestinian control, there was only a limited Israeli security presence inside the sites, while actual protection was the responsibility of Palestinian police. Now, however, Palestinians attacked Joseph's Tomb, injuring an Israeli border policeman who was stationed there. The Israeli commander in charge of this area decided not to send in a rescue force lest this incite the Palestinians even further. Instead, he contacted his Palestinian counterpart and arranged that the Palestinian authorities should rescue the trapped soldier. But he was left to bleed to death, an event that came to signify a serious breakdown of Israeli–Palestinian working relations.

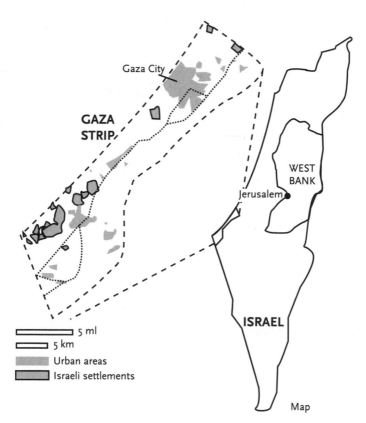

Gaza City

GAZA STRIP

WEST BANK

Jerusalem

ISRAEL

5 ml
5 km
Urban areas
Israeli settlements

Map

*Map 8* The Gaza Strip

## A summit in Paris

Appalled by this turn of events, US President Clinton tasked his Secretary of State Madeleine Albright with trying to put a lid on the violence. She summoned Prime Minister Barak and Chairman Arafat, on 4 October, to conduct ceasefire talks at the US embassy in Paris.[5] These were tough negotiations. Barak complained that, 'the Palestinian police continue to fire [on our forces]' and he demanded that 'Arafat must control the weapons [and] their distribution'; he also insisted that cessation of Palestinian violence must come first, before the Israelis made any concessions.[6] Arafat, for his part, insisted that a UN-led team should be appointed to investigate the causes of the outbreak of violence, with a senior figure such as Nelson Mandela presiding over it. They failed to bridge the gaps, the Paris Summit collapsed and, on the ground, Palestinian riots escalated, with shooting attacks taking place in the mixed city of Hebron, along several main roads leading to Jewish settlements, at Gilo, a suburb of Jerusalem, and elsewhere. On 6 October, at the end of the Friday prayers – always a sensitive time in the occupied territories, as the muftis often use them to incite fervour in the crowds – Palestinians raised the PLO and Hamas flags on Temple Mount, and hurled stones onto the plaza in front of the Wailing Wall where Jews gathered to pray. From there riots spilled into Jerusalem's Muslim Quarter, and the Israeli police station at the Lions Gate was torched. Barak instructed the police not to intervene but rather to let the violence exhaust itself.

On 7 October there was another violent day in the occupied territories – Palestinians attacked, again, Joseph's Tomb in Nablus, vandalizing it and painting it green, the colour of Islam. In a tit-for-tat response, Israelis in Tiberias, in northern Israel, attacked and vandalized an ancient mosque. Five days later, on 12 October, Palestinians attacked the Shalom al Yisrael Synagogue in Jericho, where holy books were burned and an ancient mosaic was damaged. Indeed, the *Al-Aqsa intifada* acquired a religious dimension which was less obvious during the first *intifada*.

## Israeli Arabs

The use of guns by Palestinians and an increase in attacks on holy sites were not the only new features of the insurgency; another was the greater involvement of Israel's Arab citizens in the actual war. True, during the first *intifada* the Arab citizens of Israel took an indirect part in the insurgency; they donated blood, food and money to Palestinians in the occupied territories, but they never-theless refrained from taking direct action against Jews. This time, however, upon hearing the calls of their Imams in the wake of Sharon's visit to the Haram to defend the sacred compound of Jerusalem, Israel's Arab citizens, who by that time comprised 17 per cent of Israel's total population, answered by rioting throughout Galilee, northern Israel, and in Israel's various mixed towns and cities where Jews and Arabs lived side by side. Israeli police reacted massively, and its forces, which also included snipers, opened fire on the Israeli Arab rioters, killing 13 and wounding many others. These dramatic events poisoned Arab–Jewish relations. While the Israeli Arabs were upset with the police's heavy handling of the situation – never before had police opened fire on Israeli demonstrators – the Israeli Jews, on the other hand, regarded the joining of Israeli Arabs to the *Al-Aqsa intifada* as a betrayal; in polls, 55 per cent of Israeli Jews reported that their opinion of Israeli Arabs had deteriorated. As a result, there were renewed calls to expel Israeli Arabs, an idea that had gathered pace over the years preceding the insurgency; in a poll conducted in March 2002, 31 per cent of Israeli Jews were in favour of forcibly transferring Israeli Arabs out of the country, up from 24 per cent in 1991; 60 per cent said they favoured encouraging Arabs to leave Israel.[7] Many Israeli Jews, however, came to realize that the riots by Israeli Arabs were not only in solidarity with their brethren under military occupation, but also a reaction to the historic prejudice against them within Israeli society. Now, Israeli Jews came to see that 'our Arabs', as they often dubbed the Arabs of Israel, had been treated as second-class citizens, discriminated against, their average income the lowest of any other ethnic group in the country and their infant mortality rate almost twice as high as for Jews (9.6 per 1,000 births, compared with 5.3).

In hindsight, the *Al-Aqsa intifada* signalled a new phase in Jewish–Arab relations in Israel proper which, at the time of writing, is characterized by growing tensions that are only likely to increase further in the coming years, perhaps even leading to an *intifada* in Israel proper.

## Lynching in Ramallah

Back in the occupied territories, a significant escalation occurred on 12 October when Palestinians in Ramallah lynched two Israeli reservists. The two took a wrong turn en route to their army base and wandered by mistake into the West Bank town of Ramallah, where they came across a funeral procession for a 17-year-old boy shot the day before by Israeli troops. A rumour spread among Palestinians that the reservists belonged to Israel's so-called Arabized forces, troops who disguised themselves as Palestinians, who mingled among them and arrested individuals on Israel's wanted list. The Palestinian police took the reservists into a nearby police station and, for a time, kept the gathering mob at bay. But some of the vigilantes entered through a second-floor window – an Italian TV crew filmed as the Palestinians stabbed and pummelled the Israelis inside. One of the attackers returned to the window and showed his blood-soaked hands to the jubilant crowd. Moments later, the body of one of the reservists came flying out of the window and smashing into the mob below, who danced, beat it some more and celebrated before parading the corpse through the streets of Ramallah. Palestinian police handed over the other badly mutilated soldier to a nearby Jewish settlement, where he died shortly afterwards. These horrifying pictures were shown on television in Israel and round the world.

In the Defence Ministry in Tel Aviv, the Prime Minister chaired a special emergency meeting with his security chiefs to go through their options; it was unanimously agreed that a massive retaliation was needed. Barak gave his instructions:

> The IDF would compile a list of targets to be attacked and present it to me; use of helicopters only with my permission; I see a great importance in destroying the Palestinian radio station because of its role in inciting Palestinians against Israel. In addition, curfews, checkpoints and so on should be implemented according to instructions from the [IDF] Chief of Staff.[8]

Barak instructed his aide Danny Yatom to warn the Palestinians of an imminent attack so that they could evacuate the targeted buildings; the Prime Minister was determined to punish the Palestinians for the brutal lynching, but wanted to refrain from hurting innocent people.

Before going into action, at 3.05 p.m., Barak spoke to President Hosni Mubarak of Egypt, to let him know of the coming military strike against Arafat's Palestinian Authority. It was vital to keep Mubarak in the picture, as Egypt had peace with Israel and played a leading role in the Arab world. 'There are pictures that can't be tolerated,' Barak told Mubarak, 'one of the bodies was dragged in the streets . . . like a dog – this is unacceptable.'[9] The Prime Minister asked Mubarak to urge Arafat to rein in his extremists and calm the streets down, and he also asked Mubarak to 'use your influence with Arafat so he picks up the phone and makes two telephone calls to the heads of Tanzim [the paramilitary organization linked to Arafat's Fatah Party and which was responsible for much of the violence] . . . and bring Arafat back to the [negotiation] table'.¹⁰

Barak then gave the green light to the IDF whereupon Cobra attack helicopters went into action, for the first time in the *Al-Aqsa intifada*, striking at the police station in Ramallah, where the lynching took place, as well as several police vehicles, the Voice of Palestine radio station and three transmitters. In Gaza the Israelis attacked a building used by Arafat's forces, destroyed five military vehicles, attacked the headquarters of the Tanzim, and sunk coastguard vessels, among other targets; the attack went on for 45 minutes.

## Attempts to stop the war – Sharm and Gaza

Another summit aimed at stopping the violence in the occupied territories took place on 16 October in Sharm el-Sheikh, Egypt. It was hosted by President Mubarak, and included US President Clinton, UN Secretary-General Kofi Annan, Jordan's King Abdullah and Javier Solana, representing the European Union. Progress was slow and somewhat painful; the atmosphere tense and unpleasant. Bloodshed had hardened positions on both sides and so wide were the gaps between the parties that after 28 hours of talks, all President Clinton could do was squeeze an oral ceasefire plan from the two leaders. The Prime Minister agreed to ease military restrictions on the Palestinians by reopening Gaza airport, end border closings which prevented goods from getting into the Gaza Strip and pull back troops and tanks from the edge of Palestinian towns and cities to positions held before 28 September, the start of the *Al-Aqsa intifada*. Arafat, in turn, committed himself to stopping the riots and gun battles, cracking down on anti-Israeli incitement and putting Islamic militants in jail. It was also agreed that there must be a pathway back to negotiations and the resumption of efforts to reach permanent status agreement based on the UN

Security Council Resolutions 242 and 338 and subsequent understandings. While Arafat's insistence on an international investigation into the causes of the events was rejected, the conference decided on an American-led fact-finding commission (later to be known as the Mitchell Commission or the Sharm el-Sheikh Fact-Finding Commission) with members from the US, Turkey, Norway and the UN to investigate the causes of the violent events and propose ways of preventing their recurrence. However, the commitments made at Sharm el-Sheikh were not implemented on the ground, where violence flared up as soon as news of a deal spread and was to continue in the days and weeks ahead. By now, the combined death toll had passed 100.

On 21 October, the Prime Minister held a security meeting at his Jerusalem residence where he said that given the continuing Palestinian violence, the army should tighten the screw. He instructed the military to 'try and upset Palestinian ability to broadcast TV and Radio [to stop incitement against Israel] . . . Cut off their electricity supplies for six hours [a day] . . . Stop petrol [getting through] . . . Stop buying their agricultural products.'[11] Barak hoped that making life harder for ordinary Palestinians would drive a wedge between them and their leadership, forcing Arafat's Palestinian Authority to curb violence in order to enable a return to normality. The army did as it was instructed and increased its pressure on the occupied territories, but to no avail. On 30 October, two Israeli security guards were shot in East Jerusalem, and the body of a resident of the Gilo neighbourhood was found: he had been murdered by Palestinians.

Upset by the continuing war, one of Barak's ministers, Shimon Peres, the brain behind the Oslo Agreements and the winner of a Nobel Peace Prize for his founding role in the peace process, travelled to Gaza on 1 November to meet with Arafat. When he got back, Peres reported to the Prime Minister on a deal he had struck with the Palestinian leader, whereby the Palestinians would stop the shooting – though not the stones and the Molotov cocktails – and, in return, the IDF would pull back tanks and troops from certain flashpoints in the West Bank and the Gaza Strip. Arafat and Barak, according to the deal that Peres had worked out, would make a simultaneous radio broadcast to call on their respective peoples to calm down the situation. Barak accepted the deal, but on 2 November, just before he and Arafat were due to broadcast their statements, at around 3.00 p.m., a car bomb exploded in the heart of Jerusalem, killing two Israelis and wounding ten; it also killed the proposed ceasefire.

Later that night, the French President, Jacques Chirac, phoned the Prime Minister to give his condolences. A furious Barak told Chirac:

> This is really humiliating . . . Arafat wasn't speaking to some taxi driver, but to Shimon Peres . . . The [Palestinian] shooting has been resumed in full force tonight . . . they are firing on us endlessly . . . The incitement also continues . . . [Palestinian] people are getting out to the streets incited . . . Arafat behaves like a gang leader . . . I'm biting my lips in the face of my nation's anger . . . I'm facing calls to respond . . . That's the last chance . . . If there is no serious drop in Palestinian violence we'll have to respond.[12]

To his Cabinet the Prime Minister said, 'There's a basic understanding between the state and its people [that the state should] protect them.' He emphasized that he was determined to do just that, but he would not divulge to them his decision to resort to an old tactic.

## Assassinations

Even before the establishment of the state of Israel in 1948, Jews would often resort to a policy of assassination to deal with their opponents. In 1944, for instance, Jewish activists assassinated, in Cairo, Lord Moyne, Britain's Resident Minister in the Middle East. In September 1948, the Stern Gang, a small extreme Jewish organization, assassinated in Jerusalem Count Bernadotte, a UN mediator who put forward peace proposals which they believed would hurt Israel's interests. On 11 July 1956, Israeli agents assassinated Egyptian Colonel Mustapha Hafez, who organized and dispatched militant Palestinians to strike at Israel.[13] On 10 April 1973, Israeli commandos, led by a young Ehud Barak, assassinated in Beirut three PLO officials whom Israel held responsible for the killing of 11 Israeli athletes at the Munich Olympic games. In 1985, Israeli agents killed, in Tunis, Yasser Arafat's deputy, Abu Jihad; and there were many more such assassinations.

Now, with the *Al-Aqsa intifada* under way and the Israelis desperate, and so far quite unsuccessful in stopping it, the Prime Minister decided to resort to a policy of liquidation, which the Israeli military termed 'targeted killing', 'pinpointing attackers', or 'neutralizing the organizers of attacks', namely the Palestinian activists affiliated to Fatah, Hamas or Islamic Jihad. The aim was fourfold: to weaken Palestinian command; to deter Palestinians from joining the ranks; to pre-empt attacks on Israel; and to raise fledging morale in Israel. The methods to be used in these killing operations were to range from sniper fire, through tank-fire and bombs planted in cars, to missiles fired from helicopters and bombs dropped from aeroplanes.

The killing of Hussein Abayat, on 9 November 2000 at Beit Sahour near Bethlehem by anti-tank missiles fired at his car from helicopters, was the first known assassination carried out by

Israel since the onset of the *Al-Aqsa intifada*. Imad Jamil Fares, a resident of Beit Sahour, recalls:

> My house is about 10 metres from where Abayat was killed. At around 11.45 in the morning, I suddenly heard an explosion . . . The windows of my house were broken and the shutters damaged. When I looked out I saw a grey Mitsubishi on fire and the burnt body of the driver [Abayat]. Two women were lying on the ground near the car and appeared to be critically injured. Their faces were black, completely burnt and still bleeding.[14]

But this would not stop the insurgency. On 20 November, an explosion near a bus stop close to the Gaza Strip killed two Israelis and wounded 11 children. The IDF responded by launching attacks in the Gaza Strip and, on 22 November, went on to assassinate Jamal Abed Al-Razeq, a 30-year-old Fatah activist. Again, this did little to stem the flow of Palestinian attacks – on the same day a car bomb went off in Israel's northern town of Hadera, killing two and wounding 55. The next day Israel assassinated Hamas activist Ibrahim Bani Audi in Nablus by planting a bomb in his car and, on 11 December, killed Anwar Mahmoud Humran by sniper fire. Mayada Jum'a, an 18-year-old student, later recalled:

> At around 1.30 p.m., while doing some studying in the balcony of my flat, I saw a man standing in the street, at a distance of about 10 metres from my house. He was on his own and appeared to be waiting for a taxi . . . Suddenly I heard two gunshots and saw that a bullet had hit the man in his leg. He fell on the ground and started screaming. The shots to his body continued however and did not cease . . . The shooting came from the Israeli army outpost . . . he must have been hit by twenty bullets or more.

On the next day, 24 November, another Palestinian activist, Yousif Abu Swaye, was assassinated by Israeli snipers just outside his father's house in the village of Al-Khader in the West Bank. His father, Ahmad Abu Swaye, later recalled:

> I was expecting my son and his wife for the Iftar – the breaking of the fast during Ramadan. She arrived first; Yousif had stopped at the Suleyman Pools for prayer and would arrive shortly. At about 2.30 p.m., I heard gunshots. When I went out to see what was happening I heard five more gunshots and saw a man lying on the ground. At that stage I did not realize that the young man was my son. I rushed to help him but when I reached him he did not move. He was already dead. Twenty-one bullets hit him all over his body including the head, the neck and the chest.

On 13 December, the Israelis assassinated 26-year-old Hamas activist Abas al Awiwi while he was standing in front of a shoe factory, and on the next day went on to kill 31-year-old Hamas activist Hani Abu Bakra while he was driving a van with passengers on board near Gaza City.

The assassination policy was still failing to prevent suicide attacks on Israel – on 28 December yet another bomb exploded on a bus near Tel Aviv wounding 13 Israelis – but Israel continued the targeted killings regardless. On 31 December, Dr Thabet Thabet was the target; his wife, Dr Siham Thabet, later recalled:

> My husband was killed when he was reversing his car outside our home in Tulkarem . . . from a distance of about 250 metres. Over twenty bullets hit him. Later it was found that three different kinds of ammunition had been used . . . I myself heard machine gun fire when I was on my way to work at the dental clinic. I would, however, never have imagined that what I heard was my husband being gunned down.

Denying that they had assassinated Dr Thabet, the Israelis claimed he was killed in 'an exchange of fire'.

On 2 January 2001, the Knesset Foreign Affairs and Defence committee met to discuss the 'liquidation' policy. Some members openly questioned the legal and moral basis of this policy, in which victims were killed without trial and without the chance of a fair legal process to defend themselves against the allegations brought against them by Israeli intelligence agencies, often based on information from paid Palestinian informants. A senior Israeli security official, trying to justify the killings, said in this meeting:

> We attack terrorists who set out to attack [Israeli civilians]. We identify the heads of squads and district commanders and attack them. This frightens and quiets a village, and as a result there are areas in which [Palestinian activists] are afraid to undertake activities.[15]

The Prime Minister added his defence of the policy of assassination, saying it was justifiable on the grounds that Israel was at war and had to fight terror with all available means. He said, 'If people shoot at us and kill us, then our only option is to attack them.' Chief of Staff Mofaz, also present at the meeting, referred to a legal opinion issued by the military advocate, Menachem Finkelstein, in which he had said that in 'exceptional' circumstances it was permissible to kill 'Palestinian terrorists'.

Violence continued in the occupied territories and in Israel proper. On 1 January 2001 a car bomb went off in West Jerusalem injuring a Jewish woman and, on 8 February, two more cars exploded in West Jerusalem. Five days later, on 13 February, Maso'oud Ayyad, a senior officer in Arafat's presidential guard, known as Force 17, was assassinated when his car was hit by three missiles fired from an Israeli helicopter gunship in the Gaza Strip.

# ENTER ARIEL SHARON

In February 2001, Ariel Sharon, who had sparked the *Al-Aqsa intifada* with his visit to the Temple Mount in Jerusalem on 28 September 2000, was elected Prime Minister of Israel in a landslide victory over Ehud Barak, receiving 62.5 per cent of the vote compared to Barak's meagre 37.5 per cent. Whilst his predecessor had sought a sweeping peace deal to end the Arab–Israeli conflict, Sharon's goals were more modest. He wanted to end Palestinian violence, restore stability and – providing that the calm held – to open negotiations on a limited interim agreement with the Palestinians. Sharon faced the wrath of the insurgency almost immediately. On 1 March, an Israeli was killed and nine injured by a bomb in the north of the country; on 4 March, three more Israelis were killed and 60 injured by a suicide bomb in Netanya; on 27 March, two bombs on Jerusalem buses killed one and wounded 28. On 18 May, again in Netanya, a Palestinian suicide bomber blew himself up killing five Israelis and wounding over 100. Sharon ordered a massive retaliation, dispatching F-16 warplanes to attack targets in Nablus and Ramallah; but to no avail.[16]

On 20 May, an opportunity to calm the conflict emerged with the publication of the Mitchell Report. Former majority leader of the United States Senate George J. Mitchell had chaired the commission set up at the October 1999 summit meeting at Sharm el-Sheikh (which had otherwise been something of a failure), following his successful mediation in the Northern Irish conflict. The commission's purview was to investigate the causes of the *Al-Aqsa intifada* and to propose ways of ending it. After visiting both Israel and the occupied territories the commission found out that 'despite their long history and close proximity, some Israelis and Palestinians seem not to fully appreciate each other's problems and concerns'. It also realized that, 'Fear, hate, anger, and frustration have risen on both sides' and that 'so much has been achieved', but also 'so much is at risk' and that if the parties were to succeed in completing their journey for peace then 'agreed commitments must be implemented, international law respected'.[17]

The Mitchell Report suggested a series of specific steps to be taken by each side, beginning with a cessation of hostilities through a cooling-off period and the implementation of confidence-building measures, gradually leading up to a resumption of peace talks between Israelis and Palestinians. It called on Arafat's Palestinian Authority to make clear to Palestinians and Israelis through concrete action that terrorism was unacceptable and to make a '100 per cent effort to prevent terrorist operations'. The Israelis were called upon to freeze all settlement activity on the disputed land and to be more measured and careful in their use of force. The report urged the Palestinian Authority to prevent gunmen from using Palestinian populated areas to fire upon Israeli populated areas and IDF positions, a tactic which 'places civilians on both sides at unnecessary risk'. The report also called on Israel 'to lift closures, transfer to the Palestinian Authority all tax revenues owed, and permit Palestinians who had been employed in Israel to return to their jobs and to ensure that security forces and settlers refrain from destruction of homes and roads, as well as trees and other agricultural property in Palestinian areas'. Both sides, in the light of the damage that had been inflicted on holy sites, were called upon to consider a joint undertaking to preserve and protect holy places.

It was a balanced report with sensible recommendations. Prime Minister Sharon responded swiftly by declaring, on 22 May, a unilateral ceasefire, pledging that the IDF would only shoot in self-defence. The response from the Palestinians on the ground, however, was less than forthcoming. On 25 May, two suicide bombers blew themselves up, one at the Israeli town of Hadera, the other at a security outpost in the Gaza Strip, between them wounding at least 65 Israelis. Two days later, 30 Israelis were injured by a bomb in Jerusalem. Realizing that the Palestinians were not going to match his response to the Mitchell Report, Prime Minister Sharon said, at a meeting with Chief of Staff Shaul Mofaz and other security personnel: 'We have to strike at the Palestinians everywhere . . . simultaneously. The Palestinians should wake up every morning to realize that 12 of them are dead . . . without realizing how this had happened.'[18] Sharon now made the war on the Palestinians the military's top priority, telling Mofaz: 'That's your war. Don't keep your gear in warehouses for a future war with Syria. Your test is in victory over the Palestinians.'[19]

Violence reached a peak when, on 1 June in a Tel Aviv nightclub, a suicide bomber blew himself up killing 21 Israelis and wounding more than 80, mostly teenagers. That night, a Friday, the Prime Minister gathered his Cabinet and urged ministers to approve a plan to 'remove' Arafat – perhaps to expel him. But ministers were opposed, fearing that an expelled Arafat would become a martyr and decided only to define him as someone who 'supports and activates terrorism'. In the meantime, international pressure was mounting on Arafat to declare an immediate ceasefire, which he finally did on 2 June. He insisted, though, that he regarded himself as responsible for the ceasefire only in areas under his full control and that he would not arrest Hamas and Islamic Jihad militants, who were largely responsible for the suicide attacks in Tel Aviv and elsewhere in Israel. Now, with both sides still fighting, but having agreed to a ceasefire, US diplomacy stepped in to attempt to stabilize the situation.

## The Tenet ceasefire plan

US President George W. Bush dispatched his CIA Director, George Tenet, to the region. His mission was to merge the two ceasefires separately declared by Sharon and Arafat, restore security cooperation and create the basis for the implementation of the Mitchell Report, leading ultimately to political peace talks. After six days of intensive negotiations, the so-called 'Tenet Ceasefire Plan' or 'The Tenet Understanding' emerged. Along with the Mitchell Report, this plan became the blueprint to end the *Al-Aqsa intifada* and return to a political process. Here are some of its main points:

1   The GOI [Government of Israel] and the PA [Palestinian Authority] will immediately resume security cooperation.

   — A senior-level meeting of Israeli, Palestinian and US security officials will be held immediately and will reconvene at least once a week, with mandatory participation by designated senior officials.
   — . . . As soon as the security situation permits, barriers to effective cooperation – which include the erection of walls between the Israeli and Palestinian sides – will be eliminated and joint Israeli–Palestinian patrols will be reinitiated.
   — US-supplied video conferencing systems will be provided to senior-level Israeli and Palestinian officials to facilitate frequent dialogue and security cooperation.

2   Both sides will take immediate measures to enforce strict adherence to the declared ceasefire and to stabilize the security environment.

   — Israel will not conduct attacks of any kind against the Palestinian Authority . . .
   — The PA will move immediately to apprehend, question and incarcerate terrorists . . .

— Israel will release all Palestinians arrested in security sweeps who have no association with terrorist activities.
— ... the PA will stop any Palestinian security officials from inciting, aiding, abetting or conducting attacks against Israeli targets, including settlers.
— ... Israeli forces will not conduct 'proactive' security operations in areas under the control of the PA or attack against innocent civilian targets.
— The GOI will reinstitute military police investigations into Palestinian deaths resulting from IDF actions ... in incidents not involving terrorism.

3 Palestinian and Israeli security officials will use the security committee to provide each other, as well as designated US officials, with terrorist threat information ...

— Legitimate terrorist and threat information will be acted upon immediately ...
— The PA will undertake pre-emptive operations against terrorists, terrorist safe houses, arms depots and mortar factories ...
— Israeli authorities will take action against Israeli citizens inciting, carrying out or planning to carry out violence against Palestinians ...

4 The PA and GOI will move aggressively to prevent individuals and groups from using areas under their respective control to carry out acts of violence ...

— ... Palestinian and Israeli security officials will identify and agree to the practical measures needed to enforce 'no demonstration zones' and 'buffer zones' around flashpoints to reduce opportunities for confrontation ...

— ... Palestinian and Israeli security officials will make a concerted effort to locate and confiscate illegal weapons, including mortars, rockets and explosives, in areas under their respective control ... intensive efforts will be made to prevent smuggling and illegal production of weapons ...

— The Israeli Defence Forces (IDF) will adopt additional non-lethal measures to deal with Palestinian crowds and demonstrators, and, more generally, seek to minimize the danger to lives and property of Palestinian civilians in responding to violence.

5    The GOI and PA ... will forge – within one week of the commencement of security committee meetings and resumption of security cooperation – an agreed-upon schedule to implement the complete redeployment of IDF forces to positions held before 28 September 2000.

6    Within one week of the commencement of security committee meetings and resumption of security cooperation, a specific time line will be developed for the lifting of internal closures as well as for the reopening of internal roads, the Allenby Bridge, Gaza Airport, Port of Gaza, and border crossings. Security checkpoints will be minimized ...

— The parties pledge that even if untoward events occur, security cooperation will continue through the joint security committee.[20]

Israel accepted the plan on 12 June with 'some reservations' and the Palestinians gave their 'conditional approval' on the 13th.

But comprehensive as this plan was, it still failed to halt the vicious circle of violence. Adopting his predecessor's policy of assassinations, Prime Minister Sharon authorized, on 31 July, the assassination of two senior Hamas operators in Nablus – Sheikhs

Gamal Mansur and Gamal Salim. In response, on 9 August, a Hamas suicide bomber attacked the crowded Sbarro pizzeria in central Jerusalem, killing 15 and wounding 130. On the next day Israeli police seized Orient House, the unofficial Palestinian headquarters in Jerusalem and a symbol of Palestinian aspirations for an independent state; they also closed down nine other buildings used by the Palestinian Authority. Additionally, two F-16s fired rockets at police headquarters in Ramallah, destroying it completely, and tanks levelled a Gaza Strip police position. A suicide bomb attack on 13 August at the Wall Street café in Haifa left 15 Israelis injured.

The Palestinians who carried out the attacks in Jerusalem and Haifa had come from Jenin, a Palestinian town in the West Bank, security control over which had been handed to the Palestinian Authority in 1995 under the interim peace accord which was called 'Oslo 2'. Jenin now became the prime target of Israeli forces and, on 14 August, troops, tanks and attack helicopters moved into the town, accompanied by specially armoured bulldozers, which they used to demolish a Palestinian police station and two checkpoints and to threaten the governor's residence before pulling out of town.

On 27 August, an Israeli helicopter gunship fired two missiles through the window of the second-floor office of the Popular Front for the Liberation of Palestine (PFLP) in Ramallah, decapitating the 63-year-old Ali Mustafa, the factions' Secretary General, who was sitting at his desk. The Israelis claimed that the strike was in response to the Sbarro pizzeria suicide bombing and other shooting attacks for which the PFLP had claimed responsibility. The killing of Mustafa was significant as he was a political leader rather than a militant, and killing him took the Israeli counter-insurgency tactics up to a new level, which in turn pushed the Palestinians to upgrade their response.

On 17 October, at the Hyat Hotel in Jerusalem, two Palestinians, Hamdi Koran and Basel Asmar, watched Israeli Tourism

Minister Rehavam Zeevi – one of Israel's most hardline politicians – having breakfast. At around 7.00 a.m., the minister returned to his room on the eighth floor, where the two Palestinians were waiting for him. They shot him twice in the face; his killing, so the PFLP later stated, was a tit-for-tat retaliation for Israel's assassination of Mustafa.

But rather than admitting any responsibility for having brought about the assassination of Zeevi – not only a minister but also a personal friend – Sharon threw the blame entirely on the Palestinian Authority and led his Cabinet in issuing an ultimatum to Arafat to arrest and hand over to Israel the 'murderers and their senders'. On the next day, at a special Knesset session, the Prime Minister stated, 'Everything has changed ... the responsibility is Arafat's alone, as someone who has carried out and is carrying out acts of terrorism and never took steps against it.'[21]

The very nature of Sharon's public demands of Arafat made it impossible for him to fulfil them – how would the Palestinian public regard him if he was seen to follow Sharon's dictates? Arafat thus dragged his feet and did not respond to Sharon's ultimatum – in fact, he called on Israel to abandon its policy of assassination of Palestinian leaders. Sharon therefore ordered the military to conduct an invasion and reoccupy cities and towns under direct Palestinian Authority control.

Tanks and troops, supported by helicopters, rolled into areas of Ramallah, Jenin, Bethlehem, Beit Jala, Beit Sahour, Qalqilya, Tulkarem and elsewhere, where they attacked Palestinian positions, seized buildings, imposed curfews, conducted patrols and arrested militants. This provoked worldwide condemnation and a call from the US President, upset that the continuing violence in the occupied territories was undermining his efforts in his war against terrorism, to stop the operation.

Gradually, the Israelis began to pull their forces out, and to transfer the lands they had seized back to Palestinian security forces, though they pledged to return should the Palestinians fail to stop terrorism against Israel, which still continued. In the course of this military operation, 85 Palestinians were killed, of whom 15 were specifically assassinated, and hundreds more were injured. But the Palestinians were determined to hit back – on 27 November two suicide bombers killed three Israelis and wounded 30 others in Afula, northern Israel, and two days later, three more Israelis were killed as a suicide bomber exploded a bomb on a bus near Hadera. This was followed, on 1 December, by a double suicide bomb attack in Jerusalem, which left 11 Israelis dead, mostly teenagers, and injured 180.[22] And so it continued: on 2 December, 15 Israelis were killed in a suicide bombing in Haifa; on 9 December another Palestinian suicide bomber struck again in Haifa; on 12 December, an attack on a bus near the Jewish settlement, Emanuel, on the West Bank left ten Israelis dead and 30 wounded. For Prime Minister Sharon this was the last straw. He picked up the phone and ordered Defence Minister Ben Eliezer to retaliate there and then. The military bombed Arafat's headquarters in Gaza and other government facilities, destroying Arafat's entire helicopter fleet. In Cabinet, Prime Minister Sharon and his ministers decided that, 'Chairman Arafat has made himself irrelevant . . . no contacts will be maintained with him.'[23]

### Karine A

But despite whatever the Israeli Cabinet may have decided, Arafat was still relevant in Palestinian eyes. In Ramallah, on 16 December, he called 'for a complete halt to all operations, especially suicidal operations [against Israel]', and went on to warn: 'we will punish all those who carry out and mastermind each operation'. [24] It led to an almost total end to attacks on Israel (except on settlers and settlements in the occupied territories, which were regarded as legitimate targets) – including those by Hamas and Islamic Jihad. As a result, there was a dramatic drop in casualties on both sides: in December 2001, before Arafat's ceasefire, 69 Palestinians and 39 Israelis were killed; after, in January 2002, the number of Palestinians killed dropped to 30 and Israelis to 17.[25] Having thus demonstrated his relevance to the Israelis, they in turn were about to demonstrate to the rest of the world something about Arafat that he would rather have kept secret.

The *Karine A*, previously known as the *Rim K*, was a ship flying the convenience flag of the Pacific island of Tonga.[26] Omar Acawi, a colonel in the Palestinian Naval Police, was its commanding officer, and it had a crew of 13. The ship was purchased for $400,000 in Lebanon by Adel Mughrabi, a major buyer in the Palestinian weapons-purchasing system, with the assistance of Hezbollah. With Iranian help, Fuad Shubaki, Head of the Finance Administration in the Palestinian Authority and Arafat's confidant, arranged the $15 million necessary to pay for the 50 tonnes of arms and ordnance which were loaded onto the *Karine A* on the Iranian island of Kish. The destination of the ship – and the weapons – was the Gaza Strip.

According to the 1993 Oslo Agreement, the Palestinians were limited to certain numbers and types of weapons and ordnance for their police force, and although they had more arms than the agreement permitted, the Israelis had looked the other way as long as the excess weapons were limited to small arms. But on the *Karine A* there were 80-km-range rockets, 122mm mortars, anti-tank and anti-aircraft missiles, Katyusha rockets and explosives. All of these went far beyond what Oslo permitted and, if turned on Israel, could have inflicted serious damage. The Palestinian plan was for the *Karine A* to unload its weapons in sealed barrels just off the beaches of Gaza; the cargo would then be collected by the commander of the Palestine Naval Police, Juma'a Ghali, and his executive Fathi Ghazem. Smuggling this consignment into Palestinian land constituted a serious violation of the Oslo Agreement, one to which Israel would not turn a blind eye.

Israeli intelligence had found out about the *Karine A* as early as the spring of 2001 and kept an eye on her whereabouts. When she was seen sailing for the Suez Canal on her way to her final destination, the Israelis decided to board the ship. First, though, they had to be absolutely sure that this was the right target – seizing the wrong ship would have been very embarrassing. Therefore, as Chief of Staff Mofaz recalled in an interview with the author, 'I demanded a hundred per cent identification of the ship . . . [My Naval Intelligence people] asked me, "What do you mean by a hundred per cent identification"? I said, "I want to see a ship with the name *Karine A* on it."' Twenty-four hours later, Naval Intelligence put a picture on his desk and said: 'Sir, you have a picture, this is the ship, it has the name *Karine A* on it.'[27] With the ship's identity certain, Mofaz took personal charge of the operation from a command aircraft overhead. He recalls how, 'I sat between the Commander of the Air Force and the Navy . . . we had monitors that gave us a picture . . . and when we identified the ship among many others sailing in the Red Sea and we saw the name and it fit the name we had from our Intelligence, I gave the green light for the operation.' With that, in the early hours of 3 January 2002, 'Operation Noah's Ark' got under way. Navy commandos swooped down on the deck of the *Karine A* from helicopters and took control of the ship in a matter of minutes without firing a shot. For now the capture was kept secret; the Chief of Staff did not want the news to get out until the *Karine A* and its naval escort were safely in Israel's territorial waters. When the Israelis finally displayed their haul to the world's media, Arafat denied any knowledge of the ship, but given the level of involvement of high-level Palestinian Authority officials in the affair, few believed him.

## Killing the ceasefire

Israel's security forces, meanwhile, were preparing a pre-emptive strike against the man they accused of murdering 12 Israelis between January and December 2001.

Raid Karmi was 28, charismatic, brave and hugely admired by young Palestinians in his home town of Tulkarm. According to Chief of Staff Mofaz in an interview with the author, 'Raid Karmi was a terrorist with blood on his hands . . . He was involved in many terrorist attacks against us . . . he used explosives, machinegun fire against the army and striking civilians . . . we had to either arrest him or kill him. The decision that was taken was to "put Karmi on a cross"' – to kill him.[28]

It was not easy, however, as Karmi was elusive and had already survived one Israeli attempt on his life, on 6 September 2001. Defence Minister Ben Eliezer explained to the author that Karmi 'used costumes, he moved from place to place, he hid, changed locations'. But the Israelis finally discovered a weakness: Karmi used to visit his mistress every day before lunch, the wife of a Fatah official in Tulkarm. On the way back to his hideout Karmi would always use the same route along a cemetery wall. However, when this opportunity was reported to him, Defence Minister Ben Eliezer opposed attempting an assassination, as he knew that killing Karmi now would wreck the fragile ceasefire declared by Arafat on 16 December 2001. But Ben Eliezer found himself to be in the minority, as Prime Minister Sharon, who was always keen on these special operations, sided with those who favoured the killing. Ben Eliezer reluctantly agreed, but he said to the Prime Minister, as he recalled in an interview with the author, 'Arik . . . I'm not certain of this . . . I'm going to do it, but my heart is not totally in it. Because right now we are in the middle of a ceasefire . . . it is clear that it will end the ceasefire.'[29]

With the green light given, the Israelis planted a bomb at head height in the wall of the cemetery on Karmi's route home in an eastern neighbourhood of Tulkarm. On 14 January 2002, at 11 a.m., as Karmi walked past the cemetery, the bomb was detonated and killed him instantly. In response, the Palestinian militants issued a statement: 'The so-called ceasefire is cancelled, cancelled, cancelled . . . You [Israel] have opened hell on yourself. You will be burned by its fire.'[30]

## OPERATION DEFENSIVE SHIELD

March 2002 was a bloody month, claiming the lives of 239 Palestinians and, in 17 separate suicide attacks, 133 Israelis. In Israel, it was to become known as Black March. For Prime Minister Sharon, the straw that broke the camel's back was a suicide attack on the Park Hotel in Netanya on the eve of Passover. It was carried out by Muhammad Abd al-Basset Oudeh, a 25-year-old Palestinian from the West Bank town of Tulkarm. He was a deeply religious and angry man whose wish to travel to Jordan to marry his fiancée had been blocked by the Israelis and this, in turn, made him determined to become a *shahid* (martyr) and kill himself in a suicide mission, taking as many Israelis as possible with him. Al-Basset Oudeh was recruited into Hamas by Muammar Shahrouri under the auspices of Abbas Bin Muhammad al-Sayyid, the leader of Hamas in Tulkarm. With the Jewish festival of Passover approaching, he met al-Sayyid and Shahrouri in the apartment of the latter's grandfather in Tulkarm to make the final preparations for the bombing mission. The two videoed Abd al-Basset Oudeh as he read his farewell statement in front of a Hamas flag and an M-16 assault rifle; his recording would later be used to publicize the mission all over the Palestinian territories. Next, al-Sayyid equipped Abd al-Basset Oudeh with a belt that contained 10kg of explosives and demonstrated how to detonate them. The two then helped Abd al-Basset Oudeh to disguise himself as a woman, complete with a wig. Outside, Fathi Raja Ahmed Khatib was ready to drive Abd al-Basset Oudeh to Israel, as he had a fake blue ID card that would allow them to cross the border. They left at around 2.00 p.m, on 27 March, looking for a gathering of Israeli soldiers, as their preference was to attack the military rather than kill civilians. But they could not find a suitable military target, and so headed to the seaside town of Netanya, where at around 7.00 p.m., Abd al-Basset Oudeh entered the Park Hotel and walked into the main dining hall where guests were sitting around the Passover table. He stopped in the middle of the hall, pressed the switch on his explosive belt and blew himself up, instantly killing 29 and wounding 150. It was the most devastating single suicide bombing since the outbreak of the *Al-Aqsa intifada*.

In Tel Aviv, at 11.30 p.m. that night, Defence Minister Ben Eliezer gathered his military chiefs to go over their options. His preference was to strike at Hamas, whom he knew was behind the Netanya bombing. But the military chiefs argued that more radical action was required, to be directed not only against Hamas, but also against Arafat's Palestinian Authority; they wanted to reoccupy Palestinian cities, and to have boots on the ground in Palestinian areas, being proactive in preventing future terrorist attacks.[31] As Chief of Staff Mofaz recalled in an interview with the author, 'it was clear to me that we would have to go into the centres where the terrorist organizations were located . . . inside Palestinian cities . . . inside the refugee camps'.[32] Besides, argued the generals, Hamas was too elusive to be pinned down and had no hard targets which they could go after. The military chiefs won the argument. The Defence Minister and his generals then joined a Cabinet meeting chaired by the Prime Minister, which accepted their plans to occupy towns and cities in the West Bank (the military had already effectively contained the suicide-bomb threat from the Gaza Strip where a fence along the entire border proved very effective). Although final governmental approval was still needed, instructions were given to military units to start preparations for what was to be called 'Operation Defensive Shield'.

The next day, 28 March, Sharon gathered the entire government to approve the plan decided upon by the military and the Cabinet on the previous day. One item left open on the agenda was what should be done with Arafat. While some ministers wanted to expel him and send him into exile, others, particularly the powerful intelligence chiefs, who were also at the meeting, argued that Arafat in exile might cause Israel more damage than if he stayed put in Ramallah. There was also the fear that Arafat, who always carried two guns, might resist any attempt to expel him and perhaps be killed, which, it was generally agreed, would worsen the situation. Another idea discussed in the government meeting, as General Giora Eiland recalls in an interview with the author, was to 'begin [the operation] with a one-tonne bomb on [Arafat's] *muqata* [compound] in Ramallah [as] the very first move'. But attractive as it was to some, the US had vetoed killing Arafat.

After a debate lasting eight hours, the government meeting approved the military operation in the West Bank, but compromised on what to do with Arafat by defining him as 'an enemy' and ordering the military to physically isolate him at his headquarters, 'at this stage'. The latter three words were added by the Prime Minister to leave his options open for further steps against Arafat. As Defence Minister Ben Eliezer explained to the author, 'the decision was that we were getting very, very close to the *muqata*, so close we could see it with the naked eye . . . but . . . without harming [Arafat]'.

The die was cast and 'Operation Defensive Shield', a full-scale invasion of the West Bank, was approved by the whole government. General Eiland, one of those responsible for planning the operation, recalls explaining to ministers that the army would need 'complete freedom to operate according to operational considerations with absolutely no political constraints [for] at least a month'.[33] This was in order to give the military enough time to round up suspected militants, find the laboratories where explosives were produced and to impose tight control over the West Bank on a 'door-to-door basis'. Thirty thousand reservists were to be called up – the biggest mobilization in 20 years.

The attack on Arafat's compound in Ramallah, one of the prime targets of the operation, was devastating. Surrounded by tanks and troops, the compound's walls were crushed and a tight siege was imposed: troops took up positions just 50 metres away from the rooms where Arafat was sitting. From the basement of his headquarters, Arafat talked to CNN by telephone: 'They have destroyed completely seven of our buildings . . . Completely surrounding my office and firing at my office with all their armaments.'[34]

In the coming days, Israeli forces moved into other West Bank towns and cities. In Bethlehem, just south of Jerusalem, the attack was particularly fierce, forcing militants to flee and take cover in the Church of the Nativity, where they assumed the Israelis would not attack them, lest they damage the church: built in the sixth century on the site of Jesus' birthplace, it is one of the oldest and most holy in Christianity. More than 200 Palestinians were locked inside, just like Arafat in Ramallah, along with a number of monks. The siege on the Church of the Nativity would continue for over a month and prompt an international outcry over the treatment of such a holy place.

## The battle of Jenin

Dramatic though events in Ramallah and Bethlehem were, they were to be overshadowed by the bloody fight for the northern West Bank town of Jenin. Between October 2000 and April 2002, the Israelis suspected at least 28 suicide attacks had been planned and launched from Jenin, 'the martyrs' capital'. Now, the town and its adjacent refugee camp became one of the Israeli army's prime targets.

The Jenin refugee camp, occupying approximately 1 square kilometre, was established in 1953 and was the second largest refugee camp in the West Bank, home to 14,000 refugees. It was a hotbed of Palestinian militancy, and on the eve of the Israeli invasion 200 armed men from different Palestinian factions, including the Tanzim, Islamic Jihad and Hamas, were living there. Unlike in many other West Bank towns and cities, the militants of Jenin were well prepared for an Israeli invasion, as members of the different factions cooperated and were led by a single commander, Abu Jandel. He divided the camp into ten sections, each with 20 armed men to defend it; he also had houses and fields booby-trapped to slow down the advancing army, and had snipers positioned on rooftops.

With its forces encircling the refugee camp, the army requested Defence Minister Ben Eliezer to allow them to bomb the camp from the air, as this would save Israeli casualties.[35] However, fearing the large numbers of civilian Palestinian casualties that approach would cause in the densely populated camp, the minister refused, ordering a conventional battle and a house-to-house search. Troops entered Jenin on 3 April 2002, but, finding the Palestinians well prepared, progress was slow, so from 5 April attack helicopters joined the battle, locating and firing at groups of armed Palestinians. Then, on 10 April, 13 Israeli reservist soldiers were trapped and killed by Palestinian militants; the army now changed its approach to become much more aggressive. It shifted tactics from house-to-house searches and the demolition of selected houses of known militants, to a wider bombardment with tanks and missiles. To prevent further ambushes, troops now avoided the camp's narrow alleyways and moved only after the gigantic D9 armoured bulldozers had flattened paths through the densely packed houses, wreaking massive damage. In some cases, troops used civilians as human shields to accompany them during operations to search houses, check suspicious objects or just to stand in the line of fire from militants.

With the battle raging, the army declared Jenin a closed military area, imposing a round-the-clock curfew and prohibiting the press from entering the town and refugee camp. It also began mass arrests, taking hundreds of Palestinian men out of Jenin in buses for questioning elsewhere, before releasing non-militants. Left in towns, often miles away from Jenin, and with no papers, it took these people days to get home. In the meantime, reports of hundreds of people missing – presumed dead – circulated and these rumours were further fuelled as Palestinian leaders talked on television about 'a massacre' and 'war crimes' being committed at Jenin.[36] As there were no journalists there, it was impossible for these claims to be verified.

The battle was over by 15 April; 23 Israelis had been killed in total and 52 Palestinians. While these numbers are not huge, the scenes at Jenin were horrifying. When the army finally allowed journalists and international observers in they found massive destruction, particularly in the centre of the refugee camp, where an area 200 metres in diameter had been levelled and 4,000 Palestinians had been made homeless. Abu Hamid, a militant commander, remembers how, 'After the Israelis withdrew some of us came out . . . you could smell death everywhere. Some people were vomiting, it was shocking. You could see heaps of bodies . . . an arm here . . . a leg there . . . sticking out of the rubble.'[37] These scenes of death and destruction had a strong effect on Palestinians, galvanizing many of the younger generation to join the ranks of the militants ready to fight the Israelis.

On 19 April the UN Security Council unanimously adopted Resolution 1405 (2002), which resolved 'to develop accurate information regarding recent events in the Jenin refugee camp through a fact-finding team'.[38] On 22 April, UN Secretary

General Kofi Annan established the fact-finding team, but Israel refused to cooperate with the investigation and it never got off the ground.[39]

Following the arrest of certain Palestinian militants and the expulsion of others, the Israelis eventually agreed to remove the siege from Arafat in Ramallah, but they refused to withdraw their forces from the towns and cities they had occupied during 'Operation Defensive Shield'. In Bethlehem at the Church of the Nativity, following lengthy negotiations it was finally agreed that 13 Palestinians accused by Israel of having 'blood on their hands' – that is, having been directly involved in killing Israelis – would be flown to Cyprus and exiled; another group of 26, considered less dangerous, were to be expelled to the Gaza Strip; and the remaining 84 people would be released.

In hindsight, 'Operation Defensive Shield' was quite success-ful in achieving its initial aim of reducing the number of suicide bombers coming from the West Bank, not least as it enabled Shin Bet, Israel's internal security service, to infiltrate its people into the area to recruit collaborators and collect crucial intelligence. But the sieges of the Church of the Nativity and in Ramallah, and the gruesome scenes in Jenin, caused Israel much international damage, and in no way did it put an end to Palestinian resistance, galvanizing, as it did, the Palestinian youth.

## TIT-FOR-TAT

On 5 June, a car packed with explosives exploded at the Meg-iddo junction in northern Israel, killing 16 and wounding 50. Islamic Jihad claimed responsibility, as did the Al-Aqsa Martyrs Brigade, linked to Arafat's Fatah organization. Then, on 16 July, Palestinian militants ambushed a Jewish bus near the West Bank settlement of Emanuel, killing nine and wounding 18, and on the next day two suicide bombers killed five and injured 40 in Tel Aviv. In response, the Israelis decided to go after Salah

Shehadeh, one of the founders of Hamas and commander of its military wing in the Gaza Strip.

When the opportunity to strike came, on 23 July, Defence Minister Ben Eliezer was in London. He was in a cab on his way to Heathrow Airport when he received a call on his mobile from his Military Secretary Mike Herzog, who told him: 'We have Shehadeh and it may be possible to kill him.'[40] Ben Eliezer gave the green light and 'Operation Standard-Bearer' got under way.

The assessment of the IAF was that, 'a bomb smaller than a tonne would not necessarily . . . kill him', as they planned to strike Shehadeh while he was known to be inside a building.[41] They thus proposed to use a bigger bomb than would normally be used in a targeted assassination. In an interview with the author, Defence Minister Ben Eliezer explained, 'A 1-tonne bomb has an element of certainty. You can be sure it takes a person out, for sure . . . We have tried other bombs, and it turned out that there was greater chance of surviving with a quarter-tonne and half-tonne. And here the person [Shehadeh] justified use of a bomb of this kind.'[42]

But when the 1-tonne bomb was dropped on the apartment block in Gaza City it caused colossal damage, killing not only Shehadeh, but with him 14 innocent people, including his wife and daughter. When a shocked Ben Eliezer arrived back in Israel from London, he found out that the 'intelligence [we] had about a neighbouring house which was supposed to be completely empty was wrong . . . there were people there and . . . they were killed'.[43] There was no remorse, though, from the Chief of the Air Force, General Dan Halutz, who told the crew of the plane that had dropped the bomb, 'Guys, you can sleep well at night . . . I do . . . Your execution was perfect . . . Perfect.'[44]

It should be left for experts on international law to decide whether in executing this operation the Israelis committed a war crime, but there is no doubt that the decision to drop a massive bomb in a densely populated area casts serious doubt over the judgement of the Defence Minister, Chief of Staff Shaul Mofaz, his deputy Moshe Yaalon, Chief of the Air Force, and the others involved.

Neither the elimination of Shehadeh, nor any other military operations, however, put an end to Palestinian insurgency, and the vicious circle of tit-for-tat violence continued unabated. On 30 July, a suicide bomber blew himself up in Jerusalem, injuring five, and, on the next day, seven were killed and 86 injured by a bomb in a cafeteria at the Hebrew University, Jerusalem. On 4 August, a suicide bomb on a bus near Haifa killed nine and injured 50, and close to the Damascus Gate in Jerusalem's Old City, two Israelis were killed and 16 injured in a shooting incident. On 18 September, an Islamic Jihad militant killed himself and an Israeli policeman, and the next day a Hamas suicide bomber detonated a large bomb on municipal bus number 4 in Tel Aviv, killing six and injuring 70.

## Locking Arafat up again

In his frustration, the Prime Minister decided to go after his old foe Arafat once again. He blamed him for failing to stop suicide bombers, and led his Cabinet in a decision to give the IDF a green light to execute 'Operation Question of Time' to besiege Arafat in his headquarters for a second time.

On 19 September, tanks bore down on Ramallah and entered the *muqata* compound and locked Arafat, together with 200 others, inside. This second siege turned out to be even more aggressive than the earlier one in April. Tanks and bulldozers rapidly surrounded the compound and began razing the various ministries to the ground, creeping closer and closer to the main building housing Arafat, tightening the noose on him, while demands were made on him to extradite 50 wanted militants who were with him – men, Israel claimed, who had 'blood on their hands'.

In New York, on 24 September, the UN Security Council adopted Resolution 1435 (2002), calling on Israel to halt its operations in Ramallah, 'including the destruction of Palestinian civilian and security infrastructure'. Deeply upset with the Israelis, Washington refrained from using its customary veto on resolutions condemning the Israelis, and President Bush warned that the five-day-old blockade on Arafat was 'not helpful'. Clearly, Washington was annoyed because the Israelis were operating at a time when the US was making efforts to galvanize support among Arab nations for a campaign against Iraq.[45]

Outside the *muqata*, meanwhile, rumours were circulating that the army intended to bomb or storm the building Arafat was in. A tank had recently shelled the bridge connecting the Palestinian leader's building to some adjacent offices – one shell was off target and actually struck the wall of Arafat's room; he could have been killed. The ordinary Palestinians of Ramallah poured into the streets, banging saucepans in support of their besieged leader; similar protests took place in Nablus, Gaza City, Qalqilya, Tulkarm, Hebron, Bethlehem, Jericho, in the Israeli prisons holding Palestinians and in refugee camps in Lebanon.

Finally cracking under American pressure, Prime Minister Sharon, on 29 September, gave instructions to end the ten-day stand-off. Briefly emerging from his sandbagged building – one of the only three still standing in the government complex – Arafat blew kisses to his supporters and flashed a V-for-victory sign. But he still would not leave the *muqata*, lest Sharon in his absence order it to be stormed and so prevent Arafat returning to his headquarters. The *Al-Aqsa intifada* continued.

## ANOTHER FAILED CEASEFIRE

'The Gaza Agreement' of 27 June 2003 brokered between Israeli and Palestinian delegations by US diplomats, gave both sides a much needed ceasefire. While the Palestinians pledged to control militants and stop attacks on Israel, Israel agreed to pull out and transfer responsibility over the Gaza Strip and Bethlehem areas to the Palestinian Authority (which they did on 28 June). This was intended to be the first phase in the Israeli withdrawal from all areas reoccupied during the *Al-Aqsa intifada*, as long as the Palestinians could prove themselves able to maintain security and curb attacks on Israel.

On 12 August, the Israelis decided to extend the agreement and to hand over security responsibility for Qalqilya and Jericho, and, two weeks later, to transfer Tulkarm and the flagship Ramallah, where Arafat's headquarters were situated. This arrangement had still to be finalized between the two sides before the plan could be brought before the Israeli government for a final approval. But on 14 August, in spite of the ceasefire, which was holding, the Israelis assassinated Mohammed Seder, the head of Islamic Jihad's armed wing in Hebron. He had long been on their wanted list, as he was responsible for the killing of 12 Israelis in Hebron on 15 November 2002. But the attack on him killed the ceasefire as well.

Although the assassinated Seder was from Islamic Jihad, it was Hamas that was planning revenge. This came on 19 August when Hamid Mask, dressed as an Orthodox Jew, blew himself up on a Jerusalem bus, killing 23 – seven of them children – and injuring more than 100. Two days later, on 21 August Israel hit back by launching a helicopter strike in Gaza, killing Hamas official Ismail Abu Shanab. With these attacks the spiral of violence worsened. On 29 August, following a shooting attack on a Jewish family near Ramallah, Prime Minister Sharon and his Cabinet decided to end all contacts with Arafat's Palestinian Authority.

A few days later Israeli intelligence learned that the founder and spiritual leader of Hamas, Sheikh Ahmed Yassin, would be attending a meeting in Gaza on 6 September. With him, went the intelligence report, would be the entire Hamas leadership. This seemed to be a once in a lifetime chance. However, opinion was divided within the Israeli political-military establishment about whether it was wise to assassinate the Sheikh. Those who were opposed said that Yassin 'may be the leader of Hamas but he is not the operational and tactical leader . . . let's concentrate on the tactical guys'.[46] There was also concern that killing a senior leader such as Yassin might lead to fierce Hamas revenge. Those in favour said that the distinction between military and political in an organization such as Hamas was non-existent. Eventually they decided to kill the Sheikh – it only remained to be decided how.

The dilemma, as Chief of Staff Mofaz recalls in an interview with the author, was 'what weight of explosives should we drop from the air on the building [where the meeting was to take place]'.[47] The military planners recommended a 1-tonne bomb, which would be certain to kill Yassin and his associates, but still reeling from the assassination of Shehadeh using a massive bomb that had killed 14 innocent people, it was decided to use a 500-kilogram bomb.

With the green light given, an air force jet dropped the bomb on the building, destroying its third floor where it was thought the meeting took place. But the Israeli intelligence was wrong, just as it had been in the Shehadeh case; the meeting was taking place on the ground floor. The fact that Sheikh Yassin was confined to a wheelchair and it was thus easier for him if he did not have any stairs to climb to get to a meeting, seems to have been overlooked by Israeli intelligence. The Sheikh was slightly injured, along with 14 others. He later gave a warning: 'Israel will pay a high price for this crime.'

Despite this failure, Israel proceeded with the assassination policy. On 7 September an Israeli helicopter gunship attacked the home of a Hamas member, Abdul Salem Abu Musa, in the southern Gaza Strip, injuring at least 12 people. The Palestinians hit back two days later, carrying out two separate suicide attacks that left 15 people dead and scores wounded in Tel Aviv and Jerusalem. Israel struck again on 10 September, firing missiles at the Gaza City home of Mohamoud Zahar, a senior Hamas member, killing his son and a bodyguard and leaving 25 people wounded; Zahar himself escaped with minor injuries. Prime Minister Sharon, as before, blamed Arafat for the escalation of the violence, calling him, on 11 September, a 'complete obstacle to peace' and leading his Cabinet in a decision to 'remove this obstacle in the manner and time of our choosing'.[48] On 5 October, a female suicide bomber killed 19 and injured 50 in a Haifa restaurant. The war continued.

## DISENGAGEMENT

By this time, the idea of a unilateral Israeli disengagement from the Gaza Strip – a pullout on the Israelis' own terms, rather than as part of a deal negotiated with the Palestinians – was taking root in Israel. The idea was not new. In the 2001 general election, Labor Prime Minister Barak campaigned under the slogan, 'We are here, they are there.' He had called for the construction of a security barrier along a route that would annex 7 to 8 per cent of the West Bank to Israel – retaining the big blocs of Jewish settlements – and to unilaterally withdraw from the rest of the land. Barak lost the election to Sharon. In the 2003 general election, Labor leader Amram Mitzna called for a unilateral withdrawal from the Gaza Strip. Again, he lost to Sharon.

Now, however, Prime Minister Sharon was convinced that he had no one to negotiate with on the Palestinian side, and he was getting flak from his political rivals for not having a coherent plan to deal with the Israeli–Palestinian crisis. So he adopted the Labor ideas of unilateral disengagement from the Gaza Strip and the completion of a security fence on the West Bank. Before presenting his plan to the Israeli public, however, Sharon first ran the idea past the Americans at a meeting in Rome, on 19

November. With US approval in the bag, Prime Minister Sharon then, at a conference in Herzliya on 18 December, announced his Disengagement Plan to the world. He said that he did not intend to wait for the Palestinians forever and went on to explain that he was going to remove all Jewish settlements from the Gaza Strip and redeploy the IDF along new security lines. This, he said, would reduce the number of Israelis located at the heart of the Palestinian population, and therefore reduce friction. However, Sharon explained that, 'at the same time . . . Israel will strengthen its control over those same areas in the Land of Israel which will constitute an inseparable part of the state of Israel in any future agreement'.[49] It was, in other words, a plan to trade off the Gaza Strip – a 'nest of snakes', as Defence Minister Moshe Dayan described it in 1967 – for parts of the West Bank, the cradle of Jewish history.

However, before withdrawing from the Gaza Strip, the Prime Minister wanted to decapitate its militants. It was particularly important for him to show victory over Hamas, in order to prevent a repeat of the unilateral Israeli withdrawal from Lebanon in 2000, which Hezbollah claimed as a victory for their tactics. Weakening Hamas would also give Arafat's Palestinian Authority a chance to control Gaza when the Israelis were gone, as by now Hamas and other Islamic extremists seemed to have the upper hand in there, and were considered a greater threat than Arafat. As an Israeli official explained, 'If we are going to leave Gaza, let's weaken Hamas.'[50] And so the Israeli military embarked on a systematic campaign to wipe out the Hamas leadership in Gaza – not only the operational level but also the political and spiritual leadership.

Israel's collaborators in the Gaza Strip kept the army informed on the whereabouts of Hamas operatives; they kept an especially close eye on the elderly quadriplegic and spiritual leader of Hamas, Sheikh Yassin. On 22 March 2004, at 5.30 a.m., as the Sheikh was leaving a mosque in Gaza he was struck by an Israeli missile and instantly killed; the Israelis then went after his deputy, Abdel Aziz Rantissi, and killed him too. On 10 August 2005, Israel evacuated the Gaza Strip, putting an end to more than 40 years of occupation.

In hindsight, this unilateral withdrawal opened a new phase in the Israeli–Palestinian *intifada* which saw the gradual weakening of the secular Palestinian Authority, a process that gathered pace after the death of Yasser Arafat in November 2004 (he died of a mysterious illness, or, it is said, was poisoned by the Israelis) and reached its peak when Gaza was taken over by Hamas in 2007, after winning municipal elections there in 2006. With that, Hamas and other extremists in the Gaza Strip embarked on a new tactic to attack Israel – firing rockets and missiles into Israeli territory.

At the time of writing, the *Al-Aqsa intifada* continues.

# 8

# THE SECOND LEBANON WAR

## 2006

On 12 July 2006 at 9.03 a.m., Hezbollah guerrillas attacked an IDF border patrol on the Israeli side of the border with Lebanon, killing three soldiers and capturing two others. Hezbollah planned to hold the two captives to ransom, wishing to exchange them for Lebanese held in Israeli prisons.[1] Israeli warplanes went into action, bombing 69 bridges and other targets in south Lebanon in order to cut off Hezbollah's escape routes. An Israeli Merkava-4 tank crossed the international border in hot pursuit, but it hit a powerful bomb, which killed its crew of four.

That evening, the Israeli government met and decided to respond aggressively against Hezbollah in Lebanon, where it harboured. Responding to an attack from across an internationally recognized border was perhaps justified; however, the sheer scale of Israel's military reaction and the aims the political-military leadership sought to achieve were such that it led to an all-out war with Hezbollah.

## THE SECURITY ZONE

While the 12 July incident was the trigger to 'The Second Lebanon War' – what Hezbollah calls 'Harb Tamuz', or 'The July War' – the causes of this confrontation go back more than two decades. We should recall that in the first Lebanon War of 1982, Israeli forces moved up to Beirut and the Beirut–Damascus road where they fought against, and expelled, PLO guerrilla fighters and also clashed with regular Syrian forces in the Beka'a valley in the eastern sector of Lebanon. The Israelis then gradually withdrew – in 1983 to the Awali river and then, following a governmental decision, further south.

The Israeli government Resolution 291 of 14 January 1985 ignited a fierce debate within the IDF General Staff, where two schools of thought clashed. One, led by then Chief of Staff Moshe Levi, advocated a military deployment on Lebanese territory in a security zone that would physically separate towns and villages in northern Israel from Lebanon, making it difficult for Israel's enemies to launch attacks into Israeli territory. In this buffer zone, Israeli troops, working closely with the South Lebanon Army (SLA), a Lebanese militia group allied with, trained and financed by Israel, would patrol and maintain outposts. It is worth mentioning that by 1985 Israel was already facing Hezbollah ('the party of God'), the Iranian-backed radical Shiite organization, which operated mainly in southern Lebanon, with ridding Lebanon of Israeli occupation top of its agenda.

The opposing school of thought was led by then Director of Military Intelligence General Ehud Barak, a future Prime Minister of Israel. He argued that the best way to protect northern Israel was by getting troops out of Lebanon and deploying them instead along the Israeli–Lebanese international border, from where they could, if necessary, launch cross-border raids to tackle Hezbollah. In a General Staff meeting on 13 February 1985, General Barak said:

> It is very important . . . that we fully withdraw from Lebanon . . . We do not need any fortifications [on Lebanese territory], nor any outposts . . . We should move in [Lebanon] . . . whenever there's anything to justify it . . . And it might be that in some cases we'll move in with tanks for a week . . . but we [must not] build strongholds . . . nor invest in sand barriers . . . because the damage [of deploying on Lebanese territory] will be bigger than the benefit.[2]

On 15 March 1985 the General Staff met again at the Chief of Staff's office in Tel Aviv. Scrutinizing the transcript of this debate shows that by then most of the General Staff favoured a deployment in a security zone in Lebanon proper, and relying on the support of the SLA to fight Hezbollah and protect northern Israel. General Barak seems to remain the only voice still calling for full disengagement from Lebanon and casting doubts over the effectiveness of the SLA in defending northern Israel. 'The SLA', General Barak argued,

> doesn't have any chance of being an efficient security filter. Indeed, the SLA if 'hugged' by us . . . will turn into a target [for Hezbollah] . . . In the end we'll deploy south of the international border [with Lebanon] with all our forces and . . . this is the right thing to do . . . If we fail to fully disengage [from Lebanon] . . . we will reach . . . a dangerous [situation] where we will have to intervene more and more in order to protect what we have already sent inside [Lebanon].

It was a heated debate. Barak, losing ground to those wishing to stay put in a security zone in southern Lebanon, raised his

voice. The following exchange has never before been
published:

GENERAL ORI OR [to Barak] Don't shout.
GENERAL BARAK I want it be recorded . . . we don't realize what's
   going to happen [if we stay in Lebanon] . . . Lebanon with all
   the entanglements and complications . . . we've got to get our
   forces out of there.

Asked how he would deal with incoming rockets from Lebanon,
Barak replied, 'When I know where the rocket came from [then]
I'll try to destroy it . . . if it comes from a [Lebanese] village then
I'll try to hit the village . . . I'll blow up some houses there.'³

General Barak, however, did not get his way; the IDF did not
make a complete withdrawal. Instead, a 1,100-square-kilometre
security zone was established in southern Lebanon, the depth
of which ranged between 3 and 12 miles, and which included
168 towns and villages. In this zone, the IDF deployed two
headquarters, one in Marjeyoun, the other in Bint Jbail, in
charge of 12 company-size fortified outposts. These two IDF
headquarters worked closely with the SLA, which deployed 30
company-size fortified positions and organized itself into two
brigades: the Western brigade, which had three battalions –
the 70th Shia battalion and the mixed (Christian and Shia)
80th and 81st; and the Eastern SLA brigade, which was composed of the mixed 10th and 30th battalions and the 90th
Druze battalion; the SLA also deployed armoured and artillery
battalions.

## GUERRILLA WAR

But despite the Israeli generals' best intentions, the security zone
gradually became one large battleground, scene of repeated

*Map 9* Israel's security zone in South Lebanon

clashes between IDF and SLA troops on the one hand, and Hezbollah guerrillas on the other. For Hezbollah, the rocky, hilly landscape of southern Lebanon, which is essentially infantry country, proved an ideal testing ground for their guerrilla tactics, providing their fighters with a natural advantage over the heavy armour of the IDF, and diminishing the Israeli technological advantage. Tanks, for instance, the backbone of the Israeli army that had been so effective in previous conventional wars fought in open spaces, struggled to operate effectively in southern Lebanon, where manoeuvring was restricted; indeed they became sought-after targets for the guerrillas. Lebanese villages in the security zone, the majority of which were populated by Shiite Muslims, generally supported the insurgents, harbouring them and providing Hezbollah with intelligence and hiding places for weapons.

It is worth mentioning that until 1987 Hezbollah did not use proper guerrilla tactics; rather they launched ad hoc attacks with car bombs and even direct frontal attacks on IDF and SLA outposts. But following an unsuccessful attack on an IDF stronghold on 18 April 1987, where Hezbollah lost 38 men, it shifted tactics, developing 13 principles of warfare which they believed would be efficient in defeating the relatively fixed, though technologically advanced, IDF. These principles were:

1　Avoid the strong, attack the weak – attack and withdraw!
2　Protecting our fighters is more important than causing enemy casualties!
3　Strike only when success is assured!
4　Surprise is essential to success. If you are spotted, you have failed!
5　Don't get into a set-piece battle. Slip away like smoke, before the enemy can drive home his advantage!
6　Attaining the goal demands patience, in order to discover the enemy's weak points!

7    Keep moving; avoid formation of a front line!
8    Keep the enemy on constant alert, at the front and in the rear!
9    The road to the great victory passes through thousands of small victories!
10   Keep up the morale of the fighters; avoid notions of the enemy's superiority!
11   The media has innumerable guns whose hits are like bullets. Use them in the battle!
12   The population is a treasure – nurture it!
13   Hurt the enemy and then stop before he abandons restraint![4]

In responding to Hezbollah's guerrilla tactics, the IDF proved itself to be as conservative as most other conventional armies, taking some time to adapt to the new reality, where its troops were fighting neither conventional armies (as they had done in previous wars), nor against children and women (as they had done in the occupied territories), but instead had to tackle determined insurgents, operating mainly in small groups from within populated areas. When this mental transformation eventually took place, the IDF started to get its grip on the situation by fortifying its outposts, opening new roads and brushing up its counter-insurgency tactics, not least by establishing a school for guerrilla warfare and looking at the ways other armies, notably the British army in Ireland, were operating against insurgents.

While Israel's security zone in southern Lebanon was quite effective in stopping cross-border incursions, it was less successful in stopping Hezbollah's firing of rockets into Israeli towns and villages. In response to continuing Hezbollah rocket fire, the IDF unleashed 'Operation Accountability', from 25 to 31 July 1993. This operation was aimed, among other things, at exerting pressure on the Lebanese government so it would rein in

Hezbollah and also to drive a wedge between the Lebanese and the insurgents. To achieve these aims, the IDF precipitated a humanitarian crisis in Lebanon by forcing an exodus of south Lebanese refugees to the capital Beirut; in the course of 'Operation Accountability', 200,000 Lebanese of 120 southern Lebanon villages were displaced and thousands of homes were completely or partially destroyed; 140 Lebanese including 13 Hezbollah guerrilla were killed and 500 were wounded.

While the attack led to a relatively quiet period and a reduction in the number of rocket attacks on Israel, the effects of the operation did not last for long: three years later – again in response to rocket attacks on Israeli towns – the IDF embarked on 'Operation Grapes of Wrath', from 11 to 27 April 1996. Like 'Operation Accountability', it was aimed at putting indirect pressure on Lebanon, and indeed on Syria which supported Hezbollah, to rein in the insurgencies and to undermine Lebanese popular support for them. In the course of this massive operation, 250 Lebanese were killed, hundreds of thousands were displaced and 7,000 homes were completely or partially destroyed in southern Lebanon. Israeli shells also killed scores of innocent Lebanese who took shelter in a UN camp near a village called Qana, leading to international condemnation and outcry. This in turn led to an indirect ceasefire between Israel and Hezbollah ('The April Accord'), but this proved merely a temporary lull and the fight soon restarted.

In hindsight, 1997 was a turning point in the fate of Israel's security zone in southern Lebanon. On 4 February 1997, two helicopters ferrying soldiers to the Lebanese front crashed, killing 73 troops on board. Although just an accident, this was nevertheless an unusually large number of casualties for the Israeli public to stomach. On 4 September 1997, 12 more troops were killed in Lebanon after falling into a well-planned Hezbollah ambush; the ferocity of this skirmish, where Hezbollah collected bodily remains, including severed heads and limbs, which they would later exchange for detainees in Israeli prisons, disgusted Israelis and stimulated a debate regarding the military purpose and viability of the security zone. Citizen groups opposing the continuing stay in the security zone emerged, notably the Four Mothers Movement, and although this protest never became a mass movement (not like those in the United States during the Vietnam War, or those in the UK during the 2003 invasion of Iraq), it nonetheless seemed to symbolize a shift in thinking and was a constant reminder to the Israelis of the grim reality in southern Lebanon. It is perhaps worth noting that until 1997 the Israeli public had been almost oblivious of the situation in southern Lebanon. First, because only a relatively small number of Israeli troops, up to 1,200, served there at any one time, and, overall, they suffered a low number of casualties, on average (excluding accidents) 20 to 25 troops died there each year, which even for a small country like Israel was still a bearable toll (see Table 8.1). Second, unlike previous wars where reservists were called up to fight, and then returned home to report news from the front, the war against Hezbollah was fought almost exclusively by regular soldiers, who tended not to complain, as military service in southern Lebanon was regarded as more prestigious than policing missions in the occupied territories. But, as shown, the relatively large number of casualties in 1997 lent momentum to the call to get out of Lebanon. The final tipping point would come two years later.

## A UNILATERAL WITHDRAWAL

In the summer of 1999, Ehud Barak, a former IDF Chief of Staff, was elected Israel's Prime Minister. In his election campaign Barak pledged to get Israeli forces out of Lebanon by July 2000. We should recall that in the fierce debate that took place in the

*Table 8.1* Israel defence forces' combat casualties in south Lebanon (June 1985–April 2000)

| Year | Killed | Wounded |
|------|--------|---------|
| 1985 | 2 | |
| 1986 | 9 | 193 |
| 1987 | 20 | |
| 1988 | 21 | |
| 1989 | 2 | 30 |
| 1990 | 8 | 14 |
| 1991 | 10 | 19 |
| 1992 | 13 | 48 |
| 1993 | 26 | 67 |
| 1994 | 21 | 58 |
| 1995 | 23 | 98 |
| 1996 | 26 | 96 |
| 1997 | 38* | 83 |
| 1998 | 24 | 101 |
| 1999 | 13 | 62 |
| 2000 | 9 | 22 |
| *Total:* | 265 | 891 |

*Source:* Dalia Dassa Kaye, 'The Israeli decision to withdraw from southern Lebanon: political leadership and security policy', *Political Science Quarterly*, 117, 4 (2002–3) 570.
* This figure does not include the 73 IDF deaths of February 1997.

General Staff in the early 1980s, Barak – then Director of Military Intelligence – had led the school of thought that called for a full withdrawal from Lebanon. Now, as Prime Minister, his preference was to pull out of Lebanon, but to try to link the move with an agreement with Syria, whereby Damascus (which regarded Lebanon as its backyard and had troops deployed there) would show flexibility in peace talks regarding the Golan Heights and, as a reward, Israel would get out of Lebanon, turning a blind eye to the continuing presence of Syrian troops there; Syria would also rein in Hezbollah. Although Barak would not reveal his cards to government colleagues or army command, he was determined to withdraw from Lebanon even without a deal with Syria, as for him the security zone was a liability rather than an advantage. An end to the Israeli occupation of southern Lebanon, Barak believed, would deprive Hezbollah of its legitimacy – after all, Hezbollah claimed that it was fighting the Israeli occupation – and thus if it went on to provoke Israel even after an Israeli withdrawal then the international community would back Israel in hitting back at the organization.

On 14 October 1999, IDF Chief of Staff Shaul Mofaz presented 'Operation New Horizon' to Barak, detailing how the IDF would withdraw from the security zone to the Israeli–Lebanese international border; Mofaz's assumption was that the IDF withdrawal would take place within a framework of a peace agreement with Syria. In the official meeting where 'New Horizon' was presented, the Prime Minister emphasized, yet again, that all preparations for the pull-out should be made in the context of an Israeli–Syrian deal, but, in a four-eyes meeting with Mofaz afterwards, Barak told him to be ready for all eventualities, including a unilateral withdrawal. This was the first time Barak had revealed his real intentions – he would pull Israel out of Lebanon even without a deal with Syria. Of course, Barak had to tell the IDF Chief of Staff this, as from a military point of view a withdrawal which was not part of a deal with Syria would require more preparation, as there could be no guarantee that Hezbollah would not open fire on the retreating forces, or begin to take over the evacuated areas, turning them into launching pads to attack Israel. Barak still asked the Chief of Staff not to start official preparations for a unilateral withdrawal from Lebanon, fearing that this could leak and lead to an unnecessary debate in Israel; anyway, he still hoped that talks with Syria would bear fruit.

On 24 December 1999, the Prime Minister held another meeting with the military to discuss the expected withdrawal from Lebanon and he approved a budget of 200 million shekels for preparations. The fate of SLA troops and their families was also raised in this meeting. We should recall that for years the SLA had worked closely with the IDF, but now the Israelis were concerned that following an Israeli departure from Lebanon, Hezbollah would wreak vengeance on SLA troops and their families who had collaborated with the IDF. The Prime Minister said the SLA should be encouraged to remain in Lebanon, or emigrate abroad, but those wishing because of personal security concerns to emigrate to Israel should be allowed to do so.

While secret preparations to pull out of Lebanon were taking place, the fight in the security zone continued unabated, and Israeli warplanes carried out strikes on Hezbollah both in southern Lebanon and elsewhere. On 7–8 February 2000, warplanes carried out 'Operation Robust Torch', attacking Hezbollah power stations and logistical centres in Baalbek in eastern Lebanon; this was the first air strike in Lebanon during Barak's tenure as Prime Minister.

When it became apparent that peace talks with Syria were not going well and that it would be difficult to link a withdrawal from Lebanon to a deal with Syria – and that the IDF might have to withdraw from Lebanon without a Syrian guarantee to rein in Hezbollah – Prime Minister Barak called Chief of Staff Mofaz to a meeting. Barak told him:

> At the time I prohibited the IDF from preparing any papers regarding a [unilateral] withdrawal, but I also said that as IDF Chief of Staff you need to prepare the army to pull out [even if we fail to reach] a deal [with Syria]. That was before negotiations with Syria. I did everything I could to make [these peace talks] succeed. But we failed. I will now prepare for a last-ditch attempt [to clinch a deal with Syria]. If I can't meet [Syria's President] Assad, then [US President Bill] Clinton will meet him. I don't know when it will take place, but it's clear

that we need to be ready for the prospect that the meeting will fail.[5]

The Chief of Staff replied, 'Do you mean that I can now formally start planning for a [unilateral] withdrawal [which is not linked to] a deal [with Syria]?' Barak was still cautious. The IDF General Staff, he knew, was overwhelmingly opposed to a unilateral withdrawal, believing that this would result in Hezbollah chasing the IDF up to the international border, and bringing more Israeli towns and villages into range of its missiles. The General Staff also believed that a withdrawal without a political agreement with Syria would be considered to be an Israeli surrender to terror and encourage Palestinian organizations, notably Hamas, to adopt Hezbollah's violent methods. So now Barak advocated a gradual approach. 'You don't have to do [the preparations] in one go,' Barak told Mofaz, 'but gradually . . . you can say [to your subordinates in the army] that the preference is to withdraw as part of a deal [with Syria], but that in parallel we [also] start preparing ourselves for a withdrawal without a deal.' Also, acknowledging that rumours of an imminent Israeli withdrawal might damage morale and perhaps even lead to the collapse of the SLA in southern Lebanon, the Prime Minister warned his Chief of Staff that, 'It is necessary that the SLA not know [of our preparations to withdraw unilaterally].' After this meeting, the Chief of Staff, on 21 February 2000, circulated a document among the General Staff where he instructed among other things, that,

The code name for [a withdrawal from Lebanon and] . . . IDF deployment along the international border [which is *not* linked to an Israeli–Syrian] agreement is 'Morning Twilights'. The code name for a deployment along the international border which is part of an agreement [between Israel and Syria] remains 'New Horizon'.

Thus, for the first time, the General Staff was formally notified that there might be a unilateral withdrawal from Lebanon.

## Resistance in the General Staff

On 27 February 2000 the Prime Minister gathered his ministers to debate his plans to withdraw from southern Lebanon and the possibility that this might, after all, be unilateral, not linked to a peace agreement with Syria. He had to tread carefully, as ministers were aware that within the IDF General Staff there was an almost unanimous opposition to a unilateral pull-out. In the Israeli system, the Director of Military Intelligence provides ministers with a 'national assessment', a sort of appraisal before important decisions are made. Aware, however, that his Director of Military Intelligence, General Amos Malka, opposed a unilateral withdrawal from Lebanon, the Prime Minister did not invite him to the debate and no 'national assessment' was given to the government. On 5 March, the debate continued, and at its end the ministers decided that,

> A. The IDF will redeploy along the international border with Lebanon by July 2000 and from there guarantee the security of [Israel's] northern settlements . . . [as part of an Israeli–Syrian peace] agreement. B. In case the conditions are not ripe for an IDF deployment which is part of an agreement [with Syria], the government will meet in due course to decide how to implement the decision mentioned in the article A above.

Article B would effectively enable the Prime Minister to convene his ministers to discuss other ways to implement the deployment along the border if talks with Syria failed, namely, to do so unilaterally. The option was now officially on the table.

By now, realizing that the Prime Minister was determined to get out of Lebanon unilaterally, the military high command was furious. This was apparent when the General Staff met on 6 March 2000 to discuss 'Morning Twilights', the military plan to pull out of Lebanon unilaterally. General Gabi Ashkenazi, head of Israel's Northern Command, who was responsible for the security zone and who would be in charge of IDF withdrawal when it happened, said, 'How is it that [the government] takes such a major decision without listening to our views . . . I've always been against a unilateral withdrawal.' Chief of the Air Force General David Ivri said, 'The government doesn't understand, or at least not all those in government fully understand, the implications of [a unilateral withdrawal].' Chief of Staff Mofaz commented, 'I would like to ask you not to criticize the political level, let alone in my presence . . . It is wrong that in such a meeting of 18 generals we criticize the political level.' In the meantime, the Prime Minister's Military Secretary warned Barak of the rebellious atmosphere and the growing 'bitterness' in the military high command and advised him to meet up with them. Barak did so on 10 March. It was a charged meeting where the Prime Minister made it clear that, in his view, 'it was wrong to stay [in Lebanon] . . . We'll know what to do [if Hezbollah attacks Israel after our withdrawal from Lebanon].'

As early as mid-March 2000, head of Northern Command started removing bits and pieces out of the security zone, using what came to be known as the 'the weekly vehicle'; empty vehicles would accompany supply convoys into south Lebanon and soldiers would then secretly load them with supplies to take back to Israel. At the same time, on the Israeli side of the border with Lebanon, a massive operation was underway to prepare a new line to which forces would deploy after getting out of the security zone: new outposts were constructed and defensive obstacles put in place; electronic monitoring devices were installed and new roads were built. Chief of Staff Mofaz personally supervised this logistical effort, and he began instructing his troops to call the pull-out from the security zone 'an exit' rather than 'a withdrawal'. He also ordered preparations for 'Power Castle', a war game to take place in mid-April aimed at examining operational plans to exit from Lebanon and redeploy along the new line; in the event, a delay to 29 May meant that the war game would never be played as the withdrawal itself would precede it.

On the diplomatic front, on 26 March 2000, US President Clinton held a summit with President Assad of Syria in Geneva in a last-ditch attempt to strike a deal between Israel and Syria, part of which would be an Israeli withdrawal from Lebanon and a tacit agreement that Syria would be allowed to remain there as long as they reined in Hezbollah. But the summit collapsed and the entire political-military effort was now shifted to prepare for a unilateral withdrawal.[6]

What Prime Minister Barak had in mind was a pull-out in line with UN Security Council Resolution 425 of 1978 which called on Israel to 'withdraw forthwith its forces' and for the United Nations Interim Force in Lebanon (UNIFIL) to confirm the withdrawal and secure the border areas. Although this would require a formal affirmation by the Security Council, the Israelis assumed that the Security Council would approve the same line to which the Israelis had pulled back on 13 July 1978 following the Litani campaign, a withdrawal which was also in line with UN Security Council Resolution 425. This resolution also called for the dismantling of the SLA, Israel's proxy militia in south Lebanon, and to deal with that the IDF, on 18 April 2000, issued a document entitled, 'The future of SLA as part of implementation of UN Resolution 425'. It outlined the principles which, on the one hand, would enable Israel to dismantle the SLA in line with UN Resolution 425, but on the other hand, let it continue to exist as small SLA 'civilian' units, secretly financed and supported by Israel, to operate in southern Lebanon and ensure that 'no foreigners', a reference to Hezbollah, penetrated into the area close to the international border.

In the meantime, however, faced with growing criticism that

he was ignoring military advice not to pull out unilaterally from Lebanon, the Prime Minister eventually agreed that the Director of Military Intelligence should appear before ministers, which he did on 27 April 2000. General Malka warned ministers against the dangers of a unilateral withdrawal and went on to emphasize that after the withdrawal Hezbollah would find excuses to attack Israel, and that the legitimacy among the international community that Israel would enjoy after fulfilling UN resolutions calling for withdrawal would diminish over time, making it increasingly difficult for the IDF to respond forcefully to Hezbollah's provocations. But this assessment did not deter the Prime Minister, who continued to push hard to get troops out of south Lebanon.[7]

Following the collapse of the summit between Bill Clinton and President Assad of Syria in Geneva, Prime Minister Barak wanted to ensure that Damascus did not increase its support for Hezbollah. On 28 April he approved military plans to signal to Syria that assisting Hezbollah might lead to Israeli strikes against Syrian targets. He instructed his commanders to 'choose Syrian targets that by attacking them we will send a signal to Syria',[8] but he also emphasized that attacks on Syria should be limited in scope so as not to cause 'a deterioration [in Israeli–Syrian relations]'. Barak explained that, 'the signal [to Syria] should demonstrate our determination to act, even to escalate, but at the same time not to humiliate the Syrians . . . the target could be in Syria proper not necessarily in Lebanon . . . we should be ready to do so even before we hit Lebanon as a result of growing Hezbollah [hostile] activities'. Two days after this discussion, Hezbollah struck Israeli and SLA targets and the Prime Minister instructed the military to respond by hitting four targets: two power stations in Lebanon; Hezbollah ammunition dumps; and also the Beirut–Damascus road. The latter was the signal to Syria that it should stop bolstering Hezbollah's military capacity. Warplanes went into action on 5 May 2000.

## The security zone crumbles

With the pace of IDF preparations to get out of Lebanon grow-ing, it became impossible to hide the truth from the SLA, who became concerned that they were about to be left on their own to face the wrath of Hezbollah. The SLA 70th battalion, which was operating in the central sector of the security zone, was the weakest link as its men were Shia, some with links to Hezbollah; early in May troops of this battalion started to desert and returned to their villages. On 11 May, Prime Minister Barak summoned the SLA's commander, General Antoine Lahd, to the Defence Ministry in Tel Aviv. It was a tense meeting where the Prime Minister repeated Israel's commitment to the SLA. At the end of the meeting Barak said to Lahd, 'You can now go to Paris,' a not-so-subtle hint that it was time for the Lebanese general to get out of southern Lebanon. Advising Lahd to leave at this critical moment did nothing to improve morale among SLA troops, who sensed that the IDF's departure was imminent. Their suspicions were strengthened by the transfer, on 14 May, of the IDF-held strongholds Taibe and Rotem to SLA control. That day, acknowledging that the SLA was on the verge of collapse, head of Northern Command, General Ashkenazi, sent a letter to the IDF Chief of Staff urging him to bring forward the withdrawal. He wrote:

> It would be logical to bring [the withdrawal] forward ... the pressure on the SLA is growing and the remaining time [until our departure would] enable Hezbollah to organize itself better to cause casualties [to the IDF] during the exit ... [I] recom-mend implementing the exit plan [now] ... we are ready for that.[9]

The Prime Minister, however, was not keen on an earlier exit, as he first wished to receive formal UN approval of the line of withdrawal, to ensure that Hezbollah could not claim later that the Israelis were still occupying Lebanese territory. But by 18 May it was apparent that the gap between Barak's political requirements and the situation on the ground in the security zone had become somewhat wider, as the number of SLA troops deserting their units grew alarmingly and Hezbollah fire at SLA and IDF outposts intensified. On 20 May, IDF Northern Command distributed a document among its units warning them that, 'by now it seems that Hezbollah has thoroughly taken to heart the fact that the IDF has already started its exit [from Lebanon] and this is likely to lead to fear among SLA troops and cause even more desertions'.[10]

Sunday 21 May started quietly in the security zone, but towards midday Hezbollah activists and south Lebanese villagers started marching in the direction of SLA strongholds. They proceeded to climb over the fortresses, and quickly – and peacefully – took them over before raising Hezbollah flags. One of the strongholds that fell into Hezbollah hands was Taibe, the one the IDF had transferred to the SLA the week before. Taibe was in a critical strategic location, in the narrow part of the security zone; losing it to Hezbollah meant the zone was severely weakened. Furthermore, the fall of Taibe set off a domino effect that soon resulted in ever-growing numbers of strongholds falling into Hezbollah hands.

The next morning, 22 May, Prime Minister Barak was handed an intelligence document titled, 'A rapid crumbling of the SLA', which made it apparent that the collapse of the demoralized SLA was gathering momentum and that the security zone was on the verge of total disintegration. The SLA 70th battalion had collapsed and its commander abandoned his post and fled to Israel; the 80th battalion had also collapsed, and Hezbollah activists surrounded the SLA Western brigade headquarters in Bint Jbail. SLA troops were an integral part of the Israeli deployment in the security zone and without them IDF troops were in danger as their outposts could become isolated, their flanks exposed to Hezbollah's attacks.

In an urgent meeting with Prime Minister Barak, IDF Chief of Staff Mofaz warned that, 'it would be impossible to continue holding the security zone without reinforcement' and he proposed to get out of Lebanon at once. Head of Northern Command, General Ashkenazi, added, 'Prime Minister . . . [by now] there are two options: either to stay on [in the security zone] and reinforce it with two brigades, or get out. I join the recommendation of the Chief of Staff – to get out . . . it is better to get out now. There won't be many casualties . . . Hezbollah is not ready . . . we'll surprise everyone.'[11] The Prime Minister was facing a dilemma. On the one hand he still wanted to see the UN formally conclude their discussions and approve the exact line of IDF withdrawal, but on the other hand, being a professional soldier himself, he understood that the situation was so critical that it would be better not to linger. He thus instructed the military to get out from 'problematic areas', namely from those positions where, given the collapse of the SLA, Israeli troops had become isolated, or were vulnerable to Hezbollah attacks. He also instructed to start implementation of 'Operation Shield and Oak', which was aimed at giving sanctuary to SLA troops and their families, as well as collecting their tanks, artillery and other abandoned vehicles and equipment before Hezbollah could grab them. Throughout the day the state of the SLA became even more desperate and chaotic as its troops deserted in droves; by the evening the SLA had only two functioning battalions in the eastern sector of the security zone.

That night the Prime Minister conferred with his Chief of Staff and it was at this meeting that he effectively ordered the final withdrawal from southern Lebanon. Barak said to Mofaz, 'The Cabinet will be asked to provide the IDF with the freedom to decide when to get out [from Lebanon] to the international border in accordance with [UN Resolution] 425.' At another meeting in the early hours of the morning Barak asked Mofaz: 'Can you get out tonight? Is Gabi [Ashkenazi, OC Northern Command] ready?' Mofaz replied: 'We can exit tonight.' Barak said: 'OK, I allow you to get out.' Mofaz later got back to the Prime Minister to say that their forces would need an extra 24 hours to clear the area and he asked for permission to pull out from Lebanon on 23–24 May. Barak agreed: 'We [will do it] tomorrow night.' He told Mofaz, 'I'll have a telephone round with Cabinet ministers [asking them to agree] to leave the freedom of decision regarding the exact timing of withdrawal to the IDF. Of course they will not know of the arrangement between us that the exit should take place tomorrow.' The code name given to the emergency withdrawal was 'Operation Patience'.[12]

It was quiet in southern Lebanon on the morning of 23 May, with no Hezbollah marches on strongholds, but by midday hundreds of Hezbollah activists had suddenly swamped the eastern sector of the security zone and, as they had on the previous day, took over SLA positions, planting their yellow flags atop the fortifications. As word of the disintegration of the final remaining SLA units in the eastern sector spread, southern Lebanese civilians, who years before had been removed from their villages in the security zone by the IDF and forced into north Lebanon, began moving in large numbers towards their former homes. The commander of the SLA Eastern brigade abandoned his headquarters, collected his family and fled to Israel, and soon after, the SLA 30th Druze battalion collapsed and abandoned its outposts, thus forcing the Israelis to abandon their own outposts in order not to become isolated in the area. By 5 p.m. the SLA had ceased to exist as an organized military body and Israel's security zone in southern Lebanon was no more.

That night the IDF withdrew from Lebanon. They were attacked sporadically, but otherwise the exit went according to plan; occasionally, warplanes went into action to bomb abandoned outposts and equipment. By 5 a.m. on 24 May, most troops were already in Israel proper and at 6.48 a.m., OC Northern Command, General Ashkenazi, reported to the Chief of Staff that the last troops had left Lebanon. At 7.30 a.m., Chief of Staff Mofaz announced: 'After eighteen years, the IDF has ended its presence in Lebanon.' The exiting forces then deployed along the 'Blue Line', a 79km line demarcated by a United Nations cartographic team, along which 14 border stones were put. On 16 June 2000, the UN Secretary General reported to the Security Council that Israel had withdrawn fully from Lebanon, in line with Security Council Resolution 425.

## Hezbollah prepares for war

In the years following the Israeli withdrawal from southern Lebanon, Hezbollah armed itself and erected bunkers close to the border with Israel, from where it collected intelligence on IDF movements. Deeper in southern Lebanon, it constructed an impressive defence system of concealed bunkers connected by tunnels, following the Vietnamese model, complete with electrical wiring, reinforced concrete ceilings and enough water, food and ammunition to withstand a sustained siege. It built protected rocket launchers into the ground and trained launching squads to use pneumatic lifts to raise and lower the rockets from their underground shelters. In friendly villages, Hezbollah built positions and used civilian homes to stockpile weapons, including rockets, and other supplies. All these preparations – the underground facilities, arms dumps, food stocks and training – were made with the help and supervision of North Korean and Iranian instructors.

Although Hezbollah became a semi-military organization, it continued to base its methods on small, self-sufficient units, capable of operating independently and without direction from central headquarters. Troops were equipped with AK-47 or

M-16 rifles, some with M-4 Carbines, as well as with anti-tank missiles, and were deployed in locations throughout southern Lebanon. Their mission, in case of open combat with the IDF, was to try and bleed the Israelis and slow them down in order to give Hezbollah's rocket squads time to fire missiles into Israel until the conflict's end to create the appearance that Israel's actions were not having their desired effect. By the summer of 2006, Hezbollah units – well trained, well armed and highly motivated – were ready in southern Lebanon to face the IDF.

## WAR

The IDF response to the 12 July 2006 incident, mentioned at the opening of this chapter, was so overwhelming that it took Hezbollah totally by surprise. Its leader, Hassan Nasrallah, later admitted that, 'We had not foreseen . . . that the hostage taking would lead to a war of that scope.' He went on to explain that:

> Because of several decades of experience, and because we know how the Israeli acts, it was not possible that a reaction to a hostage taking reaches such proportions, especially in the middle of the tourist season [in Israel]. In the history of wars, it never happened that a state launches a war against another for a few apprehended soldiers and a few others killed.[13]

Indeed, by analysing the pattern of Israeli reactions to Hezbollah provocations from 2000 to July 2006, Hezbollah could reasonably have concluded that the Israelis tend to react in a measured and limited scope. For instance, their reaction to the abduction by Hezbollah on 7 October 2000 of three Israeli troops on Mount Dov (Sha'aba Farms) was low key: IAF warplanes went into action against some Hezbollah targets and a Syrian radar station in Lebanon, but later the Israeli government agreed to a deal whereby they would release Lebanese prisoners in return for the soldiers. Hezbollah may have expected a similar deal to be reached in 2006, though, if so, they had missed two nuances in the situation: in October 2000 the second Palestinian *intifada* was in full swing and the Barak government was reluctant to open a new front with Hezbollah in Lebanon; by 2006 the Palestinian front was relatively quiet. Also, in October 2000 Prime Minister Barak had only just pulled Israeli forces out of Lebanon four months earlier in May, and was reluctant to hit back forcefully at Hezbollah as this might suggest that he had been wrong in withdrawing from southern Lebanon in the first place. Barak's successor, Ariel Sharon, had initially adopted the same measured policy vis-à-vis Hezbollah. Like Barak before him, his first priority was to sort out the Palestinian *intifada*, and also Sharon was particularly encumbered with bad memories of Lebanon; he had been the architect of the 1982 Lebanon fiasco that had resulted in the massacre of innocent refugees at Sabra and Shantilla, forcing his resignation as Defence Minister (indeed he was later barred by Israeli law from ever holding that post again – this did not stop him becoming Prime Minister, however). He was clearly reluctant to become re-entangled in the Lebanese quagmire. Thus, in the six years since the withdrawal from Lebanon successive Israeli governments had adopted a strategy of containment, whereby they would react in proportion to Hezbollah's border provocations and hit its Syrian patron, but at the same time would try not to rock the boat.

Now, however, the new Israeli government led by Prime Minister Ehud Olmert clearly thought it was time to take sharp action against Hezbollah, to discourage them from their cross-border raids. Although taken aback by the scale of the Israeli response, Hezbollah did not lose its nerve and responded by launching 22 rockets against towns and villages in Galilee, northern Israel. This was not the first time Israel's populated areas had come under rocket or missile attack – in the 1991 Gulf War Saddam Hussein fired 39 Scud missiles into Israel – but here, in July–August 2006, sustained and continuous rocket and missile strikes against the Israeli home front turned into the backbone of Hezbollah's tactics – they had rightly identified the home front as Israel's soft belly.

Israel's air campaign continued unabated on the next day (13 July), and in 'The Night of the Fajrs', warplanes carried out a lightning 34-minute strike, dropping laser-guided precision munitions and destroying almost all of Hezbollah's arsenal of 240mm Fajr-3 missiles, which were armed with a 45-kilogram warhead and had a range of 45km. In the coming days the IAF would also wipe out most of Hezbollah's 320mm Fajrs-5, which had a range of more than 75km. These were impressive successes for the IAF, demonstrating their professionalism and technical ability – it was also a success for Israel's intelligence services, which had correctly identified the targets. Indeed, in the years leading up to the war, Israeli intelligence managed to gather detailed data on Hezbollah's weapons and their exact locations from a network of human intelligence operating in southern Lebanon, as well as from interception of Hezbollah communications, and satellite and aerial reconnaissance through cooperative arrangements with the US. Still, despite pulverizing air strikes, Hezbollah continued to carry out rocket attacks, firing, on 13 July, 125 rockets, some of which hit Haifa, Israel's third-largest city.

Sustained air strikes were aimed at depleting Hezbollah's military ranks and arsenals (including, vitally, their stocks of rockets and launchers), but also at damaging their morale. Israel also targeted Lebanon proper: its roads, bridges, power stations and most notably Beirut International Airport, a transfer point for weapons and supplies to Hezbollah; here the aim was to compel the Lebanese government to turn on Hezbollah, and also to weaken support for Hezbollah among the Lebanese population. The IDF's Chief of Staff, Dan Halutz, a former pilot and Chief of the IAF who had learned the lessons of the air campaigns in

Bosnia and Kosovo, strongly believed that air strikes alone would be sufficient to bring Hezbollah to its knees.

Israel and Hezbollah continued to trade blows on 14 July. Israeli warplanes pounded Beirut's southern suburbs, mainly the densely populated Dahia residential neighbourhood, the nerve centre of Hezbollah, from where it was assumed their leader Hassan Nasrallah was running the war; Hezbollah, in turn, fired a barrage of 103 rockets into Israel, killing six and injuring 21. From the sea, Israel's navy, which in previous wars had played only a marginal role, attacked Lebanese targets including petrol stations in the area of Sidon. Hezbollah, however, struck back by launching a C-802, an Iranian version of a shore-to-ship missile originally developed in China, which hit the Israeli naval vessel *Hanit*, one of the IDF's latest and most capable ships; the ship was not using active countermeasures and the strike caused substantial damage – four sailors were killed. Taking an Israeli vessel out of action had a minimal impact on the overall Israeli war machine, but in a war where symbols were as important as tangible military achievements this was a significant score for Hezbollah.[14]

On 15 and 16 July, the IAF continued its blitz – striking both Hezbollah and Lebanese targets to increase pressure on the Lebanese government to tackle Hezbollah. They dropped leaflets on seven south Lebanese villages, urging villagers to leave their homes and move northwards in the direction of Beirut. This exodus, the Israelis assumed, would cause a humanitarian crisis, forcing the Lebanese government to feed and house scores of refugees at a time when essential resources, notably petrol, were running low; soon three-quarter of a million Lebanese were on the move. But this did not deter Hezbollah, who, over these two days, fired 147 rockets ever deeper into Israel, targeting the city of Tiberius, where eight were killed and scores injured, and also Haifa. On 17 July, while 92 rockets landed on Haifa and other cities, the IAF scored yet another major achievement when it destroyed 18 out of the estimated 19 to 21 600mm Zelzal-2 launchers, which had a range as far as Tel Aviv and beyond and a massive warhead of 400 to 600 kilograms.

In the Knesset, on 17 July, Prime Minister Olmert delivered what many dubbed a 'Churchillian' speech, where he stated Israel's goals in the conflict: namely, to retrieve the two captured soldiers; cease rocket attacks on Israel; a request that Lebanon deployed its army in southern Lebanon; and the ousting of Hezbollah from the area. He vowed that, 'We will not suspend our actions [before these aims are achieved].'[15] In hindsight, these were overambitious aims that would be difficult to achieve, particularly from the air alone. Indeed, while the IAF was quite successful in obliterating most of Hezbollah's medium- and long-range missiles, it failed to deal effectively with the short-range missiles which could reach between 18 and 28km into Israel. These had small warheads and were easy to operate, hide and resupply; it was estimated that Hezbollah had between 10,000 and 16,000 such rockets.

The only way for Israel to tackle the problem of these smaller rockets was to embark on a full-scale ground assault into southern Lebanon, either by crossing the international border and moving northwards to search out and destroy the rockets and their launching pads, or by landing forces from the sea, or by transporting troops by helicopters as deep as the Litani river and then moving them south to surround and cut off Hezbollah. Transferring the war into the enemy's territory has always been one of the main tenets of the IDF Doctrine of Warfare. Moving the battle onto the enemy's territory ensured that the damage was done far from home, and it forced the enemy to protect itself, thus leaving it little time to strike at Israel. However, there was little appetite in the Israeli political-military establishment to embark on such an operation at a time when it was still believed that decisive attacks from the air, coupled with artillery and naval fire and other measures such as a blockade of

Lebanon's sea- and airports, would gradually degrade Hezbollah's military capabilities and motivation to prevail. The IDF believed that instead of the classical concept of military victory – conquest, capturing of territory and destroying enemy's forces – victory could be achieved by employing massive fire from the air combined with limited ground raids when needed, all of which could effectively cripple the enemy's capability to act.

The reluctance to move troops on the ground into Lebanon also reflected the 'Israeli Lebanese trauma', as it was often described. Past experience had taught Israelis that Lebanon was a quagmire and it would be wiser to keep out of there, not least given that a ground assault would be bloody and messy, and would not be tolerated, so it was assumed, by the Israeli public.[16] The IDF's Chief of Staff, Dan Halutz, opposed a major ground assault so strongly that he would not even initiate a reserve call-up lest it encourage the government to use the troops to invade Lebanon. But, responding to growing pressure to deal with Hezbollah's continuing rocket attacks, the Chief of Staff permitted limited incursions into Lebanon in areas adjacent to the border, emphasizing, however, that the operating forces should be small, and that they should direct their attacks against small targets in order not to endanger the troops.[17] Appearing before the Cabinet on Wednesday 19 July, Halutz emphasized that his wish was to avoid as far as possible a deep ground assault into south Lebanon; he was supported by the Prime Minister himself, who was not keen on authorizing a ground operation either.[18] That day, the Israeli home front – the ordinary citizens of towns in northern Israel, who lacked proper bomb shelters and felt increasingly exposed – came under an intense attack of 116 rockets that killed four and wounded 33.

## Stalemate

After one week of fighting, the war had reached a stalemate. In a meeting with his Prime Minister, Defence Minister Amir Peretz said, 'It is necessary to decide whether to start preparations for a ground operation . . . it would not be possible to continue along the current lines.'[19] But again the Chief of Staff would not have it, saying to Peretz, on 20 July, that, 'We . . . should not . . . move deep [into Lebanon, but continue], to degrade their front line . . . degrade their willingness to keep on fighting.'[20] Although he himself was not keen to order an invasion into Lebanon, a frustrated Prime Minister complained that, 'I can't see . . . the military giving me the victory I need.'[21] Thirty-four rockets landed on the home front on that day.

On the ground in Lebanon, on 21 July, the entire front was split between two IDF divisions: the 91st division, which was charged with the Western sector of southern Lebanon; and the 162nd division in the eastern sector. Forces were then tasked with carrying out incursions against Hezbollah on the first ridge-line overlooking Israel. These limited assaults – swift entry and exit rather than lengthy occupation – came under the code name 'Operation Webs of Steel' and were the main ground method the IDF employed as a compromise between the inability of the IAF to stop the incoming rockets and the lack of military-political motivation to carry the ground war deeper into Lebanon.[22] However, for the operating forces these turned out to be tough battles, as the narrow village streets and rough terrain of southern Lebanon negated their advantages over Hezbollah's small and flexible units, who were able to swiftly change tactics, and endure repeated air and artillery shelling, by retreating into pre-prepared bunkers. The Hezbollah fighters were particularly successful with their anti-tank missiles, destroying a number of Israeli tanks, and shattering the myth of the indestructible Israeli Merkava-4 tank.[23] Israeli troops – too careful and lacking the decisiveness and boldness which so much characterized the IDF in previous wars – failed to achieve their military aims in these limited assaults. Still, the Chief of Staff continued to support the small incursions saying that, 'these [enter-and-pull-out incursions] will serve to strengthen our deterrence'.[24]

Ten days into the war, frustration grew in Israel as it became apparent that the limited ground operations and sustained air campaign had failed to render Hezbollah powerless, as it was simply impossible for the IAF to eliminate thousands of small and mobile rockets from the air. Hard pressed to deal with these rockets, the Chief of Staff, on 24 July, informed Defence Minister Peretz that he had instructed his staff to plan a deep ground assault into Lebanon aimed at clearing the area of the short-range rockets.[25] But the Chief of Staff was still torn and on the next day he continued to argue that, 'we should proceed with the activities we are doing at the moment of degrading [Hezbollah's] forces . . . on the ground and from the air'.[26] But the tide among the political-military leadership was clearly moving in the direction of a big operation. On 26 July, Amos Gilead of the Defence Ministry recommended to Defence Minister Peretz that, 'either you go to a large ground operation . . . or find a way to stop [the war]'.[27] The head of Shin Bet, Israel's internal security agency, said that, '[a ground operation] seems the most reasonable option'; and General Gabi Ashkenazi, Director of the Ministry of Defence, who led the IDF out of Lebanon in May 2000, argued that the IDF had so far failed to deliver and that it was necessary, 'to go to the government with a recommendation to have a ground operation . . . we should get at least to the Litani [river, to deal] with these short-range [rockets]'[28] But it would still be difficult to persuade the Chief of Staff. That evening, at a meeting with ministers, Halutz said, most reluctantly, that 'as Chief of Staff [I] can't but recommend to be prepared for a larger military move [into Lebanon]', but he still emphasized that this was not his preferred option. 'At the end of the day', he argued, 'I believe that the right mix is a gradual mix . . . my recommendation is not to do a large ground operation at this stage.'[29] On 27 July, the Cabinet approved the call-up of two to three divisions of reserves in preparation for a possible large-scale incursion.[30] Throughout this period rockets continued to rain on Israel (see Table 8.2).

The little momentum the IDF still had in Lebanon was lost on Sunday 30 July when an air strike on Qana – where during 'Operation Grapes of Wrath' in April 1996 more than 100 inno-cent Lebanese had been killed by Israeli artillery fire – caused a building to collapse, burying 28 people under its rubble, including 17 children; Hezbollah responded by firing 156 rockets into Israel, causing scores of casualties. Mounting international pressure forced Israel to suspend air operations for 48 hours as of 31 July at 2.00 a.m. to allow an investigation into the Qana killing.

### 'Change of Direction'

At a meeting on 4 August 2006, the Director of Military Intelli-gence, Amos Yadlin, an influential member of the General Staff, admitted that, 'I believed that two weeks of work from the air would bring us elsewhere, but today I think differently. I think the only way to clear these Katyusha [rockets] . . . is by launch-ing a significant ground assault [deep into Lebanon].'[31] When asked why it had taken him so long to reach this conclusion, the Chief of Staff replied, 'The Israeli public was not ready to accept a penetration into Lebanon on 12 July.'[32] He added that he would now recommend to the government that the IDF 'expand our ground operation. [In the] first stage [to invade Hezbollah's rocket] launch sites . . . [and then] move northwards . . . up to the Litani [river]'.[33]

By now, however, criticism of the IDF's strategy in Lebanon had grown. At a Cabinet meeting on 6 August, minister

*Table 8.2* Number of missiles and rockets fired at Israel from 12 July to 14 August 2006

| | |
|---|---|
| 12 July | 22 |
| 13 July | 125 |
| 14 July | 103 |
| 15 July | 100 |
| 16 July | 47 |
| 17 July | 92 |
| 18 July | 136 |
| 19 July | 116 |
| 20 July | 34 |
| 21 July | 97 |
| 22 July | 129 |
| 23 July | 94 |
| 24 July | 111 |
| 25 July | 101 |
| 26 July | 169 |
| 27 July | 109 |
| 28 July | 111 |
| 29 July | 86 |
| 30 July | 156 |
| 31 July | 6 |
| 1 August | 4 |
| 2 August | 230 |
| 3 August | 213 |
| 4 August | 194 |
| 5 August | 170 |
| 6 August | 189 |
| 7 August | 185 |
| 8 August | 136 |
| 9 August | 166 |
| 10 August | 155 |
| 11 August | 123 |
| 12 August | 64 |
| 13 August | 217 |
| 14 August | 0 |

Benyamin Ben Eliezer complained that, 'the one who came to this table [meaning the Chief of Staff], telling us that one blow by the air force and we are done, misled us'.[34] The Prime Minister, perhaps trying to justify why the move into Lebanon was being planned at such a late stage, commented that, 'all along there was no request, or a suggestion by the military to embark on a [big] ground assault [deep into Lebanon] . . . up to now the army has not come to the political level to ask for approval of an operation beyond the lines where we are today'.[35] At a later meeting with the Defence Minister, the Chief of Staff reassured him that, 'We are now working on the big move [to invade south Lebanon].'[36] This rush of preparations to invade Lebanon, it is worth noting, came at a time when the UN Security Council was locked in frantic discussions on a ceasefire resolution aimed at stopping hostilities in Lebanon.

On 7 August, the military reported that preparations for an invasion were complete and that it was ready to launch the offensive on 9 August. That day Prime Minister Olmert, accompanied by his Chief of Staff, visited Northern Command, where he defended his decision to go into Lebanon at this late stage by saying, 'I want you to know that today was the first time – am I right Chief of Staff? – that an operation plan to [get] to the Litani area was put before us [by the military].'[37] Later, at a meeting of the General Staff, the Chief of Staff said, 'On Wednesday night [9 August], at a time to be decided between Northern Command and the General Staff . . . [we will] attack [Lebanon].'[38]

But the diplomatic clock was ticking fast; on 8 August the Lebanese government agreed, for the first time, to send 15,000 of its troops to south Lebanon to put an end to Hezbollah's attacks, and the UN Security Council was moving in the direction of agreeing on its ceasefire resolution. In Israel, the Chief of Staff reassured his General Staff that the ground operation would go ahead regardless of any diplomatic developments. 'The army will set off . . . Full stop,' he said, adding, 'This spring is now stretched and will be released tomorrow . . . this move is aimed at reducing the firing of short-range rockets . . . not to smash [Hezbollah, but only] *to reduce* [the number of rockets launched into Israel].'[39] The operation to invade southern Lebanon was code-named 'Clear Direction', which later changed to 'Change of Direction'.

But there was no escape from the question the government was facing: does it make any sense to embark on a large-scale invasion at a time when diplomacy seemed to be closer than ever to securing a ceasefire? But Israel had so far failed to achieve its war aims and the IDF's effectiveness as a deterrent had suffered a massive blow with the continuing stalemate and the sustained fire of rockets onto the home front. What further increased pressure on the Israeli decision makers was the presence of thousands of troops, the vast majority of whom were reserves, who were waiting to be sent into action; Defence Minister Peretz expressed the dilemma when he said that, 'the most difficult problem will be if we have to tell the combat forces that the operation is postponed'.[40]

On 9 August the Cabinet convened to discuss the planned entry into Lebanon. Prime Minister Olmert explained that as international diplomacy to end hostilities was gathering pace there might be only a short time to run the proposed operation, even less than the minimum 96 hours estimated to be required to achieve its first phase, namely reaching the Litani river. But the Chief of Staff, who for so long had opposed any ground operation in Lebanon, was adamant that the army should be given the green light anyway. He said, 'We are at a time when we've got to go to a large military move, [up] to the Litani – we must.' Foreign Minister Tzipi Livni, who was involved in Security Council talks to end the fighting and was aware just how advanced these efforts were, asked the Chief of Staff, 'Doesn't the army have a plan that would take less time [to complete]? Don't you have such an animal?' The Chief of Staff replied: 'No such animal.' Asked by a minister why the large operation had not been carried out earlier, Defence Minister Peretz said, 'The army did not put forward operational plans [for a deep invasion into Lebanon].'[41] When the Chief of Staff disagreed, Prime Minister Olmert intervened by saying, 'All along . . . the military . . . said "we don't recommend a ground operation".'[42] Clearly, the war between the politicians and the military over who would be held responsible for the poor outcome of the war in Lebanon was well underway even before the main invasion had begun.

The military plan the Chief of Staff proposed called for an all-out invasion by a large force composed of three divisions, whose task would be to reach the Litani river. Then, over a period of three to four weeks, forces would clear out the area, searching for and destroying Hezbollah's rockets. Minister Shaul Mofaz, a former IDF Chief of Staff, objected to the proposed military plan. He said: 'The timetable is short . . . and I ask: are we going to send in thousands of reservists and regulars to a very difficult area, when we know that at a certain stage [the UN Security Council] will ask us to get out? And then we will not only fail to achieve our objectives, but it would be said, "the IDF has failed".'[43] Instead, Mofaz proposed to land forces at the rear of Hezbollah and 'to make a quick move . . . a move which is both surprising and that would have an impact . . . the advantage of this move is that first you've surrounded Hezbollah in southern Lebanon and you tell them: "Gentlemen, we're going to grad-ually roll our forces down to each of the [rocket] launching areas . . . taking our time . . ." and at the same time you leave freedom of action to the political level'.[44] This was an ingenious and a most original plan which, if implemented and successful on the ground, could have saved the day and restored the reputa-tion of the IDF as an imaginative and bold military machine. But Defence Minister Peretz – who regarded Mofaz as a political rival – would not agree to any proposal coming from him and, supported by the Chief of Staff, he insisted that there was one military plan on the table. The other ministers, reluctant to move against their Defence Minister and the Chief of Staff, approved the IDF 'Change of Direction' plan, although the majority of them saw the logic in the plan proposed by Mofaz. The Cabinet then granted the Prime Minister and Defence Minister the authority to decide on the exact timing of the operation.[45] On that day, 166 rockets landed on Israel.

By now, with large numbers of troops waiting in limbo, the military became impatient to take action. At 5.45 p.m., the Defence Minister phoned his Prime Minister to urge him not to delay the operation as '[the commanders] say they can't hold the troops in such a situation [any longer]'. But Prime Minister Olmert now prevaricated, knowing that he might have a Security Council ceasefire resolution at any moment. For if it was a good resolution, with terms favourable to Israel, then perhaps it was best not to embark on the offensive and endanger the troops after all. He thus ordered the Defence Minister to keep the forces waiting, and 'If there is no [Security Council] decision by tomorrow at 6 p.m. then . . . [we'll] act . . . I'll not wait any longer.' The Defence Minister repeated, 'There's huge pressure [to act, the military] say ". . . you either let us attack, or we start wrapping it all up".'[46] At 6.55 p.m. the Defence Minister phoned again to ask the Prime Minister whether, 'we can tell the troops that if there is no [Security Council] agreement they will embark on the operation tomorrow?' To that Olmert agreed.[47] That night, at 11 p.m., the General Staff issued update number 2 to 'Change of Direction', delaying the operation for 24 hours.

The next day, 10 August, the Prime Minister talked to his Defence Minister at 1 p.m. telling him that there would have to be yet another delay. It was a tense conversation where the Defence Minister, under ever-growing pressure to act from the military, said to the Prime Minister, 'Ehud, we can't delay,' to which the Prime Minister replied, '[we have] no other option

. . . I'll not endanger [a Security Council resolution] that we have a good chance of getting.' The Defence Minister replied, 'Yes, but yesterday we said the same.' Olmert said, 'It's very fragile [if we invade Lebanon now] . . . things might stop [at the Security Council] . . . and then it will take time to resume it . . . and by then we'll have . . . 100 soldiers killed.' [48] To calm the military down, the Prime Minister personally phoned his field commanders explaining the situation and the need to delay action. On that day, 155 rockets landed on the home front.

The draft UN Security Council resolution, passed to Israel on 11 August, proved to be a disappointment for them. The 20,000-strong international force the Israelis wanted deployed in southern Lebanon to patrol the area had been cut down to 15,000; the surveillance regime aimed at monitoring the transfer of weapons into Lebanon, particularly from Syria, was not as harsh as they had hoped for; and reference to the two abducted soldiers – the pretext for the whole war and the release of whom was one of Israel's primary war aims – was only declarative. Against this background, the Defence Minister phoned his Prime Minister at midday urging him to 'give [the IDF] the order to move'.[49] Fifteen minutes later they talked again and the Defence Minister urged Olmert to give the green light as, 'we can't keep waiting any longer'.[50] The Prime Minister replied, 'I urge you to be patient . . . I want to consult some ministers before we set off.' But the Defence Minister would not give up: 'There's no point in more consultations . . . there isn't time for consultations . . . These are moments of leadership. We've got to take the decision and I suggest giving the order to the forces to set off tonight.' [51] They met in the afternoon and the Defence Minister said, 'We must embark on the operation. We mustn't lose time.'[52]

At 4.40 p.m., with a deficient Security resolution draft in his hand and his forces impatient, Prime Minister Olmert finally gave the green light to act. By now, however, it was apparent that

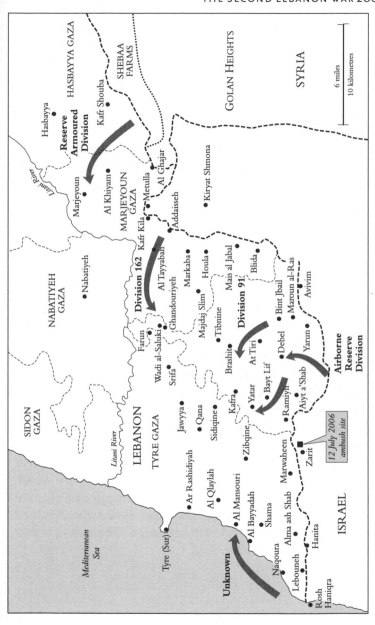

*Map* 10  Israeli attack on Lebanon, 2006

rather than the 96 hours the army needed to get up to the Litani, it would have no more than 60 hours. At 8 p.m., the Chief of Staff issued his orders to invade Lebanon, and at 9 p.m., the IDF assault began, with 9,800 troops moving across the border.

The next day, Saturday 12 August, the IDF was still operating in Lebanon, but their advance was slower than expected. At around 7.30 p.m., the Security Council passed Resolution 1701 calling for a halt to hostilities, and promising to send 15,000 armed observers to south Lebanon; the Lebanese government accepted it. On that day, Hezbollah fired 64 rockets into Israel.

The next day the Israeli government accepted Resolution 1701 and the UN announced that the ceasefire would come into effect on Monday 14 August at 8 in the morning. That day Hezbollah fired a massive barrage of 217 rockets into Israel to show that it was keeping up the bombardment right up until the end of the war.

On the morning of Monday 14 August, before the ceasefire came into effect, the IAF launched its last attack against Dahia, where Israel assumed Hassan Nasrallah was still hiding. Israeli troops, however, failed to reach the Litani river and their achievements on the ground were minimal; in the course of this last-minute, meaningless operation the IDF had lost 33 men and a Sikorsky CH-53 helicopter, which had been shot down by Hezbollah fighters.

In line with Security Council Resolution 1701, the UN sent forces into south Lebanon, which arrived there in three waves. Between 17 August and 2 September, 3,500 troops joined 2,000 UNIFIL personnel already in Lebanon; 3,500 more joined between 3 September and 5 October; and a last batch of 3,000 deployed until 4 November.

## THE BALANCE SHEET

In 34 days of battle Israel lost 154 people of whom 109 were soldiers and 45 civilians; many more were wounded. Out of the 400 tanks involved in battle, 108 were hit; 5 Merkava-4 were completely destroyed. Close to 4,000 rockets landed on Israel's home front causing much damage and severely disrupting day-to-day life (see Table 8.2). More than 1,000 Lebanese were killed during the war and scores more were wounded. In spite of the Israeli denial that it had attacked Lebanese infrastructure, it did destroy 46 petrol stations, 92 bridges, 82 communication lines, 14 radar systems and 52 tunnels all across Lebanon.[53] More than 170,000 artillery shells landed on Lebanon (in comparison, during the Yom Kippur War against the two regular armies of Egypt and Syria the IDF fired 75,000 shells).

Yet, in spite of this massive amount of fire rained down on Lebanon, Israel failed to achieve most of the goals it had set for itself at the onset of the war: the two soldiers Hezbollah had captured were still in captivity; Hezbollah was still in good shape and, as shown, continued to fire rockets into Israel until the last day of the war, and most certainly retained the capability of doing so again in the future; and Israel's deterrence had suffered a major blow, though whether or not deterrence against Hezbollah worked we will only know in the future. Overall IDF performance was poor. Indeed, the Winograd Commission, set up by the government to investigate both the political and the military leadership of the war, concluded that, 'The IDF . . . failed to fulfil its missions . . . in most cases . . . the IDF demonstrated . . . powerlessness . . . in its contest with Hezbollah.' The exception was perhaps the IAF, which, as we have shown, had some unprecedented successes, most notably in destroying Hezbollah's medium- and long-range missiles. Still, it failed to stop the vast majority of the incoming short-range rockets which continued to rain on Israel's home front until the end of the war.

Perhaps because too many air force personnel played a leading role in the General Staff (from the Chief of Staff, through the Director of Military Intelligence to the Chief of the Air Force), the IDF had been too reliant on air power and had unrealistic expectations of what air power could accomplish. The Winograd Commission said that the war in Lebanon proved, 'the limitations of air power' and that, 'the expectation that was held by some of the IDF command, that fire [from the air] . . . could decide the face of battle − was not correct'.[54] Indeed, it seems that embracing air power at the expense of a classic ground-manoeuvre campaign was a major factor in the IDF's lacklustre performance in Lebanon.

When the IDF did send ground troops in to operate − first just north of the border and then a full-scale invasion only at the last moment − their performance was disappointing and in most cases they failed to accomplish their missions. This, perhaps, should not have surprised anyone, given that since 1987 the IDF had only really been engaged in policing activities in the occupied territories, and their soldiers had not undergone any serious training in counter-insurgency warfare. This seriously diminished their conventional war-fighting capabilities at a time when Hezbollah had embraced a new doctrine, transforming itself from a predominantly guerrilla force into a formidable quasi-conventional army. The IDF troops' equipment was often obsolete and ill adapted to the war they were called upon to fight − the result of severe cuts in the budget for ground forces, particularly of reserve units, over the years. In the event, a semi-military organization of a few thousand people, carrying relatively primitive weapons, was able to survive against what was regarded as the strongest army in the Middle East, which had total air superiority and a huge technological edge. The war, as the Winograd Commission wrote, was 'a severe missed opportunity . . . [and] the responsibility to explain the missed opportunity . . . rests on the army's shoulders'.[55]

# 9

## CONCLUSIONS

Wars between Arabs and Israelis have taken place from the day the state of Israel was established on the land of Palestine in May 1948, and have since dominated both the headlines and books about Israel. When viewed from a historical perspective, these separate, short wars can be seen as one continuous conflict where territory – first the land of Palestine and then lands seized by Israel in subsequent wars – is the main, though not exclusive, trigger to repeating conflagrations. The balance sheet, after more than 60 years of Israeli–Arab conflict, indicates that on the battlefield there has been no clear victor – neither Arab nor Israeli.

In the war of 1948, the first contest between the parties, Israel held its ground and even defeated Egypt and Lebanon. But the Jordanians and Syrians did well; the former managed to seize the West Bank and the latter to cross the international border and occupy lands which had been allotted to the Jews by the UN in the 29 November 1947 Partition Plan (Chapter 1). Then in 1956, Israel struck hard at Egypt (Chapter 2), and 11 years later in the war of June 1967 Israel defeated Egypt, Jordan and Syria (Chapter 3). However, in the 1968–70 War of Attrition along the Suez Canal, there was no clear winner (Chapter 3), as was also the case in the October 1973 Yom Kippur War, where Egypt and Syria managed to win an important battle in the initial phase of the war but were later forced to yield their gains to the victorious Israelis (Chapter 4). In the war of 1982 in Lebanon, Israel struck hard at the Syrians and the PLO, forcing the latter out of the country and into exile in Tunis; but this war was still considered a disastrous failure, especially after the assassination of Israel's protégé Bashir Gemayel, and the subsequent massacre of Palestinians in the refugee camps of Sabra and Shatilla (Chapter 5). Then, during the years of the *intifada*, Israel failed to contain the disturbances, and the Palestinian uprising which began in 1987 ended temporarily after the signing of the Oslo Agreement in 1993 (Chapter 6). But it restarted with much more ferocity in 2000 (Chapter 7) and at the time of writing it is still continuing, with the Israelis seemingly unable to stop it. In the 2006 Lebanon War the Israelis failed to gain a clear victory over a paramilitary organization, Hezbollah (Chapter 8). But at the time of writing, the border between Israel and Lebanon is quiet, and it might be that Israeli actions in 2006 did succeed, after all, in deterring Hezbollah from further provocation of Israel.

Wars, however, are a clash not only of arms but of words too, and if there was no clear victor on the battlefield, then there was at least a clear victor in the war of words, and this was, until the mid-1980s, Israel. For many years Israel's leaders had managed – most successfully – to instill in the minds of their fellow Israelis, and in the minds of observers in the wider world, the idea that Israel was always the injured party, the victim of Arab aggression. But this was only partially true, for while in 1948 the newborn state of Israel was indeed the victim of Arab attempts to destroy it (Chapter 1), eight years later it was Israel who, together with France and Britain, initiated and launched a war against Egypt (Chapter 2). Then in 1967, it was again Israel who forced war upon Egypt and Syria – Jordan was the only country to attack Israel in this war (Chapter 3). However, immediately after this conflict, it was President Nasser of Egypt who imposed a War of Attrition on Israel, and later, on Yom Kippur in 1973, it was Egypt again – now led by Nasser's successor Sadat – who, along with Syria, opened fire first, attacking Israel on two fronts (Chapters 3 and 4). In the summer of 1982, it was again Israel who started a war, this time in Lebanon (Chapter 5); but five years later it was the Palestinians in the West Bank and the Gaza Strip who began a stone-throwing war against the Israeli occupying forces (Chapter 6), and in 2000 it was the Palestinians again who repeated this exercise though now with more lethal arms (Chapter 7). In 2006, Israel was clearly provoked by Hezbollah into a war in southern Lebanon, and this was accepted by the world community and Israelis (Chapter 8).

These wars cost all sides a fortune – in money, and in physical and emotional damage to the people of the region. If we include the constant necessity to prepare for war, even when there is no resulting conflict, the cost to both Israeli and Arab societies rises still further. But conversely, these wars have also proved to be the bond – the very cement – which has helped keep Israeli society together. For, especially during the first decades of the state, Israel was the gathering place for Jewish immigrants from the four corners of the earth, and rather than forming a homogeneous society, the country was more an assembly of diverse communities and people, some of whom were still 'adding up the grocery bill in Arabic; others dreaming in Yiddish and singing to their children lullabies in English or Russian'.[1] And, as shown in Chapter 2, it was the establishment of a military system where almost every citizen – male and female – was a trained soldier and a reservist, that transformed these disparate groups of people – the Israeli-born *Sabra*, the Orthodox Jew from New

York, the scientist from London, the silversmith from Yemen, the lawyer from Egypt and the small shopkeeper from Morocco – from individuals into a society and one nation under arms. And above all, what kept this Israeli organism together and helped rally Israelis round the flag and their leadership, was a deep sense of external danger and the fear that the Arabs would try to destroy Israel, and that to cope with this problem Israelis must stick together and take up arms whenever they were called upon to do so. As Abba Eban, an intelligent and well-informed eyewitness, wrote in his book *My Country*: 'The Israeli scene is often turbulent, contentious and effervescent but when *danger threatens* . . . the ranks tighten.'[2]

Indeed, throughout the formative years of the state of Israel the country's leadership had a tendency to exaggerate the external threat in order to engender a sense of insecurity among Israelis, which in turn made them willing to fight in wars and to finance the large military budget; the frequent bellicose threats of Arab leaders merely reinforced this. But, as I have shown, during the mid- to late 1970s there were many changes in Israel, most notably a growing sense that its place in the Middle East was now more secure, and that the external threat was diminishing. This change of mood came about not only because the IDF had managed to prove its efficiency and ability to defend the country, it was also the result of the beginning of a process of reconciliation between Israelis and Arabs, evidenced not least by the signing of a peace accord between Israel and Egypt in 1979, which meant that Egypt – the strongest of Israel's foes – was removed from the circle of war; with this, the danger to Israel's existence declined dramatically (Chapter 4). In a 1986 survey, 89 per cent of Israelis expressed confidence in Israel's long-term existence, and in 1987 this figure rose to 96 per cent.

The experience of the Holocaust, which had taken place just a few years before Israel was established, had a strong impact on attitudes in Israel during the first decades of the state. Indeed, within Israeli society the Holocaust survivors provided living testimony to what could be the fate of Israelis if they failed to defend themselves. Just how strongly this trauma affected Israelis is shown by *The Seventh Day: Soldiers Talk about the Six Day War*, a book in which returning soldiers talked about their experiences and thoughts, which became a bestseller in Israel after the 1967 war. One of these soldiers, Yariv Ben-Aharon, seems to represent the general mood in Israel at the time:

> People believed [before the outbreak of the June 1967 war] that we would be exterminated if we lost the war . . . We got this idea – or inherited it – from the concentration camps . . . Genocide – it's a feasible notion . . . This is the lesson of the gas chambers.[3]

But with the gradual disappearance of the Holocaust generation, and with Israel's victory in the Six Day War, the over-sensitivity of Israelis to the danger of total extermination slowly diminished. For many of the older generation of Israelis, the Holocaust was the central experience of their lives, and their thoughts and actions were dominated by the knowledge that what had happened once could happen again, an idea which was much used by Israeli politicians throughout the years in order to rally the people. But the younger generation, those born in the 1970s and later, saw the world in less threatening colours than their parents did. They may have heard anecdotes of the Holocaust from their elders, but they were more likely to learn of it from books, and it did not dominate their actions and world-view as it did their parents'. For the sons and daughters of non-European Israelis, the Holocaust seemed an even more remote event. In a survey carried out in 1986, 82 per cent of Israelis thought there was absolutely no chance (42 per cent) or only little chance (40 per cent) that the Jewish people would face another Holocaust.

Over the years another important change took place within

Israel, namely a shift from collective ideals and priorities to individual ones. While the early generation of Israelis – the builders and founders of the state – possessed an ideological sense of mission and took it for granted that the state came before the welfare of the individual, the younger generation saw things differently. For them, individual priorities often seemed more important than collective ones, and in contrast to their parents they were motivated by their individual achievements rather than by patriotic values. Thus, while the older generation were willing to pay a heavy price in terms of taxation and sacrifice of social services in order to subsidize expensive wars, the younger generation were much more reluctant to do so. In 1987, two-thirds of Israelis stated that they would not support cuts in social services in order to increase the defence budget, and in 1992 only 24 per cent of Israelis said they would be willing to finance increased defence spending.

The perception of a decreased external threat, the disappearance of the Holocaust generation and a shift from collective ideals and priorities to individual ones, resulted in the emergence of a more confident Israeli nation, less fearful for its existence and less traumatized and haunted by its past. This also meant that this new society was less single-minded and more reluctant to take up arms or make personal sacrifices, as was clearly demonstrated in Lebanon in 1982 and during the years of the Palestinian uprising in the occupied territories between 1987 and 1993, and as of 2000. It is interesting to observe the current generation of political and military leaders in Israel talking up the threat posed by Iran. Will this growing sense of danger – potentially once again to the very existence of Israel as a state should Iran acquire nuclear weapons – see Israeli society regress to that earlier, more fearful and more aggressive form? It is, as yet, too early to say.

# NOTES

## PREFACE TO THE 2010 EDITION

1 Ahron Bregman, *A History of Israel* (Basingstoke, 2002); Uri Bar-Joseph, 'The Intelligence Chief who went fishing in the cold: how Maj. Gen. (res.) Eli Zeira exposed the identity of Israel's best source ever', *Intelligence and National Security*, 23, 2 (April 2008) 226–48.

## 1 THE 1947–9 WAR

1 J. K. Galbraith, *The Great Crash 1929* (London, 1961), 25.
2 *The Complete Diaries of Theodor Herzl, Vol. I* (New York, 1960), 343 (entry for 12 June 1895).
3 A. Koestler, *Promise and Fulfilment, Palestine 1917–1949* (London, 1983), 5.
4 Letter of Ben Gurion to his wife Paula, as quoted in A. Shlaim, *Collusion across the Jordan* (Oxford, 1988), 17.
5 Interview with Hazem Zaki Nuseibeh, 28 February 1997, Amman, BLA [Brian Lapping Associates, interview carried out by this production company and kept at the Liddell Hart Centre, King's College, London].
6 J. Vatikiotis, *Among Arabs and Jews* (London, 1983), 59.
7 R. Fisk, 'Flirting with the enemy', *Independent*, 20 February 1999.

8    D. Ben Gurion, *Diary of War* (Tel Aviv, 1982), entry for 23 February 1948 (Hebrew).

9    Interview with Hazem Zaki Nuseibeh.

10    D. Ben Gurion, *Diary of War*, entry for 19 December 1948 (Hebrew).

11    D. Ben Gurion, *Diary of War*, entry for 10 November 1948 (Hebrew).

12    D. Ben Gurion, *Diaries*, entry for 27 April 1953, in Ben Gurion Archive (BGA), Sde Boker. Full details of casualties can be found in A. Bregman, 'Civil–military relations in Israel: military influence on war policy', Ph.D. dissertation (Department of War Studies, King's College London, 1993), 113, n15.

13    Gideon Rafael to author, Jerusalem, 19 January 1997.

14    D. Ben Gurion, *Diary of War*, entry for 15 May 1948 (Hebrew).

15    J. B. Glubb, *A Soldier with the Arabs* (London, 1958), 195.

16    References to the development of chemical weapons can be found in Ben Gurion's *Diary of War*, entries for 1 June, 2 June, 20 June 1948 (Hebrew).

17    General Shlomo Shamir to author, Tel Aviv, 17 December 1991.

18    B. Lapping, *End of Empire* (London, 1989), 189.

19    J. B. Glubb, *A Soldier with the Arabs*, 96.

20    Interview with Mohsein Abdel Khalek, Cairo, 19 March 1996, BLA.

21    Interview with Abdel Ghani Kanout, Damascus, 16 October 1996, BLA.

22    Interview with Adel Sabit, 23 February 1997; and with Mourad Ghaleb, 20 March 1996, Cairo, BLA.

23    J. B. Glubb, *A Soldier with the Arabs*, 79.

24    P. Bernadotte, *To Jerusalem* (Jerusalem, 1952) 132 and 137 (Hebrew).

25    *New York Times*, 23 October 1979. This censored piece also appears in A. Bregman and J. el-Tahri, *The Fifty Years War* (London, 1998), 40.

26    Interview with George Habash, Damascus, 6 October 1996, BLA.

27    Ben Gurion, in *Transcript of the Meeting of the 16th June 1948*, 21–2, in the author's archive (Hebrew).

28    Y. Rabin, *Pinkas Sherut* (Tel Aviv, 1979), 63 (Hebrew).

29    M. Dayan, *Story of my Life* (London, 1976), 146.

30    The number 5.4 million (of them about 1.5 million children) instead of the commonly known figure of 6 million Jews, is based on the fact that at least 10 per cent of the Jews who were massacred in the Holocaust were Christians, i.e. Jews who had converted to Christianity. For the Nazis, however, a Jew converted to Christianity was still a 'full Jew' (*Volljude*); see B. Lewis, *Semites and anti-Semites* (London, 1986), 20. In the Holocaust about one third of world Jewry perished.

31    D. Ben Gurion, *Diary of War*, entries for 5 July, 15 July and 10 November 1948 (Hebrew).

32    G. Rothenberg, *The Anatomy of the Israeli Army* (London, 1979), 67.

33    B. Lewis, *Semites and Anti-Semites*, 23.

## 2  A NATION-IN-ARMS 1949–67

1    D. Ben Gurion, *Diary of War*, entry for 26 and 27 November 1948 (Hebrew).

2    D. Ben Gurion, speech in the Knesset, 19 August 1952 (Hebrew) (my emphasis).

3    D. Ben Gurion, as cited in G. Rothenberg, *The Anatomy of the Israeli Army*, 71.

4    A. Yaniv, *Deterrence without the Bomb* (Massachusetts, 1987), 58.

5    J. B. Glubb, *A Soldier with the Arabs*, 303.

6    On the Gaza raid, see Ariel Sharon to author, Jerusalem, 7 April 1991; Sharon to author, Havat Ha'shikmim, 1 March 1997.

7    On 'Operation Kinneret', see Ariel Sharon to author, Jerusalem, 7 April 1991.

8    A. Eban, *My Country: the Story of Modern Israel* (London, 1973), 125–6.

9    M. Dayan, *Diary of the Sinai Campaign* (London, 1965), 60–1; for more on the planning of the campaign with the French and British, see Shimon Peres to author, Jerusalem, 11 March 1991.

10    A. Eban, *My Country*, 141.

11    Y. Rabin, *Pinkas Sherut*, 97 (Hebrew).

12    G. Rothenberg, *The Anatomy of the Israeli Army*, 116.

## 3  THE SIX BAD YEARS 1967–73

1    Memorandum of conversation, 31 January 1967, LBJ Library, E.O.12356, sec. 3.4, NEJ, 93–120.

2    E. Haber, *Today War Will Break Out: The Reminiscences of Brig. Gen. Yisrael Lior, Aide-de-Camp to Prime Ministers Levi Eshkol and Golda Meir* (Tel Aviv, 1987), 146 (Hebrew).

3    Nasser's speech at UAR Advanced Air Headquarters, 25 May 1967, in W. Laqueur and B. Rubin (eds) *The Israel-Arab Reader: A Documentary History of the Middle East Conflict* (London, 1995), 144–9.

4    Interview given by Moshe Dayan in 1976 to Rami Tal and published in *Yediot Aharonot*, 27 April 1997 (Hebrew).

5   Interview with Egyptian general Ahmed Fakher, Cairo, 27 February 1997, BLA.
6   Interview with Mohammed Fawzi, Cairo, 28 February 1997, BLA.
7   Interview with Syrian general Abdel Razzak Al-Dardari, Damascus, n.d. BLA.
8   A. Eban, *My Country*, 198.
9   Interview with Evgeny Pyrlin, Moscow, March 1997, BLA.
10  'Soviet official's comments on Soviet policy on the Middle East war – CIA report of conversation with Soviet official re June War', LBJ Library, 82–156, doc. 8420.
11  Nasser to Eric Rouleau, *The Times*, 19 February 1970.
12  Nasser's speech at UAR Advanced Air Headquarters, 25 May 1967; also interview with Nasser, *World in Action*, 29 May 1967.
13  Quoted in S. Segev, *Sadin Adom: The Six Day War* (Tel Aviv, 1967), 51 (Hebrew).
14  A. el-Sadat, *In Search of Identity: An Autobiography* (New York, 1977), 172.
15  A. el-Sadat, *In Search of Identity*, 173.
16  Interview with King Hussein, Amman, 2 March 1997; also an interview with Jordan's Prime Minister Zaid al Rifai, Amman, 6 March 1997, BLA.
17  R. Gilo (ed.) *Ba'machane – The IDF Journal: 30 Years to the Six Day War*, 11 (Hebrew).
18  Nasser's speech to Arab trade unionists, 26 May 1967, in W. Laqueur and B. Rubin (eds) *The Israel-Arab Reader*, 149–52.
19  Uzi Narkiss to author, Jerusalem, 21 January 1997.
20  Former general Matityahu Peled to author, Tel Aviv, 7 April 1991.
21  A. Eban, *My Country*, 214.
22  About how and why, see Miriam Eshkol to author, Jerusalem, 30 January 1997.
23  M. Dayan, *Story of my Life*, 341.
24  Aharon Yariv to author, Tel Aviv, 27 March 1991; also letter from Aharon Yariv to author, 2 June 1992, Tel Aviv (Hebrew).
25  Interview with Minister of War Shams el-Din Badran, London, 5 June 1997, BLA.
26  Interview with Pavel Akopov Sememovich, Moscow, March 1997, BLA. Akopov was present at the meeting between Kosygin and Badran. He was a Soviet diplomat and worked for the Middle East desk of the Politburo.
27  Interview with President Nasser, 29 May 1967, *World in Action*, tape

number 1148; see also interview with Minister of War Shams el-Din Badran.

28  Interview with Egyptian Minister of War Shams el-Din Badran.

29  From Amit's report to the cabinet, Meir Amit's archive.

30  Meir Amit to author, Ramat Gan, 20 January 1997; also interview with Robert McNamara, 21 April 1997, Washington, BLA.

31  Yitzhak Rabin to author, Tel Aviv, 21 March 1991.

32  Ezer Weizman to author, Jerusalem, 3 March 1997.

33  Interview with King Hussein of Jordan, Amman, 2 March 1997, BLA.

34  J. Lunt, *Hussein of Jordan* (London, 1989), 144.

35  The conversation between Nasser and the King can be found in A. Bregman and J. el-Tahri, *The Fifty Years War*, 90; also an off-the-record interview with the King, Amman, 28 January 1997, in the author's archive; also an interview with Zaid al-Rifai, Amman, 6 March 1997, BLA.

36  Interview with King Hussein of Jordan, Amman, 2 March 1997, BLA.

37  Quotes are from The Report of the Israeli Examining Judge – Yerushalmi.

38  Interview with General Reshetinikov Vassily Vassilievich, Commander of Strategic Aviation Corps, Moscow, 27 September 1996 (in the author's archive).

39  Chief of IAF Mordechai Hod to author, Tel Aviv, 21 January 1997.

40  Interview with Syrian General Abdel Razzak Al-Dardari.

41  A. Eban, *My Country*, 279.

42  A. M. Farid, *Nasser: The Final Years* (Reading, 1994) 6–7. For 11 years, until 1970, Abdel Magid Farid had served as Secretary-General of the Egyptian presidency with the rank of minister, and attended all of Nasser's meetings on domestic and international affairs.

43  *ibid.*, 14.

44  *Al-Ahram*, 21 January 1969.

45  A. M. Farid, *Nasser: The Final Years*, 135.

46  *ibid.*, 135–6.

47  Haim Bar Lev to author, Jerusalem, 19 March 1991.

48  Ezer Weizman to author, Caesaria, 17 February 1992.

49  Former Chief of IAF Mordechai Hod to author, Lod, 8 April 1991.

50  'Dayan outlines Israel's military strategy', *Financial Times*, 29 January 1970.

## 4 WAR AND PEACE 1973–9

1   Interview with Joseph Sisco, Washington, 19 March 1997, BLA; also interview with Alfred 'Roy' Atherton, who had accompanied Sisco on this visit, Washington, 19 October 1996, in the author's archive.

2   Interview with General Saad el-Din Shazli, Cairo, 24 February 1997, BLA.

3   Interview with General Saad el-Din Shazli and with Field Marshal Abdul Ghani el-Gamassy, Cairo, 24 February 1997, BLA.

4   On this visit to Moscow, see M. Heikal, *The Road to Ramadan: The Inside Story of how the Arabs Prepared for and almost Won the October War of 1973* (London, 1975) 83–90; also E. Zeira, *The October '73 War: Myth Versus Reality* (Tel Aviv, 1993), 87 (Hebrew).

5   A. el-Sadat, *In Search of Identity*, 318 (my emphasis).

6   Interview with Pavel Akopov, Moscow, March 1997, BLA.

7   Interview with Field Marshal Abdel Ghani el-Gamassy.

8   S. el-Shazli, *The Crossing of Suez: The October War: 1973* (London, 1980), 122.

9   The above conservation is mentioned in A. el-Sadat, *In Search of Identity*, 241.

10  Much of the following information has never been published before and is still one of the most guarded secrets in Israel. It is based on lengthy interviews with people who were close to the events and are very reliable, but whose names, for obvious reasons, cannot be revealed.

11  A. el-Sadat, *In Search of Identity*, 318.

12  A. el-Sadat, *In Search of Identity*, 241.

13  Interview with Field Marshal Abdel Ghani el-Gamassy.

14  Interview with Egyptian general Fuad Awidi, *Ma'ariv*, 24 September 1993 (Hebrew).

15  Interview with Syrian general Abdel Razzak Al-Dardary; see also Interview with Egyptian general Bahieddin Noufal. Noufal was the Chief of Staff of the joint Egyptian–Syrian federal operation.

16  Interview with Egyptian general Saad el-Din Shazli.

17  Interview with Syrian former minister of information George Saddeqni, Damascus, 16 October 1996, in the author's archive.

18  Interview with George Saddenqni.

19  Interview with former Jordanian prime minister Zeid Rifai.

20  This document was first published in A. Bregman and J. el-Tahri, *The*

*Fifty Years War*, 118–19. By publishing this rare document we have managed to confirm for the first time rumours of the King's visit to Israel.

21    Interview with Egyptian general Bahieddin Noufal.

22    Interview with Syrian Minister of Defence Mustapha Tlas, Damascus, 3 July 1997, BLA; Interview with General Saad el-Shazli, Cairo, 28 September 1996, in the author's archive; also interview with Field-Marshal Abdel Ghani el-Gamassy; also interview with general Bahieddin Noufal.

23    A. el-Sadat, *In Search of Identity*, 246.

24    Interview with Egyptian general Saad el-Din Shazli and interview with Egyptian general Bahieddin Noufal.

25    Interview with Syrian Minister of Defence Mustapha Tlas.

26    Haim Bar Lev to author.

27    Yitzhak Hofi to author, Ramat Gan, 21 October 1996.

28    Interview with former Syrian Minister of Information George Saddeqni.

29    G. Meir, *My Life*, 358.

30    A. Braun, *Moshe Dayan and the Yom Kippur War* (Tel Aviv, 1992), 86 (Hebrew).

31    S. el-Shazli, *The Crossing of Suez*, 150.

32    Interview with Field Marshal Abdel Ghani el-Gamassy.

33    S. el-Shazli, *The Crossing of Suez*, 157.

34    Yisrael Tal to Uri Milstein, 8 January 1984, Yad Tabenkin Archive (YTA), 25/60/2 (Hebrew).

35    Yisrael Tal to Uri Milstein.

36    M. Dayan, *Story of My Life*, 488.

37    M. Dayan, *Story of My Life*, 494.

38    M. Dayan, *Story of My Life*, 503.

39    S. el-Shazli, *The Crossing of Suez*, 162.

40    M. Heikal, *The Road to Ramadan*, 227.

41    Yisrael Tal to author.

42    A. Sharon, *Warrior: The Autobiography of Ariel Sharon* (London, 1989) 311; also Ariel Sharon to author.

43    M. Dayan, *Story of My Life*, 590.

## 5 WAR IN LEBANON 1982

1    Interview with King Hussein of Jordan.

2    Shimon Peres to author, Tel Aviv, 9 July 1997.

3    A. Naor, *Begin in Power: Personal Testimony* (Tel Aviv, 1993), 253 (Hebrew).

4 A. Sharon, 'Facts as they are about the war in Lebanon', lecture at the Centre for Strategic Studies (Tel Aviv, 11 August 1987), 4 (Hebrew).

5 Former Mossad agent David Kimche to author, Ramat Ha'sharon, 3 October 1996, in the author's archive.

6 Z. Schiff, Ha'aretz, 23 May 1982 (Hebrew).

7 Y. Marcus, 'The war is inevitable', Ha'aretz, 23 May 1982 (Hebrew).

8 A. Sharon, 'Facts as they are about the war in Lebanon', 10 (Hebrew).

9 Interview with Morris Draper, Washington, 13 October 1996, in the author's archive.

10 Ariel Sharon to author, Havat Ha'shikmim, 1 March 1997; interview with Alexander Haig, Washington, 18 March 1997, BLA.

11 The above quotations are from: G. Ball and D. Ball, The Passionate Attachment: America's Involvement with Israel, 1947 to present (New York, 1992), 123.

12 As cited in H. Sachar, A History of Israel, vol. II (Oxford, 1987), 175.

13 Y. Shamir, Summing Up (New York, 1994), 132; Yitzhak Shamir to author.

14 Chief of Staff Rafael Eitan to author, Jerusalem, 20 March 1991.

15 A. Sharon, 'Facts as they are about the war in Lebanon', 14, 20 (Hebrew); former Chief of Staff Rafael Eitan to author.

16 Former Director of Military Intelligence Yehoshua Saguey to author, Bat Yam, 7 March 1991.

17 Ariel Sharon to author; interview with Karim Pakradouni, 21 Feb 1997, BLA.

18 Ariel Sharon in Yediot Aharonot, 28 June 1982, 5 (Hebrew); also A. Sharon, 'Facts as they are about the war in Lebanon', 19 (Hebrew).

19 The above quotations are based on the interview with Karim Pakradouni.

20 Avigdor Ben Gal to author, Tel Aviv, 16 January 1992; also Director of Military Intelligence Yehoshua Saguey to author.

21 Interview with OC Northern Command Amir Drori, Ma'ariv, 1 July 1994 (Hebrew) (my emphasis).

22 Minutes of a cabinet meeting, 6 June 1982, as quoted by Sharon in his speech in the Knesset, Divrai Ha'Knesset, 29 June 1982, 2936 (Hebrew).

23 Ariel Sharon to author, 7 April 1991, Jerusalem.

24 Amos Amir to author, Tel Aviv, 27 February 1997; also Dr Yosef Burg to author, Jerusalem, 18 March 1991.

25 E. Geva, in Ma'ariv, 26 September 1982 (Hebrew).

26　Interview with Lebanese Chief of Intelligence Jonny Abdo, Beirut, 1 April 1997, BLA.
27　Interview with former prime minister Shafiq al-Wazzan, Beirut, 19 February 1997, BLA.
28　Ariel Sharon to author.
29　M. Zipori, *In a Straight Line* (Tel Aviv, 1997), 305 (Hebrew).

## 6 *INTIFADA* 1987–93

1　Eitan Haber to author, Ramat Gan, 20 January 1997. Haber was Defence Minister Rabin's assistant; also former general Amram Mitzna to author, Haifa, 27 January 1997. General Mitzna was the overall commander of Judea and Samaria (the West Bank) at the time of the *intifada*.
2　As cited in D. Peretz, *Intifada: The Palestinian Uprising* (Boulder CO, 1992), 35.
3　Z. Schiff and E. Ya'ari, *Intifada: Israel's Third Front* (New York, 1989), 79.
4　Ehud Barak to author, Kochav Yair.
5　Z. Lockmann (ed.) *Intifada* (Boston, 1989) Communiqué no. 1, 328–9.
6　W. Laqueur and B. Rubin (eds) 'Hamas: Charter, August 1988', in *The Israel-Arab Reader*, 529–37.
7　General Amram Mitzna to author.
8　Z. Schiff and E. Ya'ari, *Intifada*, 150.
9　Z. Schiff and E. Ya'ari, *Intifada*, 40–1.
10　As cited in G. Frankel, *Beyond the Promised Land: Jews and Arabs on the Hard Road to a New Israel* (New York, 1996), 22.

## 7 THE *AL-AQSA INTIFADA* 2000–5

1　This was indeed the conclusion of the Sharm el-Sheikh Fact Finding Commission led by Senator George Mitchell, namely that 'The Sharon visit did not cause the *Al-Aqsa intifada*.' But the Senator also added that the visit 'was purely timed', *The Mitchell Report*, in the author's archive.
2　Ahron Bregman, *Elusive Peace: How the Holy Land Defeated America* (London, 2005), Chapter 8, 85–121.
3　Aluf Ben and Yossi Verter, 'Summit fails: PM says "dream of peace still lives"', *Ha'aretz*, 24 July 2000 (Hebrew).
4　Private source.

5 About this dramatic summit, see Ahron Bregman, *Elusive Peace*, 128–35.
6 Private source.
7 *Haaretz*, 12 March 2002.
8 Private source.
9 Private source.
10 Private source.
11 Private source.
12 Private source.
13 Avraham Dar to author, Atlit, 26 January 1997, in the author's archive.
14 'Extra-judicial executions during the *Al-Aqsa intifada*', The Palestinian Society for the Protection of Human Rights and the Environment, 25 March 2001. Other testimonies of assassinations appearing in this chapter are taken from this source.
15 *Ibid*.
16 Suzanne Goldenberg, 'War jets attack West Bank after mall bomb carnage', *Guardian*, 19 May 2001.
17 *The Mitchell Report*, in the author's archive.
18 Ahron Bregman, *Elusive Peace*, 156.
19 As cited in Amos Harel and Avi Issacharoff, *The Seventh War* (Tel Aviv, 2004) (in Hebrew), 115.
20 Text of the Tenet Ceasefire Plan, in the author's archive.
21 As cited in Amos Harel and Avi Isacharoff, *The Seventh War*, 166.
22 Avi Machlis, 'Israeli bus blast casts shadow on peace process', *Financial Times*, 30 November 2001.
23 James Bennet and Joel Greenberg, 'Israel breaks with Arafat after Palestinian assault on bus in West Bank kills 10', *New York Times*, 13 December 2001.
24 Arafat's declaration in Gaza, Palestine Satellite Channel Television, 16 December 2001, at 4 p.m. On the same day in Gaza the leader of Hamas, Sheikh Ahmed Yassin, also declared a ceasefire; interview with Diana Buttu, 26 May 2004, Ramallah, in the author's archive.
25 Amos Harel and Avi Isacharoff, *The Seventh War*, Appendix.
26 A flag of convenience is a foreign flag under which a ship is registered for tax-avoidance purposes.
27 Interview with former Chief of Staff Shaul Mofaz, 13 February 2005, Tel Aviv, in the author's archive.
28 Interview with Chief of Staff Shaul Mofaz.
29 Interview with Benyamin Eliezer.
30 See http://www.guardian.co.uk/israel/Story/0,2763,633643,00.htm.

31  Interview with General Giora Eiland, 18 September 2004, Ramat Ha'sharon, in the author's archive.

32  Interview with Shaul Mofaz.

33  Ahron Bregman, *Elusive Peace*, 187.

34  Ahron Bregman, *Elusive Peace*, 188.

35  Interview with Benyamin Eliezer and Mike Herzog, 11 October 2004, Washington, in the author's archive.

36  In an interview given to CNN on 17 April Saeb Erekat said to Wolf Blitzer: 'We have 1,600 missing men in this refugee camp. Mostly women and children, husbands and wives . . . how many people were massacred? We say the number will not be less than 500.'

37  Ahron Bregman, *Elusive Peace*, 205.

38  Tenth emergency special session, Agenda item 5, 'Illegal Israeli actions in Occupied East Jerusalem and the rest of the Occupied Palestinian Territory, Report of the Secretary General prepared pursuant to General Assembly Resolution ES-10/10'.

39  Interview with Terje Roed-Larsen, 29 June 2004, Herzliya, in the author's archive.

40  Ahron Bregman, *Elusive Peace*, 228.

41  Ahron Bregman, *Elusive Peace*, 228.

42  Ahron Bregman, *Elusive Peace*, 229.

43  Interview with Benyamin Eliezer. Fingers were pointed at Israel's General Security (Shin Bet) for failing to provide accurate information. According to Ben Eliezer, 'His wife, we knew, was a terrorist just like him.'

44  Interview with Chief Commander of the Israeli Air Force Dan Halutz, *Ha'aretz*, 23 August 2002 (Hebrew).

45  Aluf Benn, 'US telling PM that the *Muqata* siege undermining plans for Iraq', *Ha'aretz*, 29 September 2002.

46  Interview with Mike Herzog.

47  Interview with Shaul Mofaz.

48  Ahron Bregman, *Elusive Peace*, 279.

49  Ahron Bregman, *Elusive Peace*, 281.

50  Ahron Bregman, *Elusive Peace*, 282.

## 8 THE SECOND LEBANON WAR 2006

1  Hezbollah wanted to release prisoners, including Samir Kuntar, a Lebanese who in 1979 killed an Israeli man and his four-year-old daughter.

2   A General Staff meeting, Tel Aviv, 13 February 1985, private source
    (Hebrew).
3   A General Staff meeting, Tel Aviv, 15 March 1985, private source
    (Hebrew).
4   Ehud Ya'ari, 'Hezbollah: 13 principles of warfare', *The Jerusalem
    Report*, 21 March 1996.
5   This and the following quotations are based on a private source.
6   On the Clinton–Assad summit see Ahron Bregman, *Elusive Peace*,
    52–63.
7   The army did not hesitate to use the press to brief against Barak's
    idea of unilateral withdrawal. For instance, on 7 April 2000, *Maariv*
    quoted senior IDF officers who said that getting out of Lebanon uni-
    laterally was 'a dangerous gamble'.
8   Private source.
9   Private source.
10  Private source.
11  Private source.
12  Private source.
13  Hassan Nasrallah, interview on the Lebanese News TV channel, 27
    August 2006.
14  Hezbollah fired another missile at the Israeli *Romach* vessel, but it
    missed, hitting instead an Egyptian merchant ship.
15  Address by Prime Minister Ehud Olmert to the Knesset, 17 July 2006,
    The Knesset Records (Hebrew).
16  The Winograd Commission, which was appointed by the government
    to investigate the war, said that one of the IDF's considerations in
    deciding not to dispatch ground forces deep into Lebanon was the
    assumption that the public was 'not ripe' to accept the large number
    of casualties which is associated with such an operation; see The
    Winograd Report, 526 (Hebrew, henceforth: Winograd).
17  Winograd, Chapter 4, 81–2 (Hebrew).
18  Winograd, 85 (Hebrew).
19  Winograd, 91 (Hebrew).
20  A meeting in the Defence Ministry in Winograd, 93 (Hebrew).
21  21 A meeting, 22 July 2006, in Winograd, 98 (Hebrew).
22  The first of these limited operations was carried out by the 91st div-
    ision and was aimed at attacking Hezbollah in Bint Jbail; operations
    began on 23 July and ended on 29 July without the forces achieving
    their military aims. The second incursion started on 25 July and was

carried out by the 162nd division against Hezbollah forces in El Hiam; it was stopped three hours later.

23 Anti-tank missiles used by Hezbollah included the AT-3 Sagger, which was the most commonly used anti-tank missile, but also the AT-14 Kornet-E and more. Hezbollah fired anti-tank missiles against tanks and vehicles, but also against personnel, houses and shelters used by the Israelis.

24 Winograd, 101 (Hebrew).

25 Meeting between Defence Minister and Chief of Staff, 24 July 2006, Winograd, 103 (Hebrew).

26 Winograd, 109 (Hebrew).

27 An evaluation of the situation in the Defence Ministry, 26 July 2006, 26–7, Winograd, 118 (Hebrew).

28 An evaluation of the Situation, General Staff, 26 July 2006, 32–4, Winograd, 118 (Hebrew).

29 The forum the Seven, 26 July 2006, 28 and in Winograd, 121 (Hebrew).

30 Discussion of The forum the Seven, 26 July 2006, 51–2, Winograd, 122 (Hebrew).

31 General Staff meeting, 4 August 2006, Winograd, 156 (Hebrew).

32 Winograd, 156 (Hebrew).

33 Evaluation of the Situation, General Staff, 4 August 2006, 13; also Winograd, 156, 377 (Hebrew).

34 A governmental meeting, 10.00, 6 August 2006 (private source).

35 Government meeting, 6 August 2006, 45, Winograd, 163–4 (Hebrew).

36 Meeting Defence Minister and Chief of Staff, 6 August 2006, 8–9, Winograd, 164 (Hebrew).

37 Prime Minister talks to commanders in Northern Command, 7 August 2006, in Winograd, 168 (Hebrew).

38 Winograd, 170 (Hebrew).

39 Winograd, 176 (Hebrew).

40 General Staff Evaluation of the Situation Meeting, 8 August 2006, 29, in Winograd, 177 (Hebrew).

41 Cabinet meeting 9 August 2006, 45 in Winograd, 181 (Hebrew).

42 Cabinet meeting, 9 August 2006, 51 in Winograd, 181 (Hebrew).

43 Cabinet meeting, 9 August 2006, 50 in Winograd, 182 (Hebrew).

44 Cabinet meeting, 9 August 2006, 54–5 in Winograd, 182 (Hebrew).

45 Winograd, 184 (Hebrew).

46 The above quotes are from consultations between the Prime Minister and Defence Minister, 9 August 2006, in Winograd, 187 (Hebrew).

47 Winograd, 187 (Hebrew).
48 Winograd, 191 (Hebrew).
49 Winograd, 198 (Hebrew).
50 Winograd, 200 (Hebrew).
51 Winograd, 200 (Hebrew).
52 Testimony of Amir Peretz to Winograd Committee, 24 January 2007 (Hebrew).
53 O. Shelah and Y. Limor, *Captives of Lebanon* (Tel Aviv, 2007), 62 (Hebrew).
54 Above quotations from Winograd, 326, 330 (Hebrew).
55 Winograd, 394 (Hebrew).

## 9 CONCLUSIONS

1 S. Hareven, 'The first forty years', *The Jerusalem Quarterly*, 48 (Jerusalem, autumn 1988), 8.
2 A. Eban, *My Country*, 287 (my emphasis).
3 Recorded and edited by a group of young Kibbutz members: *The Seventh Day: Soldiers Talk about the Six Day War* (London, 1971), 217–18.

# SELECT BIBLIOGRAPHY

For reasons of space, this list is very selective and concentrates on works in English and books as these are more accessible.

Mahmoud Abbas, *Throuugh Secret Channels* (Reading, 1995).
Avraham Adan, *On the Bank of the Suez: An Israeli General's Personal Account of the Yom Kippur War* (London, 1980).
Musa Alami, *Palestine is My Country*, (London, 1969).
Yigal Allon, *Shield of David: The Story of Israel's Armed Forces* (London, 1970).
Moshe Arens, *Broken Covenant* (NewYork, 1995).
Asher Arian, et al., *National Security and Public Opinion in Israel* (Boulder, 1988).
Hanan Ashrawi, *This Side of Peace* (New York, 1995).
Ehud Avriel, *Open the Gates* (New York, 1975).
James A. Baker, *The Politics of Diplomacy: Revolution, War & Peace 1989–1992* (New York, 1995).
Frank Bamaby, *The Invisible Bomb: The Nuclear Arms Race in the Middle East* (London, 1989).
Uri Bar Joseph, *The Watchman Fell Asleep: The Surprise of Yom Kippur and its Sources* (New York, 2005).

Mordechai Bar On, *The Gates of Gaza: Israel's Road to Suez and Back, 1955–1957* (London, 1994).

Yaacov Bar Siman Tov, *The Israeli-Egyptian War of Attrition, 1969–1970* (New York, 1980).

Michael Bar Zohar, *Ben Gurion: A Biography* (London, 1977).

Kylie Baxter & Shahram Akbarzadeh, *US Foreign Policy in the Middle East: The Roots of Anti-Americanism* (London, 2008).

Morris Beckman, The *Jewish Brigade: An Army with Two Masters 1944–45* (London, 1998).

Menachem Begin, *The Revolt* (London, 1951).

Shlomo Ben Ami, *Scars of War, Wounds of Peace: The Israeli-Arab Tragedy* (London, 2006).

David Ben Gurion, – *Rebirth and Destiny of Israel* (New York, 1954).

—— *Israel: Years of Challenge* (New York, 1963).

—— *Israel: A Personal History* (New York, 1971).

Edward Beverley Milton, *The Israeli-Palestinian Conflict* (London, 2009).

Uri Bialer, *Between East and West: Israel's Foreign Policy Orientation 1948–1956* (Cambridge, 1990).

Ian Black & Benny Morris, *Israel's Secret Wars: A History of Israel's Intelligence Services* (London, 1996).

Jeremy Bowen, *Six Days: How the 1967 War Shaped the Middle East* (London, 2004).

Ahron Bregman, *Israel's Wars, 1947–93* (London, 2000).

Ahron Bregman & Jihan el-Tahri, *The Fifty Years War: Israel and the Arabs* (London, 1998).

—— *Israel and the Arabs: An Eyewitness Account of War and Peace in the Middle East* (New York, 2000).

—— *A History of Israel (London,* 2003).

Frank Brenchley, *Britain, the Six Day War and its Aftermath* (London, 2005).

Zbigniew Brzezinski, *Power and Principle* (New York, 1983).

Odd Bull, *War and Peace in the Middle East* (London, 1976).

John Bulloch & Harvey Morris, *Saddam's War* (London, 1991).

Jimmi Carter, *Keeping Faith* (New York, 1982).

Christopher Catherwood, *Making War in the Name of God* (London, 2007).

Sergio Catignani, Israeli Counter-Insuigency and the Intifadas: Dilemmas of a Conventional Army (London, 2008).

Helena Cobban, *The Palestinian Liberation Organization* (Cambridge, 1984).

Larry Collins & Dominique Lapierre, *O Jerusalem* (Bnei Brak, 1993).

Martin van Creveld, The Sword and the Olive: A Critical History of the Israeli Defence Force (New York, 1998).

Jay Cristol, *The Liberty Incident: The 1967 Israeli Attack on the US Navy Spy Ship* (New York, 2002).

Moshe Dayan, *Story of My Life* (London, 1976).

—— *Breakthrough: A Personal Account of the Egypt-Israel Peace Negotiations* (New York, 1981).

—— Diary of the Sinai Campaign (London, 1991).

Abba Eban, *My Country: The Story of Modern Israel* (London, 1973).

—— An Autobiography (London, 1977).

—— Personal Witness (New York, 1992).

Charles Enderlin, The Lost Years: Radical Islam, Intifada, and Wars in the Middle East, 2001–2006 (London, 2007).

Amos Elon, *A Blood-Dimmed Tide* (London, 2000).

Ismail Fahmi, *Negotiating for Peace in the Middle East* (London, 1983).

Abdel Magid Farid, *Nasser: The Final Years* (Reading, 1994).

Robert Fisk, *Pity the Nation: Lebanon at War* (Oxford, 1990).

Ziva Flamhaft, *Israel on the Road to Peace: Accepting the Unacceptable* (Boulder, 1996).

Simcha Flapan, *The Birth of Israel: Myths and Realities* (New York, 1987).

Glenn Frankel, *Beyond the Promised Land: Jews and Arabs on the Hard Road to a New Israel* (New York, 1996).

Lawrence Freedman, *A Choice of Enemies: America Confronts the Middle East* (London, 2008).

Thomas Friedman, *From Beirut to Jerusalem* (London, 1993).

Richard Gabriel, *Operation Peace for Galilee: The Israeli-PLO War in Lebanon* (New York, 1984).

Allan Gerson, *Israel, the West Bank and International Law* (London, 1978)

Martin Gilbert, The Arab-Israeli Conflict: Its History in Maps (London, 1974).

Isabella Ginor & Gideon Remez, *Foxbats over Dimona: The Soviets' Nuclear Gamble in the Six-Day War* (London, 2007).

Matti Golan, *The Secret Conversations of Henry Kissinger* (New York, 1976).

—— *Shimon Peres: A Biography* (London, 1982).

Nahum Goldmann, *The Autobiography of Nahum Goldmann: Sixty Years of Jewish Life* (New York, 1969).

Calvin Goldscheider, *Israel's Changing Society: Population, Ethnicity, and Development* (Boulder, 1996).

Arthur Goldschmidt & Lawrence Davidson, *A Concise History of the Middle East* (New York, 2005).

Gershom Gorenberg, *The Accidental Empire: Israel and the Birth of the Settlements, 1967–1977* (London, 2007).

Yosef Gorny, Zionism and the Arabs, 1882–1946: A study of Ideology (Oxford, 1987).

David Grossman, The Yellow Wind (New York, 1988).

Jill Hamilton, God, Guns and Israel: Britain, the First World War and the Jews in the Holy Land (London, 2004).

Amos Harel & Avi Issacharoff, 34 Days: Israel, Hezbollah and the War in Lebanon (London, 2008).

Alan Hart, Arafat: Tenorist or Peacemaker? (London, 1984).

Amira Hass, Drinking the Sea at Gaza (London, 1999).

Yoram Hazony, The Jewish State: The Struggle for Israel's Soul (New York, 2000).

Mohamed Heikal, The Road to Ramadan: The Inside Story of How the Arabs Prepared for and Almost Won the October War of 1973 (London, 1975).

—— Secret Channels (London, 1996).

Arthur Hertzberg, The Zionist Idea (New York, 1977).

Chaim Herzog, The War of Atonement: The Inside Story of the Yom Kippur War, 1973 (London, 1998).

Dilip Hiro, Sharing the Promised Land: An Interwoven Tale of Israelis and Palestinians (London, 1996).

David Hirst & Irene Beeson, Sadat (London, 1981).

David Hirst, The Gun and the Olive Branch (London, 1977).

Dan Horowitz & Moshe Lissak, The Origins of the Israeli Polity: Palestine Under the Mandate (Chicago, 1978).

Hala Jabar, Hezboliah: Born with a Vengeance (New York, 1997).

Clive Jones & Emma Murphy, Israel: Challenges to Identity, Democracy and the State (London, 2002).

Dov Joseph, The Faithlul City: The Siege of Jerusalem, 1948 (New York, 1960).

Michael Karpin, The Bomb in the Basement: How Israel went Nuclear and What that Means for the World (New York, 2006).

Samuel Katz, Days of Fire (New York, 1968).

Arthur Koestler, Promise and Fulfilment: Palestine 1917–1949 (London, 1983).

Teddy Kollek, For Jerusalem (London, 1978).

Dan Kurzman, Genesis 1948: The First Arab-Israeli War (New York, 1970).

Anton La Guardia, Holy Land, Unholy War: Israelis and Palestinians (London, 2007).

Walter Laqueur & Barry Rubin, The Israel-Arab Reader: A Documentary History of the Middle East Conflict (London, 1995).

Walter Laqueur, A History of Zionism (London, 1972).

David, W Lesch, *The Arab-Israeli Conflict: A History* (New York, 2007).

Bernard Lewis, *Semites and Anti-Semites* (London, 1986).

Barnet Litvinoff, *The Story of David Ben Gurion* (New York, 1959).

Keneft Love, *Suez* (New York, 1969).

Noah Lucas, *The Modern History of Israel* (New York, 1974).

Edward Luttwak & Dan Horowitz, *The Israeli Army* (London, 1975).

Daniel Marston and Carter Malkasian, *Counterinsurgency in Modern Warfare* (London, 2008).

Nur Masalha, *Expulsion of the Palestinians* (Washington, 1992).

Paul McGeough, *Kill Khalid: Mossad's Failed Hit and the Rise of Hamas* (London, 2005).

Peter Medding, *The Foundation of Israeli Democracy, 1948–1967* (New York, 1990).

Golda Meir, *My Life* (London, 1975).

Benny Morris, *The Birth of the Palestinian Refugee Problem, 1947–1949* (Cambridge, 1988).

—— *1948 and After: Israel and the Palestinians* (Oxford, 1990).

Donald Neff, *Warriors at Suez* (New York, 1981).

Marcelle Ninio, *Operation Susannah* (New York, 1978).

Augustus Richard Norton, *Hezboliah: A Short History* (Oxford, 2007).

Hazem Zaki Nuseibeh, *Palestine and the United Nations* (London, 1981).

Edgar O'Ballance, *No Victor, No Vanquished: The Arab-Israeli War, 1973* (California, 1997).

Ritchie Ovendale, *The Origins of the Arab4sraeli Wars* (London, 1984).

Amos Oz, *In the Land of Israel* (New York, 1983).

Judith Palmer Harik, *Hezbollah: The Changing Face of Terrorism* (London, 2005).

Ilan Pappe, The Making of the Arab-Israeli Conflict 1947–1951 (London, 1994).

Raphael Patai (ed.), *The Complete Diaries of Theodor Herzl*, 5 vols. (New York, 1961).

Shimon Peres, *David's Sling* (London, 1970).

—— *Battling for Peace: Memoirs* (London, 1995).

Don Peretz, *Palestinians, Refugees and the Middle East Peace Process* (Washington, 1993).

Kenneth M. Pollack, *Arabs at War: Military Effectiveness, 1948–1991* (London, 2004).

Terence Prittie, *Eshkol of Israel: The Man and the Nation* (London, 1969).

Naim Qassem, *Hezbollah: The Story from Within* (London, 2002).

William Quant, *Camp David: Peacemaking and Politics* (Washington, 1986).

Yitzhak Rabin, *The Rabin Memoirs* (London, 1979).

Abraham Rabinovich, The Yom Kippur War: The Epic Encounter that Transformed The Middle East (London, 2005).

Itamar Rabinovich, *The War for Lebanon, 1970–1983* (New York, 1984).

—— *The Road not Taken: Early Arab-Israeli Negotiations* (Oxford, 1991).

Gideon Rafael, *Destination Peace, Three Decades of Israeli Foreign Policy: A Personal Memoir* (London, 1981).

Jonathan Randal, *The Tragedy of Lebanon* (London, 1990).

Simon Reeve, *One Day in September The Story of the 1972 Munich Olympics Massacre* (London, 2000).

Jehuda Reinharz and Anita Shapira (ed.), *Essential Papers on Zionism* (London, 1996).

Mahmoud Riad, *The Struggle for Peace in the Middle East* (New York, 1981).

Norman Rose, *Chaim Weizmann: A Biography* (New York, 1986).

Gunther Rothenberg, *The Anatomy of the Israeli Army* (London, 1979).

Howard Sachar, *A History of Israel* (Oxford, 1987).

Anwar Sadat, *In Search of Identity: An Autobiography* (New York, 1977).

James Scott, *The Attack on the Liberty: The Untold Story of Israel's Deadly 1967 Assault on a US Spy Ship* (New York, 2009).

Edward W. Said, *The Question of Palestine* (New York, 1980).

—— Peace & Its Discontents (London, 1995).

Herbert Viscount Samuel, *Memoirs* (London, 1945).

Zeev Schiff & Ehud Ya'ari, *Israel's Lebanon War* (London, 1984).

—— Intifada, The Palestinian Uprising, Israel's Third Front (New York, 1989)

Kirsten E. Schulze, *The Arab-Israeli Conflict* (London, 2008).

Patrick Seale, *The Struggle for Syria* (Oxford, 1965).

Tom Segev, *The Seventh Million: The Israelis and the Holocaust* (New York, 1993).

Yitzhak Shamir, *Summing Up: An Autobiography* (Boston, 1994).

Ariel Sharon, *Warrior: The Autobiography of Ariel Sharon* (London, 1989).

Saad el-Shazli, *The Crossing of Suez: The October War (1973)* (London, 1980).

Gabriel Sheffer, *Moshe Sharett: Biography of a Political Moderate* (Oxford, 1996).

David Shipler, *Arab and Jew: Wounded Spirits in a Promised Land* (New York, 1987).

Avi Shlaim, *The Politics of Partition, King Abdullah, the Zionists and Palestine 1921–1951* (Oxford, 1988).

—— *The Iron Wall: Israel and the Arab World (London, 2000).*

Eric Silver, *Begin: The Haunted Prophet* (New York, 1984).

Robert Slater, *Rabin of Israel: Warrior for Peace* (London, 1996).

Charles D. Smith, *Palestine and the Arab-Israeli Conflict: A History with Documents* (New York, 2007).

Steven Spiegel, *The Other Arab-Israeli Conflict: Making America's Middle East Policy from Truman to Reagan* (Chicago, 1985).

Steward Steven, *The Spymasters of Israel* (London, 1980).

William Stevenson, *90 Minutes at Entebbe* (New York, 1976).

Christopher Sykes, *Orde Wingate* (London, 1959).

—— *Cross Roads to Israel: Palestine from Balfour to Bevin* (London, 1965).

Marie Syrkin, *Golda Meir: Woman With a Cause* (New York, 1961).

Mark Tessler, *A History of the Israeli-Palestinian Conflict* (Bloomington, 1994).

Shabtai Teveth, *Moshe Dayan* (London, 1972).

—— *Ben-Gurion and the Holocaust* (New York, 1996).

Sadia Touval, *The Peace Brokers* (Princeton, 1982).

Barbara W. Tuchman, *Bible and Sword: How the British Came to Palestine* (New York, 1956).

Brian Urquhart, *Ralph Bunch: An American Life* (New York, 1993).

David Vital, *The Origins of Zionism* (London, 1975).

Bernard Wasserstein, *Herbert Samuel: A Political Life* (Oxford, 1992).

EzerWeizman, *On Eagles' Wings* (London, 1976).

—— *The Battle for Peace* (New York, 1981).

Chaim Weizmann, *Trial and Error: The Autobiography of Chaim Weizmann* (New York, 1949).

Harold Wilson, *The Chariot of Israel* (London, 1981).

Richard Worth, *The Arab-Israeli Conflict* (London, 2006).

Ehud Ya'ari & Eitan Haber, *The Year of the Dove* (New York, 1979).

Avner Yaniv, *Deterrence Without the Bomb: The Politics of Israeli Strategy* (Massachusetts, 1987).

# INDEX

328 INDEX

Independence 32; impact of War of Independence 35–8; immigration 36, 39–41, 295; population 36–7; language problems 41, 42–3, 295; insecurity and public cooperation after 1948 48–55; Palestinian infiltration 48–51; importance of Straits of Tiran to 56–7; complacency in 1967 62–3; relations with Syria (1967) 63–6, 67–70, 72; mobilization and strategy in 1967 74–7; public anxiety during 'waiting period' 77–9; attitude to USA 88; public reactions to wars 92–3, 100–1, 142–3, 176–8, 200–3; and Lebanese civil war 148–50; pre-war operations in Lebanon 150–2, 153–5; first occupation of an Arab capital 175; demonstrations and protests by Israelis 177, 203, 260; policy on Islamic fundamentalists 193–4; measures against *intifada* 196–200; economic consequences of *intifada* measures 198–9; seizes *Karine A* 234–5; maintains presence in Lebanon 253–5, 258–9; as initiator of wars 294–5; diminishing insecurity 296–7; increase in individuality 297–8; *see also Aqsa intifada, Al-*; Gaza Strip; *intifada*; Lebanon War, first; Lebanon War, second; Sinai Campaign; Six Day War; War of Attrition; War of Independence; West Bank; Yom Kippur War
Israeli Air Force (IAF): and Six Day

War 84–5; and *Liberty* Affair 88–9; and Operation Boxer (1970) 99; deep penetration strategy 99–100; and Yom Kippur War 124, 128, 134, 135, 138, 139; attacks on PLO in Lebanon 150, 152, 157, 159; attacks on Syrians in Lebanon 154; and first Lebanon War 171, 172, 173, 174–5; and *intifada* 181; and *Al-Aqsa intifada* 225, 244–5; and second Lebanon War 276–8, 280, 281, 282, 290, 291–2
Israeli Defence Force (IDF): establishment of 28–9; reorganization of 41–5; compulsory military service 42–4; three tiers 43–4; reserves 44, 45, 49–50, 59, 176–7, 202–3, 285, 295–6; career soldiers 44, 260; intelligence service 44; exemptions 45; equipping 41, 46, 52, 53–5; training and manoeuvres 46–7; and Sinai Campaign 58–9; attack strength 75–6; and Six Day War 85, 91; and Bar Lev line 97–8; 'Blue-White' plan 115–16; in Yom Kippur War 128, 131, 133–41; casualties in Yom Kippur War 142; and Litani campaign 150; and first Lebanon War 160–4, 165–6, 168–71, 174; opposition to Sharon 174, 177; and *intifada* 179, 187, 192; not equipped for riots 187–8, 192; and *Al-Aqsa intifada* 217, 218, 219, 220, 222, 226, 229, 230, 231, 232–3, 239–40; and battle of Jenin 241; debate on Lebanon 253–5; security zone in Lebanon

Israeli measures against 48–51; Jordan's treatment of 118, 146; in Lebanon 146–8, 174–7; evacuation from Beirut 175; camp massacres 174–7, 205, 275, Pl. 4; conditions in Gaza camps 183–5; civil resistance in Gaza camps 185–7; Popular Committees 192; economic hardship 198–9; Camp David proposals and 208–9; *see also* Gaza Strip; *intifada*; West Bank

Paris summit 214

Peel, Lord 9, 12, 92

Peres, Shimon 58, 149, 219–20

Peretz, Amir 280, 281, 285, 286–8

PFLP *see* Popular Front for the Liberation of Palestine

PLO *see* Palestinian Liberation Organization

police forces: Israeli 205–6, 211, 214, 215; Palestinian 192, 212, 214, 216–17, 219, 231; *see also* Shin Bet

Popular Front for the Liberation of Palestine (PFLP) 30, 186, 189, 231–2

population 36–7, 49, 201–2

prisons and detention centres 186, 198, 246

propaganda 50, 53

Protocols of the Elders of Zion 60

Pyrlin, Evgeny 69

Qalqilya 232, 246, 247

Qana 259, 282

Quds Palestinian Arab Radio, Al 191

Rabin, Yitzhak: and War of Independence 30, 31; and Sinai Campaign 59–60; on Syria 64–5; and Six Day War 76–7, Pl. 2; and Lebanese civil war 148, 149, 150, 153; and *intifada* 181–2, 197

radio: criticisms of Nasser on Arab stations 67; Eshkol's disastrous speech 79; Palestinian stations 191, 217, 218, 219

Rafael, Gideon 105

Rahnim, Mohammed 162

Ramallah 197; lynching 216–18; *Al-Aqsa intifada* in 225, 231, 232, 233; Operation Defensive Shield in Pl. 6; Israeli attacks on Arafat's compound 239–40, 243, 245–6; and ceasefire 247

Ramat-Gan 53

Ramleh 30, 53

Rantissi, Abdel Aziz 251

Razeq, Jamal Abed Al- 222

Reagan, Ronald 152

refugees *see* Palestinian refugees

Rifai, Zeid 119

Right of Return 208

Rostow, Walt 62–3

Rotem 269

Rothenberg, Gunther 38

Ruppin, Arthur 5

Rusk, Dean 83

Russia *see* USSR

Russian Jews 4

Sabit, Adel 28

Sabra refugee camp: massacre 174, 175–7, 205, 275, Pl. 4

Sabri, Ali 103

Sadat, Anwar el-: receives Russian intelligence of Israeli moves (1967) 67; on Nasser's motives 72; importance 102; international

public reaction to 91–3, 142, 178
SLA *see* South Lebanon Army
Solana, Javier 218
Soldiers Against Silence 176
South Lebanon Army (SLA); cooperation with IDF 253, 254, 255, 257, 269; two brigades 255; and Israeli withdrawal from Lebanon 263, 264, 269–70; UN calls to dismantle 267; collapse of 269–72
Stern Gang *see* Lehi
Straits of Eilat 58
Straits of Tiran: and Sinai Campaign 56–7, 59; and 1967 crisis 70–2, 73, 76, 77, 83, 104
strikes 198, 202, 212–13
Suez Canal: and Sinai Campaign 55–6, 57, 59; and Six Day War 81, 85; and War of Attrition 93, 95, 97–101; Bar Lev line 97–9; and Yom Kippur War 102, Pl. 3; Sadat's peace intitiative and (1971) 103–7; and Yom Kippur War 122, 124–5, 126, 132–3, 139, 141; *Karine A* in 235
suicide bombers 205, 223, 225, 226–7, 231, 233, 237, 240–1, 243–4, 245, 247, 248–9
Sunni Moslems 145
Syria: and civil war 15; and War of Independence 24, 25, 26, 27, 33; refugee camps 48; and Palestinian resistance 50; relations with Israel (1967) 63–6, 67–70, 72; defence pact with Egypt 65, 66; and DMZs 65–6, 67; mobilizes in 1967 74, 78; and Six Day War 90–1; and Yom

Kippur War 112, 117–23, 125, 127–9, 130, 132, 134–7, *136*, 138; forces in Yom Kippur War 127, 128; and first Lebanon War 148, 150–1, 153–6, 160, 162, 163–5, 166–73, 175; forces in Lebanon 164, 170, 171; and *intifada* 181; and PFLP 186; support for Hezbollah 259, 261, 267, 268, 275, 288; peace talks (linked with Lebanon situation) 261–2, 263–4, 265, 268

Taibe 269, 270
Tal, Yisrael 75, 77, 98, 128, 135, 139
tanks: purchase of 53; Arabs' strength in (1967) 74, 76; Egyptian 95, 139–41; Israeli 75, 76, 137, 139, 164, 187, 257, 291; Jordanian 74, 137; PLO 165; Syrian 127, 134, 164; lost in Yom Kippur War 142; *see also* anti-tank weapons
Tanzim 217–18, 241
Taylor, A.J.P. 72
Tel Aviv: 'Red House' 21; and War of Independence 35; sabotage of US radar 88; Sadat's wish to bomb 110; terrorist attacks in 150, 227, 231, 243, 245, 248–9; Israeli protests in 177, 203
Tenet Ceasefire Plan 227–30
terrorist attacks: in 1978 150; in 1990s 200; *Al-Aqsa intifada* and 205, 222, 223, 224, 225, 226–7, 231, 233, 237–8, 240–1, 243–4, 245, 247; in Jerusalem 220, 224, 227, 231, 233, 245, 248–9; in Tel Aviv 150, 227, 243, 245, 248–9; Israeli assassination policy